STRIDES

BENJAMIN CHEEVER

STRIDES

RUNNING THROUGH HISTORY WITH AN UNLIKELY ATHLETE

RODALE

Rodale books may be purchased for business or promotional use or for special sales. For information, please write to: Special Markets Department, Rodale Inc., 733 Third Avenue, New York, NY 10017.

Printed in the United States of America

Rodale Inc. makes every effort to use acid-free ♾, recycled paper ♻.

Book design by Susan Eugster

Library of Congress Cataloging-in-Publication Data

Cheever, Benjamin, date
    Strides : running through history with an unlikely athlete / Benjamin Cheever.
      p.   cm.
    Includes bibliographical references.
    ISBN-13 978–1–59486–228–1 hardcover
    ISBN-10 1–59486–228–1 hardcover
    1. Running. 2. Marathon running. 3. Marathon running—History.
  4. Cheever, Benjamin, date I. Title.
GV1062.C54 2007
613.7'172—dc22   2007027868

Distributed to the trade by Holtzbrinck Publishers

2 4 6 8 10 9 7 5 3 1 hardcover

RODALE
LIVE YOUR WHOLE LIFE™

We inspire and enable people to improve their lives and the world around them
For more of our products visit **rodalestore.com** or call 800-848-4735

For Janet, John, and Andrew

"Everyone is an athlete.
The only difference is that some of us
are in training and some are not."

—DR. GEORGE SHEEHAN

CONTENTS

PREFACE

Shortly after my first marathon, I dreamt I was flying. The first roof I scudded over must have belonged to the house I grew up in, because the next clearly recognizable landmark was the Vanderlip swimming pool. I rocked backward and zipped up until the planet—tidy, muffled, and geometric—began to fall away.

Flying—I'd learned—was all about technique. The trick was so simple that I couldn't imagine why it had eluded Leonardo. You just needed to get down in a kneeling position, as if for prayer, put a hand—palm down—on each thigh, and lean back. Even dreaming, I knew this was going to be huge. I'd phone a lawyer, and an accountant, when I came down. For the moment, though, there were a lot of places I wanted to see.

When my Casio beeped and woke me, I resented needing to land but consoled myself with the certainty that I could do this again, whenever I wanted. I had the technique.

It turned out, of course, that in the waking world, I was as flightless as the cassowary bird, the ostrich, or the dodo.

And yet, the sensation stayed with me, the broad vistas, the possibilities that were so great as to be unthinkable.

Like dreams, road races are played out in an alternate universe. If you're in the middle of one, the earlier contests—even if they were held in a different decade or on a distant continent—return vividly to consciousness.

So when I came back to the Boston Marathon at 58 years old in 2006, I was running through a museum with France in it, and Greece, Baghdad, and my first Boston, which had been in 1979. I also ran through the halls of Boston 1980, my fastest at 2:46 and change. During that race, it came to me that while I'd sworn many dread oaths against marriage, I was going to beg Janet Maslin to marry me.

Writing this book has forced me to take a close look at one of the great hinges of my life. The history is enthralling, both just what I expected and a complete surprise.

Other runners are what made this book worth writing. These people don't just stop and pick the flowers. They stop and pick the daisies and then give the daisies to somebody else.

We have educators like Amby Burfoot, who's devoted a lifetime to the study of the sport and then to passing on his results. Navy Commander Matt Simms is another runner. He organized a 10-K in Baghdad. Or take John Manners, who seems to get his biggest kick out of landing a Kenyan kid in an Ivy League college.

These are the outsiders, the people I traveled to meet. My most gratifying expeditions have been to the parking lot behind the Sleepy Hollow High School. There, a half dozen extraordinary people could be found to fall in with for 7 or 10 or 20 miles.

I've often felt like the last honest man with his finger in the dike. Turns out, there are a lot of people with their fingers in dikes. There are a lot of leaky dikes, too, but that I had always expected. And, yes, I trust my judgment of these other men and women. Because we run, we're honest with one another.

What I hate most in this world is the absence of candor, the void left by the extraction of true humanity. A long, cheery, congratulatory voice-mail maze is like an ice pick in my heart. I'd sooner spend a decade alone in a cave dining on fat grubs than an hour with some creature half man, half public relations agency braying about how smart he is, how successful, frugal, and altruistic. These guys act as if they've got the fate of the globe in their hands, and yet I go away terrified about my future.

It's odd that I like marathons so much. Ordinarily, I don't fit in at staged gatherings. The bigger the ceremony, the less festive I feel. Crammed in with a hundred strangers who are probably as similar to me as other peas in my pod, I feel alienated, unique, and alone. Nor do I have the sort of attitude that leads to lasting connections. Soon, I'm criticizing the filet mignon, speculating out loud about how much they paid the keynote speaker. "And didn't he already publish this in a column?" A tuxedo brings out the Hamlet in me. There's something rotten in the state of Denmark.

Set this same cynic down at Fort Wadsworth on line for a toilet that really *does* smell rotten, and he's a believer. Suddenly, I respect authority. It was raining the year I saw Mayor Koch striding through a clot of runners at the start of the New York City Marathon, waving his arms above his head as if he'd just won a heavyweight bout. Nobody was cheering. Nobody. I liked him, though. I thought he looked a little silly, but also statesmanlike. This was a man who would not be ruled by the crowd. Seemed he didn't need us at all.

I like the people at a marathon. Maybe this is because as a species, we're so good at concealing ourselves. And the signals we give one another are like the feints a ball carrier might use to outwit a tackler. We hate or love our jobs, depending entirely on who's listening. We didn't mean to buy this car. "After circling the globe, I never thought I'd wind up in this town." "I didn't mean to marry him."

When you run a marathon, you mean it. We're built for running. We dream of flying. For now, though, we're built to run.

xi

CHAPTER 1

The Fat Man in Green Pajamas

"EXPECT POISON FROM STANDING WATER."
—WILLIAM BLAKE

Pheidippides is said to have run the first marathon. That was in September of 490 BC. He brought news that the Persians had been defeated. Athens was saved. Civilization was saved. "Rejoice!" he said, "We conquer!"

> *"Like wine through clay,*
> *Joy in his blood bursting his heart,*
> *He died—the bliss!"* [1]

The bliss is what I'm after.

Although mortality is part of it. I was moving in a pack of runners 20-odd years ago on a sidewalk in White Plains, New York, after a half-marathon.

Spotting others in singlets and with the distinctive post-exertion matted hair, we'd wave our bony little fists. "Good race!" we'd shout.

"Good race!" they'd shout right back.

A funeral cortege appeared suddenly on the street beside us. The contrast between this ominous procession and our own towering spirits silenced the pack and made us—for an instant—ashamed. Then one of the runners waved his fist at the hearse. "Good race!" he shouted.

When long-distance running found me 30 years ago, I had begun the transition that I hoped would be my last. I yearned to become an adult male—a full suit with a job, a lawn, and a temper. I'd sold the motorcycle. In an exact reversal of the life cycle of the butterfly, I'd stopped flapping around and had settled down to learn a skill. This done, I was reconciled to a long caterpillar-like phase of dull work capped—I fervently hoped—with solvency.

As a child, I'd felt most myself when I was out of doors. Now I lived on Edgewood Road, but I rarely plunged into the woods from which our development took its name. Although I'd sometimes lurk behind a tree smoking a clandestine cigarette. The only face time I had with Mother Nature was spent weeding the pachysandra or cutting the lawn. I was throat-deep in a marriage that didn't work for anyone, not even the pets. I was employed as the only male on the copy desk at the *Reader's Digest* magazine. My idea of exercise was cadging cigarettes from colleagues who had the conviction to buy their own. I was 28 years old and all set for a wooden overcoat.

Then I spent $11 on a tag-sale bicycle. The frame was too big for me and had been sloppily repainted in Creamsicle orange. The machine had 10 speeds, though. I'd never owned a bicycle with 10 speeds. "I'll ride it to work," I said, justifying the expense. We had only one reliable car. "Maybe I'll lose some weight." I got a two-piece outfit in lime green with a zipper down the front and zippers at the ankles. Like tuxedo pants, the bottoms had a stripe of darker material down the outer seam. I liked the look, but clearly these "warm-ups" were from the bathrobe/pajamas family, the material sheer, the zippers frail. The label said, "Dry clean only."

I drove a suit, shoes, and neckties to the office one day and left them in the closet. There was a shower in the basement at the *Reader's Digest*. I could use that.

The next morning, I stuffed a fresh shirt, socks, and underwear into a backpack along with my papers. The largest pack I owned at the time was Swiss Army surplus. Or that's what the girl at the head shop told me when I bought it during my hippie phase. It had wooden buttons, leather button holes, and fur on the outside. You could see why the Swiss had moved on.

Even today, I can visualize the blue-gray of the asphalt on that first day, when I made the left turn out of Edgewood Road and onto Route 133. This was the big road, and I could hear the big cars on it. I was frightened, and I was right to be. I hadn't bicycled since I was a child. I was slow and I wobbled. The shoulder—when there was a shoulder—was pocked with holes and littered with broken Heineken bottles.

A couple of miles out, I caught the left leg of my warm-ups in the chain. This stopped all forward motion, and I fell slowly, gracefully, into a gap in the middle of a lane of traffic. Scrabbling out of the way, I heard brakes and then a horn. "Who is this asshole?" they must have wondered. I wondered, too.

I made it, though. There were a lot of downhill stretches on the way from Ossining to the *Reader's Digest*. The ascents were gradual, almost forgiving. I took my shower and found my post at work. That afternoon, I hung my suit in my office closet and climbed back into my warm-ups. I dreaded the ride home. There was reason to dread it. The machine had 10 speeds all right, but you still had to pedal. At 5 feet 7 inches, I weighed 170 pounds. I'd been big and strong. I was still big. I couldn't make it even a third of the way up the first hill. I must have looked absurd. A fat man wearing green pajamas and walking an orange bicycle. And from a distance, it looked as if I had a dead animal tied to my shoulders.

I heard the cars driven by colleagues growling up behind me on the first steep ascent above the Saw Mill River Parkway. The road has many curves, and they were forced to wait for a chance to pass. And passing these same people in the hall, I'd see it in their eyes—recognition, a flicker of amusement, and then nothing.

I might have given up the plan immediately if I hadn't already spent $11 on that eyesore of a bicycle. I developed a wicked case of what veteran cyclists call "beginner's butt." If it didn't rain in the morning and dampen my shirt before work, then it rained in the afternoon and soaked the proofs I ferried home.

I'd watch the end of the local TV news and base my plans on the beaming meteorologist. I bicycled to work so often in the rain that I took to setting a clock radio and listening to the morning weather report. I still got wet. I kept setting the clock radio, but instead of listening to its buzzing prophecy, I'd step outside and smell the air, peer up at the sky.

Slowly, but decisively, my body began to change. A month went by. Maybe 2 months. Then one afternoon, without dismounting, I made it up that first hill. Within a week of that triumph, I was looking forward to the commute. Flying down Roaring Brook Road in Chappaqua one day, just after dawn, I was shocked to hear a cry of pleasure, a yodel really.

That was me.

CHAPTER 2

First Marathon

"AND THIS LONG-DISTANCE RUNNING LARK
IS THE BEST OF ALL, BECAUSE IT MAKES ME THINK
SO GOOD THAT I LEARN THINGS EVEN BETTER
THAN WHEN I'M ON MY BED AT NIGHT."
—ALAN SILLITOE, *THE LONELINESS OF THE LONG-DISTANCE RUNNER*[1]

Crazy for endorphins, I traded stories with the runners I met in the shower at work. Then one Saturday, I ran a mile. I was astonished. It must have been winter, because I was wearing a black crewneck sweater from the Army Navy store, blue jeans, and sneakers—remember sneakers? I stood in front of the bathroom mirror, my face crimson with the effort, and thought: *I ran a mile. Impossible!*

My experience was solitary and seemed one of a kind, but this was 1977, and I was being worked on by forces of which I was not entirely cognizant. Kenneth Cooper's *Aerobics* had been published in 1968 and picked up by the *Reader's Digest*. Frank Shorter had won a gold medal for America in the marathon at the 1972 Olympics. I was in suburban New York. Tish Hamilton was in Atlanta and 15 in 1977.

"There's a park across the street from the house where I grew up," says the woman who is now an executive editor at *Runner's World* magazine. "It took me a while to work up to running 'all the way around the park.' When I finally did, it was a really big deal. I ran all the way around the park! 'You did what? All the way around? My goodness!' Everyone in my family was impressed. I had to lie down for the rest of the day."

"I measured it later—nine-tenths of a mile. All the way around!"

Turned out that *my* mile—a circuit of the Ossining, New York, development I lived in—wasn't quite a mile either. Nor was the 7 miles I ran within the month a true seven. But here's the thing: I was an adult male—hairy, married, and stolid. I wore a necktie. Running was for children. And yet I'd just run 7 miles. I did lose weight.

I wasn't afraid anymore. I mingled with the other runners. Some of these men were way up the masthead. I was painfully aware of the disparity in status and power. Was this reaching? Was I a striver? Did it show? Then one day, I got to the basement a little late. Assistant managing editor Jerry Dole gave me a look that might actually have been stern and said, "You're late, Cheever!" Now, Jerry's exquisitely polite. He'd never have said anything if he had actually been angry. I was delighted. I repeated the exchange over and over in my mind, mimicking the affection I'd caught in Jerry's voice. In the locker room and on the roads, we would be equals.

Apparently, my transformation was noticeable, because a *Digest* colleague, Tom Lashnits, wrote an article for the *New York Times,* which began, "It all started for me when my friend Ben began to run. He's the son of a famous writer...."[2]

Since I'd read *Walden* in high school, I had been haunted by Thoreau's charge that when I came to die, I might discover that I had not lived. *If I run a marathon,* I thought, *I will have lived.* I also thought I might die. Marathon champion Alberto Salazar once said, "Standing on the starting line, we are all cowards." This was a brave and generous thing for him to say. And it's true. But we also feel like heroes.

That first year, I signed up for the 47th Annual Yonkers Marathon, in New York. It's the second-oldest 26.2-miler in the United States (after Boston), but because of the hills, this race is a whole lot less popular. I fell in beside a helpful veteran named Spencer, Spenser? I never saw it spelled, although we met each other at other races after this. I think he had a beard. Spenser was planning to break 3 hours, a good goal for a veteran, if ambitious for a first-timer. "You have to run the New York Marathon," he told me. "The crowd will suck you right up First Avenue."

We stayed together, and I moved quickly and well, until I came down into Tarrytown at about 15 miles. Then it was just as if I were a car and the fan belt had gone, just as if somebody had shattered my engine block with the .357 Magnum Clint Eastwood had introduced to the public in *Dirty Harry*. And, no, I didn't feel lucky. This was the wall.

I did finish the race in 3 hours and 31 minutes. And, no, I didn't walk, although I was more than half an hour off the time I'd need to qualify for Boston. I went to other races and reported the experiences so excitedly that civilians assumed I must be winning. When I explained that I wasn't winning, they didn't get it. Other runners got it. This wasn't about image, or fame.

The sport had its celebrities, its icons, and we adored them, but we didn't expect to replace them. Fame in running is earned in numbers, and simple math is hard to argue with.

A blowhard can write an execrable epic poem and tell his neighbors that it's splendid. "I'll never be published because I'm too brave and candid. I won't play the games." But he can't say, "I just ran an Olympic-quality 8-minute mile." So we admired Bill Rodgers, and mourned the loss of Steve Prefontaine, who—having died young—became a Christ figure for the sport. Brash as Ali, Pre was fast. At one point, he held the American record at every distance from 2,000 to 10,000 meters. "To give anything less than your best is to sacrifice the gift," he said, and we were on the same page. It's just that most of us found much smaller packages under the tree.

On weekends, I took long bicycle rides with my father, and we began to repair a friendship that had been damaged and then severed by his drinking and my claustrophobic marriage. "We share an interest in rudimentary forms of transportation," he liked to say.

I spent $18 and change on a pair of Brooks running shoes, which I found marked down at Macy's. *Runner's World* had selected the Brooks Vantage with the "varus wedge" as the shoe of the year. Perfect, but they were a size too small. So I wasn't wearing socks for my first long training run. One foot was heavily bandaged when I ran a 2:59:33 in New York and qualified by a whisker for the Boston Marathon. I waited in Alice Tully Hall for the results. It was that close. Bill Rodgers won in 2:11:28. Grete Waitz set a women's world marathon record finishing in 2:32:30.

I wore my yellow New York Marathon T-shirt with childish pride. A woman stopped me in the produce section of the Millwood A&P to ask where she could get such a shirt. I paused at first, embarrassed, pondering her question. Then the majesty of my accomplishment dawned on me. "You need to run the New York Marathon," I told her.

Joy changes the landscape. My old life began to loosen around me like somebody else's shell. I felt naked, exposed. I had flashes of ecstasy, but pain was also more available to me. And not just physical pain either. I was swept with waves of remorse. And alarmingly, I also felt the stirrings of ambition. I'd stumbled into an arena where I could go all out, holding nothing back, and nobody—nobody—would be injured, or even threatened. The smell of 3-in-One oil was as nostalgic for me as the madeleine is fabled to have been for Proust. I bought a new bicycle, a Raleigh Grand Prix with the Alpine gear, and loved the music made by the click of its chain. The Grand Prix was royal blue, and I kept it in the kitchen at home and in my office at work. Life is a miraculous undertaking if you're paying attention. Glorious, but also dreadful. Look right at the sun, and you'll go blind.

And there was all this talk, a sort of buzz about how good distance running was for me. I was getting thin and fast, and—the cherry on the sundae—I might live forever.

"Most Americans are in terrible shape," wrote Jim Fixx in his just-published 1977 bestseller, *The Complete Book of Running.* "We smoke and drink too much, weigh too much, exercise too little, and eat too many of the wrong things," Fixx wrote. "A California pathologist, Thomas J. Bassler, says on the basis of autopsies he has performed that two out of every three deaths are premature; they are related to what he calls loafer's heart, smoker's lung, and drinker's liver. Thomas K. Cureton, a professor at the University of Illinois Physical Fitness Laboratory, has said, 'The average American young man has a middle-aged body. He can't run the length of a city block, he can't climb a flight of stairs without getting breathless. In his twenties, he has the capacity that a man is expected to have in his forties.'"

Bassler said that if you ran a marathon in under 4 hours, you were guaranteed not to have a heart attack. I read somewhere that when you run for longer than an hour, your body begins to adapt in miraculous ways. I couldn't actually have thought, even then, that my arteries were growing, but it was like that. I'd go for a 20 and glance down at my sternum, like a hen sitting on an egg.

But in the background, I could hear the fearsome rumbling of infuriated authority. Having come into my office on other business, one of my superiors spotted the new bicycle.

"My wife has the car," I explained.

"Tell your wife," he said, "that you can drive to work or not come to work at all." He laughed when he said this, but it was a mirthless laugh. DeWitt Wallace, who with his wife, Lila, founded and owned the magazine, believed in fitness. And Peter Canning, my immediate superior, had been running and bicycling to work for years. So I couldn't be fired.

But I was told I would soon be a couple of inches shorter. That my hips might be damaged, my retina detached. Lots of people saw arthritis in my future, and many expected cancer. "The body isn't designed for that kind of wear."

Jerry Dole remembers motorists buzzing him, when he ran on the shoulder of the road. Riding his bicycle to work, Peter Canning was struck from behind with a fist. Running at dusk on a Friday or Saturday, I actually wondered if it was smart to wear bright clothes and thus let the drivers see me.

I felt 10 years younger, but a week didn't pass without a perfect stranger wondering out loud about my knees. "And where do you find the time?" One well-educated colleague told me that marathons were once held in Madison Square Garden.

"What happened?" I asked, going for the bait.

"They realized how harmful marathons were for the athletes. . . . the culture moved on. There was an editorial condemning marathons in the *New York Times*." This I didn't believe, but the tidbit rankled. And I harbored doubts of my own. I was having fun, all right, but fun is not always a good sign. Was this about vanity? Were we narcissists? Did we run because we were afraid to die?

Coming up from an afternoon workout in my shorts and a T-shirt one evening, I found Temple Williams, the editor who was then my best friend, waiting in my office. At that point, I'd lost 15 pounds. My calves were suddenly prominent, and my knees had thickened dramatically. There was a new bridge of cartilage running downward from the point of my kneecap.

"You've changed your body type," Temple told me. "You're a different person now. You can't ever go back."

CHAPTER 3

Running in Prehistory,
Long-Distance Intuitions

"It has been said that the love of the
chase is an inherent delight in man—
a relic of an instinctive passion."
—CHARLES DARWIN, *DIARY OF THE VOYAGE OF H.M.S. BEAGLE*

Writers have long intuited a running past that stretches back before
written history, back before consciousness as we know it today. Colin
Smith seems to be in touch with this distant past in *The Loneliness of the
Long-Distance Runner*: "Because when on a raw and frosty morning I get up
at five o'clock and stand shivering my belly off on the stone floor and all
the rest still have another hour to snooze before the bells go, I slink
downstairs through all the corridors to the big outside door with a permit
running-card in my fist, I feel like the first and last man on the world,

both at once, if you can believe what I'm trying to say." It's dawn in the story, but also the dawn of time.

"Running is the most elemental sport there is," wrote John Jerome in *The Elements of Effort*.[1] "We are genetically programmed to do it. One might even say we are the free-ranging, curious, restless creatures that we are because of running."

The theme echoes through John L. Parker Jr.'s cult classic, *Once a Runner*. Quenton Cassidy is talking to Andrea, a girl who is sometimes bemused, but often infuriated by his commitment to the sport. She is trying to figure out how untouchable this guy really is. He's telling her about "the demons."

"They make you bolt awake in the middle of the night with an involuntary shot of your own true adrenaline, ready to run a hundred miles; we're talking when you're there, now, really there, four-minute shape or better. They make you jittery with the smell of forest, ready to hurdle fallen trees, run down game, leave gore in the bushes ..."[2]

"Run down game?" you ask yourself. "Gore in the bushes?"

Seems a little extreme, but then this connection to a savage past has been made repeatedly in running fiction. And nonfiction as well. Science is beginning to fall into line.

Dr. Dennis M. Bramble of the University of Utah and Dr. Daniel E. Lieberman of Harvard see distance running as a significant step in the development of the species. Dr. Bramble is a professor of biology and a specialist in the biomechanics of animal locomotion. Dr. Lieberman is a paleontologist. Both are students of evolution. Both runners.

"When I was an undergraduate at Harvard," Dr. Lieberman told me, "I took a class with a super-famous guy named Dick Taylor, maybe the premier physiologist of locomotion in the last century. Just an amazing guy. Taylor completely discounted the human capability to run. Pointed out that we're lousy runners. And he was typical at that time, because most people think about running in terms of sprinting. And there's absolutely no question that humans are lousy sprinters. By all kinds of criteria. We have low maneuverability and stability. We're up there with penguins in terms of the energy costs of running.

"The fastest human can run about 10 meters a second for about 10 seconds," Dr. Lieberman said. "Your typical squirrel can double that for 4 or 5 minutes. We're really pathetic. That was the story.

"When I was a graduate student, I was working on how bones respond to loading, and I was running pigs on treadmills actually, and this guy Bramble, who was on sabbatical at Harvard, walked into the lab. He was kind of watching my pigs running, and he said to me, 'You know that pig can't hold its head still.'

"I watched the pig and realized that its head was jiggling about in a kind of a funny way, whereas most animals, I mean you think about a greyhound or a horse, or even a human running, and the head locks in. That's when he told me his idea about humans being good at running."

Humans can run distance on a hot day, Dr. Lieberman told me, "when no other animal could. The bushmen, the various hunter-gatherers in Africa, will run animals to death. There's documented evidence of it. There actually was a fellow from South Africa who's been corresponding with me, and he's got GPS data and all kinds of stuff documenting it. There's not a lot published, mostly because the people who are interested in hunter-gatherers can't run to keep up with them."

Dr. Bramble and Dr. Lieberman worked together, and after a time, "we realized that we had something to write," Dr. Lieberman told me. "So he came here, and we holed ourselves up for a week and wrote that paper."

This ran in the journal *Nature* in November 2004. "We were very excited to get the paper in *Nature* in the first place, which is not, not, not easy to do," said Dr. Lieberman. "It was fun also to get the cover. But then 1,000 newspapers carried our story. I spent a week answering e-mails, and a large proportion were from runners, who sent me poems and their stories and their theories. So we obviously touched a nerve."

Dr. Lieberman, who calls himself "a really shitty runner," said, "It's interesting that most people who run are completely accepting of our idea.

It's like, 'Yeah, of course!' And interestingly, there are other people who scratch their heads and say, 'What on earth are they talking about?' And most of them are nonrunners. Because I think, I mean, you know that running is an incredibly natural human thing. Just watch a good runner go by you on the street. Or when you're running yourself, and it feels so good, and it's an amazing, beautiful motion, and we're so well adapted to it. And yet most people in the study of evolution think of humans as walkers. And they think that running is just fast walking, which is completely nonsense."

The paper in *Nature*—the paper heard round the world—gave running a crucial role in human evolution. It postulated that, while the species does not produce sprinters, we are unusually talented endurance runners.

"Judged by several criteria, humans perform remarkably well at endurance running [ER], thanks to a diverse array of features, many of which leave traces in the skeleton," the paper stated. "The fossil evidence of these features suggests that endurance running is a derived capability of the genus *Homo*, originating 2 million years ago, and may have been instrumental in the evolution of the human body form."

Dr. Lieberman and Dr. Bramble found that "No primates other than humans are capable of ER. . . .

"In contrast to apes, human legs have many long springlike tendons connected to short muscle fascicles that can generate force economically," the paper reports. These are estimated to save approximately 50 percent of the metabolic cost of running. The most important of these springs is the Achilles tendon. The arch also acts as a spring.

"There's all sorts of tendons in there that we have that chimps don't have," Dr. Lieberman told me. "And that is proof positive for selection for running. There's no other explanation."

And, of course, there's the aforementioned nuchal ligament that keeps the jogger's head from flopping around like the head on a pig.

"Running made us human, at least in an anatomical sense," Dr. Bramble told the *New York Times*. "The hypothesis that ER evolved in *Homo* for scavenging or even hunting therefore suggests," the paper said, "that ER maybe made possible a diet rich in fats and proteins thought to account for the unique human combination of large bodies, small guts, big brains, and small teeth. Today, ER is primarily a form of exercise and recreation, but its roots may be as ancient as the origin of the human genus, and its demands a major contributing factor to the human body form."

In *The Old Way: A Story of the First People*, Elizabeth Marshall Thomas observes that "we seldom think of 'early man' as running after animals. Some of the textbooks show our stereotype—a big muscle-bound guy in a leopard skin, standing with his knees bent, wielding a club or a spear. That, to us, is early hunting. Yet several important truths support the probability that we became big-game hunters by chasing animals, our potential victims getting larger as we modified our bodies for speed."

In some cases, the animals were speared, or shot with arrows, but this was not always necessary. Often the prey overheated. In other cases, chase myopathy did the job: They just freaked out and died at the end of a long pursuit.

While many suspect our ancestors also ran from predators, Elizabeth Marshall Thomas judges the theory "hardly worth the trouble to refute." If this had been the case, she says, then we would have evolved into creatures fast enough to outrun the cats. The fastest man goes approximately 18 miles an hour, whereas the cheetah goes 46. Now maybe the fastest man could fight a cheetah with a stick, but the lion goes 35 miles an hour. Figure you'll stay up north? The grizzly can reach a speed of 35 miles an hour. Dashing away wasn't just cowardly, it was futile. And so, part of the joy of the run may come from its history as a hunt. And there's some feeling that we ran in groups, maybe with dogs. We've been running for at least a million years. And when we ran, we chased. We were not being chased. Which helps explain why the questions, "Do you want to go for a run?" or "Can we get a run in?" are freighted with gleeful anticipation.

In prehistory, hunger was not an annoyance, but a warning light. People didn't get peckish before dinner—they starved to death. "Let's all go for a run," translated roughly as "Let's eat." Or try to.

CHAPTER 4

Welcome to the Club

" . . . OF ALL THE GIFTS THAT RUNNING
HAS BROUGHT ME—AND THERE HAVE BEEN
WAY TOO MANY TO LIST—THE GREATEST GIFT
BY FAR IS THE ABILITY TO CONNECT WITH PEOPLE
ON A PROFOUNDLY PERSONAL LEVEL."
—JOHN "THE PENGUIN" BINGHAM [1]

At first an ordeal and then an accomplishment, the daily run becomes a staple, like bread, or wine, a fine marriage, or air. It is also a free pass to friendship.

When I met Ray Bonner in Manhattan in the early 1980s, he was the guy who had gone to El Salvador and reported on the fighting for the *New York Times*. His dispatches infuriated both the Reagan administration and the administration it supported in El Salvador. His allegations of the El Mozote

16

massacre, while denied at the time, have since been verified. Ray was widely admired by the journalists *I* knew.

I was then an editor at the *Reader's Digest* and therefore not widely admired by the journalists I knew. But Ray and I were both runners. And so we ran together. When I met Ray on the sidewalks of Riverside Drive, I could spot him from a great distance because he's the sort of runner who bounces.

Ray had a tradition of running through Harlem early on New Year's Day. Once we came by three large men reclining on the sidewalk, and while I won't be held to the exact words, I have got the tone right. One of them said, "Better go fast, because we're three bad niggers."

If you feel like it, you run. If you don't feel like it, you run. If it's raining, you run. If it's snowing, you run. If it's Baghdad, you run.

Ray ran in El Salvador with a T-shirt that read "*El periodista, no dispara.*" Journalist, don't shoot.

"I pull on my extralong shorts," wrote *New York Times* correspondent Dexter Filkins in *Runner's World* in October 2006, "tie up my New Balance 991s, run past the barricades and blast walls that surround the compound where I live, and slip into Baghdad's anarchic streets."

Soldiers in Germany and Iraq told me they hoped always for a forward operating base large enough so that they could get in a decent run. Lieutenant Colonel Tom Graves remembered a 3-mile perimeter. "I even went for a 10-mile run once," he told me. "Felt like I was getting dizzy."

This compulsion brings with it membership in a huge and varied brotherhood, one that has members all over this country and also the world. Jogging on the shores of the Black Sea in Varna in Bulgaria, I passed another runner. I didn't speak his language. He didn't speak mine.

"Paavo Nurmi," I called out.

"Paavo Nurmi," he called back.

The process makes a wide variety of people palatable to each other. This seems to be true of all serious endeavors. The 2006 documentary *Wordplay* showed the pleasure crossword puzzle fanatics take in one another.[2]

But movement makes animals—and we are animals—less self-conscious. And running is the most absorbing sort of movement available without training. Although all sports present a neutral platform on which individuals can meet. I have wondered if there are limits to sport-induced empathy.

When a friend told me that he was playing golf with a business associate known to be a crashing bore, I said I'd rather have my toenails pulled than to spend time with said individual and not for pay.

"It's golf," he said. "I'd play golf with Adolf Hitler."

Which made me wonder, of course, would I play golf with the Führer? During the First World War, "runner" was Hitler's job and title.

"Hitler was not a runner in the sense we now think of the word," according to historian Robert Cowley. "In the days before walkie-talkies and portable radios, runners carried messages back to regimental head-quarters. They usually worked in pairs, in case one was taken out by a bullet or shell burst. Casualties were high. Before an action, Hitler would pore over trench maps, trying to figure the best way back. Then he would crouch, run, crawl, and wallow through the shell-torn landscape. He was lucky; he was also careful. Alas for the world, he survived."

Despite Hitler's title, I like most runners. "Of course you love each other," a friend once told me. "You're all high as kites." I suppose the much-ballyhooed and debated endorphins have to be factored in. Like addicts, we were a self-isolating minority that was alternately puffed and slandered. But we appreciated one another in a way drunks and addicts are less apt to do. The club was open to everyone but required a long and often tiresome apprenticeship. We shared a willingness to appear ridiculous and to pass through pain in search of ancient joys.

CHAPTER 5

Are We Designed for It?

"WE FORGET OUR BODIES TO THE BENEFIT
OF MECHANICAL LEISURE. WE ACT CONTINUOUSLY
WITH OUR BRAIN, BUT WE NO LONGER USE OUR BODIES,
OUR LIMBS. IT IS THE AFRICANS WHO POSSESS
THIS VITALITY, THIS MUSCULAR YOUTH, THIS THIRST
FOR PHYSICAL ACTION, WHICH WE ARE LACKING.
WE HAVE A MAGNIFICENT MOTOR AT OUR DISPOSAL,
BUT WE NO LONGER KNOW HOW TO USE IT."

—EMIL ZATOPEK, FOUR-TIME OLYMPIC GOLD MEDALIST
FROM CZECHOSLOVAKIA

When adults tell me they ran once and didn't like it, I ask them if they ran far enough or—and this is more important—if they ran slowly enough.

During the first great running boom of the late 1970s, a friend tried jogging. Bob Seltzer looked at the clock in his apartment building, waited for the elevator, rode it down to the lobby, and walked out onto the street. Once on pavement, he took off. I don't know for sure, but I'm guessing he ran the way a child does—full out. He ran until he was exhausted, walked disconsolately back to the apartment building, waited for the elevator, rode it up to his floor, and reentered his apartment. He looked at his clock. Twelve minutes had elapsed.

The first time I tasted malt liquor, I slurped the foam off the top of a legal friend's can of Colt 45. I had less than half an ounce of the brew. "It's bitter," I said, "and does nothing for me." Whereas, if I'd emptied the 16-ounce can, I might have understood what all the hoopla was about.

Dash around a track once after years of not running, and you could hurt yourself. Even if you don't hurt yourself, you'll be tired out before you have any fun.

Run for a while, and slowly enough to talk. Don't worry how slowly. Keep it up, and you'll begin to understand. You may even feel as if you've done something natural.

That's what I say, and yet the flu is passed around much more easily than is the running bug.

Running is stressful, and for most contemporary Americans, it isn't strictly necessary. It doesn't take great ingenuity to dodge athletic requirements. By the time you're in high school, physical fitness—never central—drops from the curriculum altogether. "Never run for a bus," advises Mel Brooks in *The 2,000-Year-Old Man*. "There will always be another."

In our imaginative life, in movies and TV shows, being fast on your feet can be crucial, but this is fiction. These are characters who live in stories. If actors and actresses didn't run quickly, many films would be 15 minutes long. The first assassin would outrun Tom Cruise, garrotte the star, and end the movie before some folks bought their popcorn and found their seats. There would be few happy endings. But few of us ever need to run for our lives.

So why do joggers feel their hobby is both essential and natural? Lord knows it doesn't look natural. Some runners are graceful and swift. Most runners are neither graceful nor are they swift.

It used to be that the more runners there are, the slower they got. Of the 395,000 Americans who completed marathons in 2005, according to Running USA, 59 percent were men and 41 percent, women. Median times for the men in 1980 were 3:32:17. For the women, they were 4:03:39. Median times for the men in 2005 were 4:20:29. For the women, they were 4:51:19. But in 2006, 410,000 Americans are estimated to have finished marathons, and the median time for men was 4:15:34, and the woman had 4:46:40. So marathon times are getting slightly faster again. But still, we're not most of us fast. Nor are most of us even marathoners.

I see them dodging broken beer bottles in the break-down lane of our highways. It doesn't look like they're having fun. On a hot enough day, they look as if they've just stepped out of a canvas by Hieronymus Bosch.

It's easy to imagine the nagging wife, or the scornful husband, behind this exercise in futility. Isn't that fat, slow man you drove past this morning courting the very heart attack he dreads?

Roads are not put in for running. If you want to get from point A to point B, I've got two words for you—*internal combustion*. Not that getting from A to B comes up, because runners rarely do get places. We go in circles. Not even lemmings go in circles. For most animals, running in circles means a spinal injury.

I ran for years with a Labrador retriever. Miranda would leap up and down and literally yelp with anticipation when she saw me pull my shorts on. But even my dog had her limits.

I had a 45-minute course I'd mapped out in the park. And if—as sometimes happened—I'd get ahead of schedule and have a few extra minutes, I'd spend these circling a clearing near my house. After the first circuit, the Labrador would plunk down on her hindquarters and refuse to move. Frantic not to lose a second of running time, I'd unleash her—breaking the law—and dash off. She'd sit perfectly still and watch the moron who dispensed the Milk-Bones. *He's going nowhere,* she'd think. *I'm a dog, but even I can see that he's going nowhere.*

And why do I insist on running? Why not use that opposable thumb the species is famous for? The fat gray squirrels in the backyard are much faster than I am.

Running is acceptable these days, but then this is not exactly comforting. If smoking were fashionable—and it once was—that, too, would be encouraged. Nonrunners have trouble containing their curiosity. "It looks *so* boring," they say. "Like a hamster in a wheel."

My own beloved father gave as an assignment in a writing class: the thoughts a runner might have over a mile. One pupil handed in a page with "One two three four. One two three four. One two three four," written over and over again. And when Pop told me the story, he was gleeful about it.

People tell me, "I'd rather just eat less." I've been asked—and more than once—why I don't simply hit myself in the forehead repeatedly with a hammer. "When you stop, it'll feel great. Be easier on your knees."

Nor has science always supported the contention that running is natural for *Homo sapiens.* Running is natural for horses, greyhounds, even deer, but for men? Not all of nature runs. Mushrooms, for instance, don't run. You almost never see a snail registering for a 10-K. Is this passion for running another of mankind's many and wrong-headed attempts to reject or alter the basic precepts of his physical self? I think of corsets, high collars, of bound breasts, bound feet, and the dearth of urinals in Manhattan.

I understand people who don't want to "give up the time."

But then it seems to me that we've already made substantial sacrifices.

Our closest living relative is the chimpanzee. Chimps walk and can even stand up, but a chimp can also use his feet to open a jar of peanut butter.

Running might well have forced the transformation of our lower hands into feet. If so, we gave up a pair of hands in order to run. It would have been possible for us to walk and have two pairs of hands. The orangutan walks and has four hands.

Awkward as we may feel starting out, the experience of the long, slow run goes back and back into the mists of time. We sense this. It's built into our tendons and muscles.

"My suspicion is that the effects of running are not extraordinary at all, but quite ordinary," wrote Jim Fixx at the close of *The Complete Book of Running*. "It is the other states, all other feelings, that are peculiar, for they are an abnegation of the way you and I are intended to feel. As runners, I think, we reach directly back along the endless chain of history."

In *Racing the Antelope: What Animals Can Teach Us about Running and Life*, Bernd Heinrich quotes from Fixx and then tells of looking under a small rock overhang in Matobo National Park in Zimbabwe. There, he discovers a pictograph—maybe 3,000 years old—of runners with bows and arrows. The lead runner has flung his arms and hands up into the air.[1] It's as if he were Steve Prefontaine just about to take his victory lap.

CHAPTER 6

Running in Ancient History

> "... THE PRIZE WAS NO MERE BEAST FOR SACRIFICE
> OR BULLOCK'S HIDE, AS IT MIGHT BE FOR ·
> A COMMON FOOT-RACE, BUT THEY RAN
> FOR THE LIFE OF HECTOR."
>
> —HOMER, *THE ILIAD*, BOOK XXII, SAMUEL BUTLER TRANSLATION

Civilization emerged 40 centuries ago in and near the suggestively titled "Fertile Crescent." Men and women with their dogs settled in numbers, planted wheat, and raised goats. Ancient human bones and ruins have been disinterred in Egypt and a place the Greeks called Mesopotamia, "Land Between Rivers." We were running there then; we are running there now.

In 2005, I ran on the streets of Camp Victory in Baghdad with Navy Commander Matt Simms. Simms had just won a marathon held for the US

Armed Services in Ur. Ur was once a great city of Mesopotamia. Two thousand years ago, King Shulgi of Ur was a runner, too, supposed to have been blindingly fast. It is written that he could catch a gazelle on foot and ran 200 miles during a hailstorm. The king's speed was taken as one proof of his divinity.[1]

The Pharaohs ran as part of the Heb-Sed festival. There are many representations of Egyptian kings running as a demonstration of their fitness to rule. The funeral complex of King Djoser, also in Egypt, includes a ceremonial running course.

And so while agriculture and the domestication of animals may have rendered long-run hunts less important, people still ran to get from one place to another, but they also ran to show off.[2]

Even in ancient times, some thought running might also contribute to fitness. Hippocrates, the father of medicine (460–377 BC), recommended "sharp runs so that the body may be emptied of moisture." He also suggested "running in a cloak," to increase body heat.[3]

Homer—if he existed—was one of the first great poets, and there's plenty of running in Homer.

Hector lost one of the first races in literature.

Achilles, "the fleet-footed Achilles," had been sulking in his tent, letting the Trojans win battles. Hence the origin of the phrase, "he's been sulking in his tent."

Finally, Achilles' great good friend Patroclus put on the hero's distinctive armor and led the Greeks into battle. He did splendidly at first, turning the tide. Then Patroclus ran into Troy's great champion, Hector. Hector slew Patroclus and took the armor for himself. Big mistake! Achilles adored Patroclus. The warriors were cousins and friends, and some people think they were lovers, while others do not.

Either way, Achilles was infuriated. He came out of his tent and slew great heaps of Trojans. But who he really wanted to slay was Hector. The "rabble of routed Trojans was thankful to crowd within the city till their numbers thronged it." Brave Hector remained outside. "'Hector, my son, stay not to face this man alone and unsupported, or you will meet death,' Priam cried."[4]

Achilles, a "plumed lord of battle," strode up to Hector. And Hector ran away.

There's some speculation that Hector ran only because Homer enjoyed a good foot race and wanted to illustrate exactly how fast these two men were. Hector wasn't the sort to run from a fight, or never had been.

Both men dashed off. The walls of Troy are thought to have been about a half mile around. Achilles warned the other Greeks not to hurt the fleeing Hector. He said the equivalent of "Leave him alone. He's mine."

"On they flew along the wagon-road that ran hard by under the wall, past the lookout station, and past the weather-beaten wild fig-tree, till they came to two fair springs which feed the river Scamander. . . . and swiftly indeed did they run, for the prize was no mere beast for sacrifice or bullock's hide, as it might be for a common foot-race, but they ran for the life of Hector."

Three times they ran around the city, and then Hector stood to fight. He lost, of course. Everybody lost to Achilles. Achilles knew the armor, he knew the place where Hector's neck was exposed. So he speared Troy's great champion through the fleshy part of the neck.

Mortally wounded, Hector begged Achilles to sell his corpse back to his—Hector's—family, so that they could burn it properly, and give him the coins he'd need to pay the boatman Charon so that he could cross the river Styx into Hades. Achilles thought not.

"Your mother shall never lay you out and make lament over the son she bore, but dogs and vultures shall eat you utterly up," he said.

Hector's father made piteous moan, and throughout the city, the people fell to weeping and wailing. Then Achilles tied Hector's dead body to a chariot and dragged it back and forth before the walls of the city.

And you have to think that if Hector had known this was going to happen, he might have lost those last 5 pounds, taken the necessary days off, and done his interval work.

Remembering, of course, that Hector didn't start the war. It was his feckless brother, Paris, who stole Helen from her husband, and even the captive Helen liked Hector. So it's a bad world. But in this bad world, it's often useful to be fast on your feet.

Back in camp, Achilles held funeral games to honor his dead friend Patroclus. The festivities included a foot race. "Forthwith uprose fleet Ajax, son of Oileus, with cunning Ulysses, and Nestor's son Antilochus, the fastest runner among all the youth of his time. They stood side by side, and Achilles showed them the goal. The course was set out for them from the starting-post, and the son of Oileus took the lead at once, with Ulysses as close behind him as the shuttle is to a woman's bosom when she throws the woof across the warp and holds it close up to her; even so close behind him was Ulysses treading in his footprints before the dust could settle here, and Ajax could feel his breath on the back of his head as he ran swiftly on." Ulysses prayed to Minerva, and "she made his hands and his feet feel light." Which might have been enough, but then Athena also had Ajax slip in the offal left by the cattle that Achilles had slaughtered. "Ulysses therefore carried off the mixing-bowl, for he got before Ajax and came in first."

Ulysses (a.k.a. Odysseus) had won his wife, Penelope, in another race, although he was more cunning than he was fast. He was the man who thought up the Trojan Horse. And wits still win races. The best runners know exactly how fast and how long they can kick at the end and time their move to the microsecond.

Like Hector, the mythological Actaeon couldn't run quite fast enough. A hunter, he came upon the goddess Diana bathing in the woods. He saw her naked, and she saw that he had seen her naked. She transformed him into a stag and took away the power of speech. Then his scent—which I guess she'd changed as well—was picked up by his own pack of hounds. Actaeon ran for his life, but not fast enough. The hounds caught him up and tore their master to shreds.

If you have a dog and if that dog has ever had "an accident" on a good rug, then you can imagine how remorseful these dogs all were. And when a statue was made of their unfortunate master, they fawned at its feet.

If the ancient men ran, then so did ancient women. Atalanta was left to die in the forest by a cruel father who had wanted a son. The babe was suckled by a bear. A hunter saw her racing through the wilderness and was astonished by her beauty and speed. He caught her in a snare. Adopted by the kind hunter, Atalanta grew into a fierce huntress, but the first man that she fell in love with was killed. She then went back to her biological father, who now wanted her to marry. Thinking that this would be a betrayal of her first love, Atalanta agreed to marry any man who could beat her in a foot race. But if a suitor lost the race, he'd lose his life as well.

Since men were not any smarter then than they are now, a lot of them accepted this challenge. And many died. In a case like this, running your own best race just isn't enough.

Finally Atalanta was approached by Melanion. Atalanta liked the way Melanion looked. She begged him not to race her. But Melanion would not be deterred. He prayed to Aphrodite for help. The goddess gave him three golden apples, which some people think were actually quinces. So when Atalanta got ahead of him, he'd throw one of the apples way off the track. Atalanta couldn't resist a golden apple, so each time, she left the track and went and picked the apple up. Melanion won the race, and they were married, happily married. Then they made love in one of Zeus's temples, and he turned them into a pair of lions. At the time of the story, it was thought that lions could not mate with lions, but only with leopards, and so it was assumed that this was the end of the affair. (Atlanta, Georgia, is named after a woman—the daughter of a governor of Georgia—whose middle name was that of the huntress and runner.)

Mythological women often ran from gods who wanted to rape them.

The nymph Syrinx was a great beauty, and ran away from the god Pan, whom she considered ugly. Syrinx wasn't fast enough and so had to transform herself into a reed in order to escape his advances. The wind through the reeds made a mournful sound. Pan then picked 10 reeds to make himself a flute.

Apollo, the god of light and music, tried to chase down a nymph named Daphne. She wasn't fast enough either, but by the time Apollo caught his prey, Daphne's father—a river god to whom she'd begged for help—had turned her into a tree. Apollo found himself embracing a laurel tree. So then he made a wreath of some twigs from the laurel, and wore it himself, which is why the winners of races are given laurel wreaths today.

The fifth labor of the mythological strongman Hercules was to clean the stables of King Augeas, who ruled in Olympia. The stables were impossibly dirty, but Hercules rerouted two rivers to wash away the filth. Augeas refused to pay for the work. Hercules sacked the city and subsequently began the Olympic Games to honor his father, Zeus.

Another version of the story has Hercules winning a race at Olympia and then deciding that the contest should be held again every 4 years. Still another version has it that the games were started by Zeus to celebrate the defeat of his father, the Titan Cronus.[5]

Held first at Olympia, the gathering moved to other cities, including Corinth and Delphi, before finally settling back at Olympia. The races took place on the grounds of a sanctuary for the gods, which included—among other attractions—a gold and ivory statue of Zeus that was almost 40 feet high. This statue was one of the seven wonders of the ancient world. The festival grew to be so regular that the term *Olympiad* came to mean a period of 4 years.

While the Olympics may have started as early as 1370 BC, the earliest records date back to 776 BC.[6] Winning was considered an act of worship. The effort was thought to appease the gods and also the dead.

The games were said to have been held at the full moon. The athletes came from city-states, often city-states that were at war with one another. While the Olympics allowed rogue nations to come together in peace, the athletic events themselves were understood to be grueling in the extreme.

"The Term 'Olympic Games' is a bad mistranslation of Greek *Olympiakoi agones*," writes David C. Young in *A Brief History of the Olympic Games*.[7] This is because our understanding of the Greek term has been filtered through Latin, and the Romans "did not take Greek Athletes seriously. But the Greek word *agones* can never refer to 'games.' Rather, it means 'struggles' or 'contests' or even 'pains.' Our word 'agony' derives from it."

The central—and at first the only—event was a foot race. This was called the *stadion*, or stade race, and it was the length of the stadion where it was held. At Olympia, this was 600 feet. Then the *diaulos,* or two-stade race, was introduced. This was an out-and-back. Ultimately, events over distances of approximately 3 miles were included.

Opinion is much divided about the distance of the longest foot race, writes Charles Russell in his 1873 book, *Wonders of Bodily Strength and Skill in All Ages and All Countries*.[8] "According to some, it was seven courses of the stadium; to others it was 20 courses, which is difficult to believe.

"This last feat too frequently repeated resulted in the loss of life, as in the case of Ladas of Lacedaemonia [Sparta], who fell dead on arriving at the goal, after having run the *dolichos,* Russell wrote.

So apparently, it was assumed in 1873, if not in ancient times, that fast running over too great a distance would be fatal.

Among the running events was the *hoplite* or "armed" race. In this contest, the competitors wore a helmet and carried a shield.

Ordinarily, the athletes ran naked except for those who wore the *kynodesme* (literally a dog leash). The word is hard to say, and the getup is ghastly to imagine. It was a leather strip tied around the foreskin and attached to a waistband. Presumably, this was to keep the penis from flopping around. In ancient times, athletes seem to have been drawn to nudity. In fact, the word *gymnasium* derives from the Greek word *gumnzein*—exercise naked.

The vase on the cover of this book is a replica—slightly altered—of a vase representing Olympic athletes thought to have been made during the 6th century BC.

We associate the ancient Greeks with democracy, but athletes had to be free men. Most sources indicate that women were not allowed to compete, and some report that while virgins could watch, a married woman caught at the games would be thrown from the cliffs of Mount Typaion.

Although—as the event grew in popularity—a women's athletic competition was initiated and actually held in the Olympic stadium. The runners wore tunics that went down almost to the knee. The right shoulder was bared.

In his history *All That Glitters Is Not Gold: An Irreverent Look at the Olympic Games*, William O. Johnson Jr. argues that we have sanitized and elevated the whole affair well beyond the rather grisly reality. A rule against finger breaking during wrestling matches was largely ignored. One champion won all his matches by breaking all the fingers of his opponents. The boxing was brutal and often fatal. The Pankration, a popular hybrid of wrestling and boxing, prohibited only gouging and biting.

When Rome conquered Greece in 146 BC, the festivities lost momentum, although Nero showed up in AD 66 with 5,000 bodyguards. Having traveled to Olympia in an attempt to improve relations with the colony, the emperor couldn't resist entering himself in multiple events. And (surprise! surprise!) he won them all. He was judged the best musician and the best singer. His 10-horse chariot was declared winner of the race he entered despite his having fallen out and very nearly killed himself in the accident.

Because of their pagan origins, the great contests—which had run for more than 1,000 years without interruption—were finally banned by the now strictly Christian Roman empire. Archeologists had concluded that the last event was staged in AD 393. Now it looks as if some sort of competition might have continued in some form for hundreds of years after that.

There were no testosterone patches, there was no blood doping, but the ancients did what they could.

"The racers of antiquity who purposed competing at the Olympic games," wrote Charles Russell, "were extremely careful that nothing should interfere with the rapidity of their pace; and with this object, they paid special attention to the condition of their spleen, believing that the unhealthy condition of that organ renders the whole body heavy and the breath short."

Some tried to shrink or to dissolve the tiresome organ with nostrums. Russell reports that "Pliny speaks of a plant *equisetum,* a decoction of which the runners drank for three consecutive days, and after having been without food for twenty-four hours...."

It was long believed that hostilities between Greek states were suspended every 4 years. This was not so, although soldiers were given time off to compete, and the warring nations agreed to grant safe passage to and from Olympia. Looking back through the filter of centuries, it is easy to imagine splendid athletes and extraordinary sportsmanship.

William O. Johnson discounts this sunny view, pointing out that you had to be rich to compete. "The truth is the athletes of ancient Greece were a pampered class, a corps of swaggering narcissists ..."

Winning was everything, Johnson reports, quoting the Greek poet Pindar who wrote, "Losers were lepers. They slink away, sore smitten by misfortune nor does any sweet smile grace their return."

"Xenophanes complained that the culture of Greece reached a point where people praised a wrestler's strength over a philosopher's wisdom." [9]

Can you imagine that?

CHAPTER 7

You Don't Need a Coach

"MAYBE I'VE BEEN WRONG ABOUT YOUNG CHEEVER."
—COACH

"Lot of smoke, no fire, Cheever." That's what the wrestling coach used to shout when I was groaning noisily in an attempt to escape from the opponent who was powering me around the mat. This was in high school, and it's when I first learned that time stops if you're anxious enough and in pain. I could look up at the clock three times during a 45-second drill.

I was supposed to escape, but I was supposed to escape carefully. It was also possible—all during a 45-second eternity—that I'd be flipped like a tortoise and pinned. (If you've never been pinned, never heard the slap, slap, slap of the ref's hand on the mat, then you can look it up in the dictionary under "M" for mortification.)

So I struggled cautiously, and when I moved, I groaned. Apparently, my groans were more convincing than my struggles were: hence the coach's comments. And yet I liked the wrestling coach. I went out for wrestling. I made it onto the wrestling team. Most sports I didn't go out for. Most coaches I didn't like.

I can still summon their hoarse masculine voices today: "Heads up, Cheever! Step into the batting box. I said *into the batting box*. Keep your eye on the pill, son. Dig it out. Hustle! Hustle! Hustle!"

There are men who had their lives saved by the attentions of a rough-hewn coach. Not me. I know boys who, when they came home from college or Vietnam, they'd stop for pie and coffee with Coach, before they stopped for pie and coffee with Ma. Not me.

I've said I hated coaches. And they hated me right back.

I thought them heartless. They thought I didn't have any heart.

It's common for runners to have failed at other sports. They're often slight, and sometimes not coordinated either.

"Remember when we were growing up, you used to read the comic books with the 98-pound weakling?" said Allan Steinfeld, the former director of the New York City Marathon. "That was me. Because I had no self-image, other than being a bright person."

Throw a ball at Allan Steinfeld, and it would bounce off his chest. Same with me. Only I wasn't thought bright either. Nor was I much of a runner.

And I hit the playing fields in the era when coaches—until then perfect autocrats—were first compelled by social mores to give every boy a chance. I was a boy, but I was not an asset.

I began my athletic career at Scarborough Country Day School in Scarborough, New York. This institution, since defunct, was built by Frank A. Vanderlip, a business titan who wanted his children to be able to go to school without having to leave the property. The campus was life-sized, but somehow also miniature. We had an auditorium modeled after the Little Theater in London. The inscriptions above its two doorways were: "Life Is for Service" and "Manners Maketh Man."

The school song included the lines: "Fight oh fight for Scarborough/ Fight with pep and vim." Vim was meant to rhyme with "win." We almost never von.

I'm not sure today if the school was small because it was elite, or if it was small because so few people wanted to go there. There were, just for instance, six of us in the sixth grade: Amy Ingersoll. Hammy Holmes. Joey Kahn. Cindy Brieant. Nichole Riche. That's five. And me. I think Norah Toohey didn't come until the seventh grade. With a student body so limited, every pupil was expected to play.

Poor Coach. I was fat, I was slow, I was uncoordinated, but it was worse than that. I was easily frightened.

Take baseball, for instance, the national pastime. There's a reason they call it hardball. The ball, or pill, it's hard. Like a stone. I didn't want to be hit by one of those. I'd as soon have jumped into a wading pool full of hammerhead sharks as to step into the batter's box. I was supposed to stand there, all tender parts exposed, while another boy hurled stones down at me from a hill or mound.

If I'd had any chance of hitting the wretched thing, I might have mustered a little courage. There was no chance. Legendary Red Sox slugger Ted Williams is supposed to have been able to see the stitching on a ball screaming across the plate. I rarely saw the ball at all. I wasn't even certain it had been thrown, until I heard it thunk into the catcher's mitt. The best I could do for my team was to get beaned and walk to first.

I have learned only recently that I have trouble with my binocular vision, which means that one eye prefers to look off to the side, as if somebody might be gaining on me. I can make both eyes work, but it's an effort. So when I need to look hard at something for any period of time, I just let the left eye peer off into the inside of my skull, while the strong one does the work. One-eyed people aren't frightfully good at judging distance.

I was at the bottom of the batting roster, and so my humiliations were brief and far between.

When the other team was up, the coach would send me deep into the outfield. Emboldened by distance and isolation, in remotest left field, I found myself wanting to play. Now that I was safely out of the action, I wanted to make a difference. I yearned to hustle. But man is—above all else—an adaptive creature. So I adapted. There was nothing for me to do. So I did nothing. I'd put my mitt over my face and look at the world through the V of the glove. I liked the cool leather on my cheeks. I liked the smell of neat's-foot oil. I'd dream. I'd breathe deeply. In...out. In...out. The Zen of baseball.

I might have settled to the ground and taken a nap, but this was frowned upon. I also learned that it was not considered cricket, or baseball, to turn around and look off into the woods. For reasons that mostly escaped me, I was supposed to face home plate.

Bored almost into a coma, I'd squint through the glove at the other players. I'd watch their distant dramas with admirable detachment. *Why are they so excited now?* I'd wonder. *I didn't know there was another Cheever on the team. Why is everyone rushing toward me? Why are their faces crimson? Why are they waving their arms in the air?*

In the eighth grade, I ran the 880 for Scarborough. We had a meet with Peekskill Military Academy. They had a 220-yard track.

When my race started, the coach wasn't there. Now it happened that three of the runners from PMA were substantially faster than I was. Yet at one stage late in the race, we were neck and neck. What my late-arriving coach didn't realize was that for the runners from PMA, this was the fourth and final lap. For me, it was the third.

Coach and a knot of others appeared just as the race became a duel. The four of us were thundering around that final curve. "Hustle!" he shouted. "Hustle, Cheever. Dig it out."

In his hoarse cry, I could hear Coach thinking, *What do you know? Maybe I've been wrong about young Cheever.*

Then we all crossed the finish. The PMA runners staggered off the course. I made the turn and headed manfully off for my final lap.

Coaches are supposed to have small and weathered hearts, something on the order of a horse chestnut. But this is the sort of performance that breaks even a chestnut heart.

My sporting achievements couldn't have been much good for my father's vitals either. The man wanted an athlete as a son.

No video games in those days. Not much TV either. So I played everything. Baseball, football, kick-the-can, even pin-the-tail-on-the-donkey.

I played everything, and I played everything woefully.

"Want to go out and toss a ball?" my father would ask me. I guess he hoped that I could be taught.

"Sure."

We'd go outside. He'd throw the ball at me. I'd drop it.

"I'm sorry," I'd say and pick the ball up and throw it back.

He'd throw the ball again. Again I'd fail to make the catch. "Sorry," I'd say and throw it back.

"For Christ's sake, stop apologizing," he'd say.

"Okay," I'd say. "I'm sorry."

Freshman year looked like my breakthrough. I made it onto the varsity squad of Scarborough Country Day School's six-man tackle football team.

Steve was first-string center. Steve was not his name. I remember his name. I can still picture the way his belly hung over the canvas belt of his uniform. I remember the way he smelled.

Steve wasn't all that big. Nor was he particularly fast on his feet. Steve had quick hands. The moment the ball was snapped, he'd reach across the line of scrimmage, grab the face guard of the opposing lineman with one hand, and with the other, he'd drive the nose he found there back into the face it belonged to.

This happened in games with other schools. It also happened in scrimmages between the first and second team. I've already told you that Steve was first-string center. I was second-string center.

A cobra is supposed to strike so quickly that it can't be seen by the naked eye. Steve's hands were that fast. I'd spend the rest of the play staggering slowly around in circles while the tears that had obscured my vision ran down my face.

But this was football, varsity football, and I, Ben, was playing.

In his third novel, *Bullet Park*, my father has Tony Nailles threaten to murder a French teacher named Mrs. Hoe when she arranges to have him cut from the football team.

"He [Tony] had not anticipated this staggering injustice. He would not cry but there was a definite disturbance in his eyeducts. She didn't know what she was saying. She knew, poor woman, much less about football than he knew about French. He loved football, loved the maneuvers, the grass work, the fatigue, and loved the ball itself—its shape, color, odor and the way it spiraled into the angle of his elbow and ribcage. He loved the time of year, the bus trips to other schools, he loved sitting on the bench. Football came more naturally to him than anything else at his time of life and how could they take this naturalness away from him and fill up the breach with French verbs?

"'You don't know what you're saying, Miss Hoe.'"

"'I'm afraid I do, Tony. I've not only talked with Mr. Northrup. I've talked with the coach.'"

"'With Coach?'"

"'Yes, with Coach.'"

I didn't like French either. Nor did I want to be cut from the team. But Tony and I had nothing else in common. I lacked his finer sensibility. I had no appreciation of the ball itself, its shape or color.

If there was a shape to my football, it was the pendulous gut of Steve, the first-string center. If there was a color, it was the red I saw after Steve had inserted his little fist into my face mask.

My father was an unusually articulate and forthright man. He used to like to say that he and I operated "on a basis of absolute candor." And there was something to this, although he didn't tell me about his bisexuality.

Nor did I tell him what it was actually like to play second-string for the six-man tackle football team at Scarborough Country Day.

He knew that I—a Freshman—was on the varsity squad. That was all he needed to know. He didn't know, for instance, that I was in the running for the coveted position of "least popular man on the squad."

If it hadn't been for Smalls—not his real name either—I would have won the title. Smalls was fat, of course, and uncoordinated. He was covered with black, oily hair. The starters used to joke that Smalls couldn't smoke cigarettes, because if his eyebrows caught fire, his entire body would burn to the ground.

Smalls was not hated for his faults, but for his virtues. Smalls was punctual. The jocks were inevitably late for practice. They forgot their equipment, they goldbricked through drills, counting two laps around the field as three.

Smalls showed up fully suited, and he showed up early. Smalls hustled. Smalls dug it out. Smalls seemed to believe that—ultimately—attitude was enough.

Coach finally gave a lecture: "Gentlemen," he said. "If Bill Smalls—who hasn't yet been on the field in a game—can make it to practice early, then I don't see why all you glory hounds can't make it to practice on time."

Next day, the starters caught Smalls while he was changing. They stripped him naked, took a locker out of its place against the wall, removed the shelves, and inserted Bill Smalls. The locker fit him like a coffin. Then they closed the door, attached a combination lock, and put the locker back against the wall upside down.

"Where's Bill Smalls?" the coach asked. "I don't know," said Steve. "I guess he's late today."

After practice, Smalls was released. His head was the color of a peeled beet.

Was this the sort of squad that Tony Nailles didn't want to be cut from?

And yet, it was a fine thing to have won my father's approval. Practice wasn't over until after the last bus had left the school. My father ordinarily hated the chauffeuring part of parenting, but after football practice, he was pleased, he was honored to pick me up. On the way home, he'd stop and buy me fresh dinner rolls at the Ossining Italian bakery. He had a phrase, a mantra really, "My son, the football player."

Fortunately, he never went to a game.

I remember him asking me if I had ever caught a pass. I told him no. I hoped he'd think that, as in 11-man football, the center was not eligible to catch a pass.

Fact is, that in six-man tackle, the center could catch a pass. Provided, of course, that he could catch a pass.

During one away game, I was sent out to run a button hook. That play was filmed, and afterward, the whole team got to watch me waddling away from the line of scrimmage, turning uncertainly towards coach, who operated the camera. The football came flying into the picture, struck my chest, and then hit the ground.

CHAPTER 8

My Varsity Football Career on an 11-Man Team: A Short Chapter

"THE RACE IS NOT ALWAYS TO THE SWIFT,
NOR THE BATTLE TO THE STRONG,
BUT THAT'S THE WAY TO BET."
—DAMON RUNYON

My varsity career playing six-man tackle football had lasted 1 year. As a sophomore, I went off to boarding school, and yes, I applied for the football team. Is "applied" the correct word here? I went out for football.

All the varsity and junior varsity football wannabes lined up in front of the cage. (*Cage*, for those of you who have not been—as I have—varsity athletes, is the term used for the room or locker in which sporting equipment is left to gather mold and grow fungi.)

A whistle was blown, and we rushed the cage. We tore off our street clothes and donned equipment. This was social Darwinism at its purest.

The toughest, pushiest boys came up with the best equipment. The shy, uncertain boys made do with what was left.

I managed somehow to secure pants, pads, and a jersey. I was still searching for a helmet when I heard the whistle. We all charged out onto the field. We were divided into squads. We ran simple drills. Then we were lined up to scrimmage.

The coach noticed me.

> Coach: "Yo."
> Me: "Yes."
> Coach: "Where's your hat, son?"
> Me: "My hat?"
> Coach: "You gotta have a hat to play ball."
> Me: "A hat?"
> Coach: "Go back in and get a hat."

Two days later, I was cut.

I was at boarding school, and contact with home was limited to letters and the occasional call made or received on the pay phone at the end of the corridor. I considered withholding the information, but the next time I called in, I blurted out the news. "I didn't make the team."

There was a silence on the other end of the line. The subject never came up again. Ever.

CHAPTER 9

Running in the Middle Ages

> "SEVERAL ITALIAN CITIES HAD FOOT-RACES
> FOR PROSTITUTES."
>
> —EDWARD S. SEARS, *RUNNING THROUGH THE AGES*

The great popularity of jogging in contemporary life throws the past into shadow, but even in the Dark Ages, races illuminated public life. And sponsors in those benighted times worked with a wild abandon not found in our more prosperous and permissive age. The Roman winter carnival—just for instance—featured contests for young men, old men, and prostitutes.

Pope Alexander VI is supposed to have hosted a foot race around Saint Peter's Basilica in Rome in 1501. The competitors were prostitutes. This is reported by Edward S. Sears in his excellent history, *Running Through the Ages*.[1] I couldn't find the story elsewhere, which doesn't make it false.

A foot race for whores within the walls of the Vatican is exactly the sort of event we've come to expect from Pope Alexander. He was a Borgia and reported to have kept a distinctive golden cup for poisoning guests. His illegitimate daughter, the oft-married Lucretzia, was also alleged to have been handy with lethal potions. The family excited the admiration of Niccolo Machiavelli, whose book *The Prince* is still—more than 500 years later—considered the absolute high-water-mark in ruthless cynicism.

Alexander did allow at least one bullfight in the Vatican and staged a party so colorful that when Alexander Gordon wrote of it in his *The Lives of the Popes,*[2] he was forced into Latin, because he couldn't bear to report what had happened in his native tongue. "The First of November, a Day dedicated for celebrating the Solemn festival of all the saints, no less than 50 City Whores were invited to an Entertainment within the Vatican; a most shocking and abominable spectacle! Et ut ad irratandum ..."

Since I can't read Latin, I'll never know what went on. I do know that whores not employed by the Pope ran in more than one Palio.

The Palio takes its name from the prize, which is a piece of fabric, often a banner of silk or velvet. The Palio at Siena, Italy, still held today, is a horse race, but in the Middle Ages, these contests were often foot races.

"Several Italian cities had foot-races for prostitutes," writes Sears. The report is taken from *Palio and Ponte: An Account of the Sports of Central Italy from the Age of Dante to the XXth Century,* by William Heywood:[3]

"The siege of Arezzo, in 1335, was marked by a strange mixture of religion and indecency; for the victorious Perugians not only caused the prostitutes who followed the army to run a palio in a peculiarly shameless way, but actually supplemented the performance with a solemn mass in the captured Cathedral, above which waved the Perugian standard, the red lion of the Party of Guelf on a white field ..."

Heywood also prints a report that in 1363 "the Pisans made an incursion even to the walls of Florence and there they halted and abode three days, doing great damage with many insults. They caused three palii to be run, well nigh to the gates of Florence. One was on horseback, another was on foot, and the third was run by loose women (*le femmine mundane*); ..."

I don't know if prostitutes felt weighted down by their spleens, but men of the Middle Ages were still fixated on the organ. In his *Wonders of Bodily Strength and Skill in All Ages and All Countries,* Charles Russell writes that for those who were not satisfied with herbal drinks, "Surgery offered other means, more efficacious but also more extreme, for the attainment of the athlete's object, viz, the removal of the organ by the knife or by fire.... The celebrated empiric Leonardo Fioravanti is said to have cured a young Greek suffering from tumor of the spleen at Palermo in 1549 by cutting out the organ, which weighed several pounds.

"It is believed," Russell continues, "that those who among the Turks adopt the profession of the couriers are subjected to the fire rather than the knife treatment. Formerly the Grand Turk always maintained eighty or a hundred runners, who were named *peichs* (lackeys or footmen), and who were generally natives of Persia.... The former ran on before their master when he traveled.... All along the road they continually cried, *Allah Deicherin*—'God preserve the Sultan in power and prosperity.'"

According to Russell, "The ancient Turkish couriers always ran with bare feet, which were so hard and destitute of feeling, that they are said to have had themselves shod, like horses, with light iron shoes."

While I've not heard of iron shoes, many aspire to have feet "hard and destitute of feeling." The *Wall Street Journal* published a story in 2006 profiling a San Diego runner named Tsuyoshi Yoshino, who was going barefoot trying to batter his feet up sufficiently so that in the future, he wouldn't need running shoes. And he was having a lot of success, at least in the battering part of the process. While the shoe provides protection and can help compensate for an awkward stride, it also restricts the natural motion of the foot. Some athletes train barefoot on grass. This makes sense to me. The foot evolved to function unshod. Abebe Bikila won the Olympic marathon in 1960 without shoes. The competitors in the ancient Olympics ran barefoot. But then the desire to protect the foot is also ancient. Cave drawings thought to be 15,000 years old picture humans with their feet wrapped in animal skins.

If shoes are unnatural, then so is asphalt and concrete.

CHAPTER 10

All Runners Are Created Equal.
Some Runners Are More Equal
Than Others.

"WE HOLD THESE TRUTHS TO BE SELF-EVIDENT
THAT ALL MEN ARE CREATED EQUAL...."
—THE DECLARATION OF INDEPENDENCE

I like to run. I'd like to win, but I don't win, which puts me in the overwhelming majority. And yet, this is not always understood by civilians. I'd been running a couple of years and was by now off the copy desk, but still a low-level editor at the *Reader's Digest*, when Jack O'Hara, then chairman of the board, appeared in my office. "Are you the hotshot runner?" he asked.

This had never occurred to me. Turned out a friend of O'Hara's who owned a bank was organizing a race and wanted runners. O'Hara handed me a sheaf of applications, grunted, and vanished. Sometimes right after the New York City Marathon, strangers will ask, "Did you win?"

Which makes me *so* tired I want to lie down immediately. It's like the question, "A marathon? How far was it?"

"It was 26.2 miles," I'll say, swallowing the hostility. "A ruler is 12 inches long, and a marathon is 26.2 miles. Not a dance marathon, or the Comrades Ultra, but most marathons are 26.2 miles. And no, I didn't win."

"But you finished?" they say.

"Yes, I finished."

"Well that's a victory," they say, immediately losing interest.

Whereas—like a great many of my peers—I had a particular goal in mind. And while there's no difference in their eyes between a 7-hour marathon and one that takes 3 hours, there's a difference for me. Right about 4 hours.

It's not an either/or situation. Either you win, or you survive. There are a lot of people running out there in the gap between winning and surviving. It's a big step to be on the road at all, a big step and a blessing. But that's not the end of it. You want to improve.

There are plenty of slow people out there running 10-Ks and even marathons. And they don't mind being slow. But neither, I suspect, would they mind getting just a titch faster. Just a titch.

We change, you know, the species over eons, and so do individuals over the course of their lives. Nor is change always accurately anticipated. You can work toward one goal and meet another.

Manned flight was once inconceivable. No, that's not right. We conceived of it. Talked about it. In the same way we talk now about world peace, or a simple cure for all cancers. But most of us had no clear understanding of what might actually happen. In *Out of Africa*, Isak Dinesen tells of coming upon a man who had lived beyond the reach of newspapers. When he asked what had changed in the world at large, they told him that men could fly.

The man wasn't surprised, but had a question: Did men who flew tuck their legs up into their chests like a thrush or trail them behind, the way storks and herons do?

If the foot race is a metaphor for a human life, there are sprints and there are ultras. When he was just a child, Elie Wiesel had to sprint to stay alive. In *Night,* the Nobel laureate runs past the infamous Dr. Mengele, who is taking down the numbers of the concentration camp victims who will be immediately exterminated. Wiesel runs by the doctor, hoping that this demonstration of health will keep Mengele from taking down his number. "I ran without looking back. My head was spinning: You are too skinny ... You are too weak ... You are too skinny, you are good for the ovens ... The race seemed endless; I felt as though I had been running for years...."

When he asked if his number had been taken, a friend said they couldn't have. "You were running too fast."[1]

That's the dash. A lot of us are going to face an ultra. We won't be starved to death, but we may well be coddled into a long, debilitated old age. It's almost as if we mated with those sofas, armchairs, and car seats we spend so much time in. Rudimentary forms of transport seem a hardship. I, too, find myself gazing covetously at parking slots reserved for the disabled. In the past 25 years the number of overweight children and adolescents has increased by 300 percent. Nearly one in five Americans under 18 is overweight.

Former Arkansas governor Mike Huckabee has shed 110 pounds since he began running. As a recovered fatty, he's deadly serious about the nation's epidemic of obesity. "When I hear Washington politicians say we have a health-care crisis," says Huckabee, "I say, 'That's baloney.' We have a health crisis."

The forgiving embrace of the sofa can be deadly, but that's not all of it. We are in peril of being divorced from nature. Which means losing touch with our origins and therefore losing touch with our essential selves.

We can't outwit death. Frailty, however, can be and often is defeated. The sedentary are rendered vital. The sick can and do make astonishing recoveries.

My son John came to watch me run the Mystic Places Marathon in Connecticut in 2000. I had assumed the race would begin and end in Mystic, Connecticut, and John would therefore have museums to go to. At the very least, he could find a coffee shop and plunk down there with his book. The start and finish, though, are in a park, and so he was bored, and cold. I was, of course, delighted to see him at the finish, and he told me how proud he was, but we were both moved beyond our two-man celebration by the runner who had crossed the line at about the same time I did. We could tell from the yells of his personal cheering section that he'd had quadruple bypass surgery less than a year ago.

As a young man, I was horrified to hear a friend from Price Waterhouse say that in his firm, nobody stayed still. It was "up or out" at Price Waterhouse. Such ferocity among accountants seemed unbecoming. Turns out that there's a truth to this that goes well beyond any single corporation's ruthlessness. If you aren't working hard at getting better, you're probably working just as hard at getting worse.

And if we get out of shape, we have more to lose now than ever before, or more time to lose it in. A 1928 government study forecast that the "natural" life span of Americans would ultimately rise to 65 years, according to Gregg Easterbrook in *The Progress Paradox*.[2] Hear that again—the natural life span would rise to 65 years. "When the Social Security system was enacted in 1935," Easterbrook continues, "this estimate was used as the basis for setting federal retirement at sixty-five, lawmakers assuming that Social Security would be economical because most people would die without ever receiving a benefit check."

And so, the bad news of Social Security's funding is the result of some extremely good news—life. More life. Now if this "life" is spent getting fed out of tubes, or trapped in a narrow room while being cared for by strangers, then it's not such a great deal.

If you can travel, read, listen to music, write a memoir, intercede usefully in the life of a younger person, well then, these extra innings are worth playing. When William Maxwell was in his nineties, and his beloved wife, Emmy, died, he decided to die as well. Writer Annabel Davis-Goff convinced him to listen one more time to Tolstoy's *War and Peace,* and yes, she'd picked the volume for its length. Annabel came to Bill's apartment every afternoon to read to him from the novel. I came sometimes to listen. And we were having fun.

Bill had been my father's editor at the *New Yorker*. In his seventies and then in his eighties, he would have me to tea and bear silent witness to a torrent of doubts and fears. One afternoon, I said to Bill, my voice creaking, "I always imagined that some day my father would take me aside and teach me how to write."

Bill paused. He had a magnificent pause. Bill could get more into a pause than I can get into a paragraph. "Well," Bill said, "obviously he has taught you how to write."

Not a font of wisdom? Then you can work happily in your garden, as my mother still does at 89. When—up until a year ago—she lived alone, I used to phone her every evening to make sure she'd gotten safely back inside after feeding the deer. In the heart of summer, this was a problem for me. I like to wake up at dawn. This means I like to go to sleep at dusk. But my mother never came in from working in the garden until it was dark. So I'd have to stay up past my bedtime in order to call my mother in from play.

What was old then is not old now. In the magnificent Katharine Hepburn–Peter O'Toole movie, *The Lion in Winter*, O'Toole plays an old king, and he's 50. His son, Richard, is taunting him, after having been—in fairness to Richard—taunted frightfully himself.

> Richard: "How's your leg today?"
> King Henry: "Better, thank you."
> Richard (with menace): "Your bad back. You're getting old, you'll have me once too often."
> King Henry: "When? I'm fifty now. Good God, boy, I'm the oldest man I know. I've got a decade on the Pope."

Fifty was old. The Lion who was 50 years old was a lion in winter.

"I shall soon have passed my fifty-sixth year," wrote the essayist Michel de Montaigne, "an age which some nations, not without reason, fixed as so proper a limit to life that they allowed no one to exceed it. Yet I still have occasional though uncertain and brief returns to health, so bright that they hardly differ from the sound and painless state of my youth ... I have made up my mind that I can no longer run; it is enough that I can crawl...."[3] He died 3 years later, an extremely old man at 59.

Unlike Montaigne, the odds are that we're going to have a big chunk of time on our hands. The old age that was once a rare blessing will soon be commonplace. There were more than 55,000 centenarians alive in the United States in 2005. I didn't even know what a centenarian was until a month ago. It's somebody who's 100 years old.

We can use that time, or we can let it use us.

Canadian Ed Whitlock ran 2:54:44.9 at the Scotiabank Toronto Waterfront Marathon in 2004. He was 73 years old.[4]

I know this makes me a sourpuss, but I think it's important for midpack runners like myself to assess our talents realistically. Manhattan's Armory at 168th Street has been transformed into a magnificent center for runners of all ages, and also a museum of the sport.

The walls are inscribed with all manner of inspirational quotes, but this is the one that got me:

"Can you become a champion? The short answer is yes. Becoming a champion starts with believing in yourself, knowing what you want to achieve, and being willing to work for it. Being realistic helps, too. It's important to pick the event that's best for you, learn what you need to train for it effectively, get good advice—and go for it! You can be a champion at whatever level you attain."

Sure you can. We're all winners, but we don't all win. Aptitude and interest are expected to be joined at the hip, so it's important here to distinguish between those who find they can run and those who find they can run fast, really fast. Those who find that, can win.

In his 1955 memoir, *The Four-Minute Mile,* Roger Bannister recalls running on the beach as a child. "No longer conscious of my movement I discovered a new unity with nature. I had found a new source of power and beauty, a source I never dreamt existed."

Sounds touchy-feely, but Bannister was not a process man. He was goal oriented. He was studying to be a doctor, while training for the Olympics. He rarely ran for more than 45 minutes a day. He did not indulge in long-slow workouts. He indulged in short, excruciating ones. "When he goes out for a run, he looks like a man going to the electric chair," a friend told Paul O'Neil, who profiled the great English miler for *Sports Illustrated*.

Looking back on races he first began to enter at the age of 11, Bannister writes, "I always finished in the last stages of exhaustion, but I refused to let anyone beat me.... Over the last half-mile there was a steep hill, and I used to make an alarming noise like an hysterical girl sobbing as I gasped for breath. It worried people...."

America's runnerati—and there is such a group—is studded with men and women who are fast and were faster. Most of them have accomplished a solid life's work when not running. But still it turns out that they were fast. One suspects that each and every one of these people had a mother, a father, or lover who feared they would not survive.

"Oh Quenton," Andrea tells Quenton Cassidy in *Once a Runner*, "I wonder sometimes if you know how I really feel about you. How much I'd like for it to work out. If there was only some compromise, some ..."

"Well," he responds, "there you have touched upon something, Andrea, because that's it right there: The thing itself is the absence of compromise. There are no deals available. I wish there was some way to explain that. The thing doesn't dilute." [5]

Frank Shorter won a gold medal in the marathon at the 1972 Munich Olympics. He was the first American to win an Olympic gold medal over that distance in 64 years. This, after the slaughter of the Israeli athletes. This, after it looked as if the games would be cancelled altogether. This, after the schedule was changed. After all of that, Shorter still went out and ran 26.2 miles faster than anybody else could that day. Correction: Who knows how fast another runner might have gone? Shorter ran faster than anybody else did. He's a licensed lawyer. He's written a book. He's kept on running and helped shepherd thousands of others into his sport.

In *Olympic Marathon: A Centennial History of the Games Most Storied Race*, author Charlie Lovett speculates that Shorter might have cut 7 seconds from his time, and broken Abebe Bikila's Olympic record. Lovett wonders if Shorter slowed because he knew the former champion, since crippled in an auto accident, was in a wheelchair in the stands.

There are fat diet doctors. There are bankrupt financial advisers and nutty therapists. Many of those who mean to save the world torture their personal staff. Runners are apt to practice what they preach. They don't just like to talk about running, they like to run.

Roger Robinson is a scholar of Robert Louis Stevenson and emeritus professor at Victoria University of Wellington, New Zealand. He is also a great historian of the sport. Nothing there to imply speed, but it turns out that he's represented England and New Zealand in world championships and had record breaking age-group victories in the Boston and New York Marathons. He's married to Kathrine Switzer.

K. V. Switzer is what she wrote on her application for the Boston Marathon. If you watch marathons on TV, you've probably seen Robinson and/or Switzer at a microphone. In 1967, she became the first woman to run the Boston Marathon with the numbers that mark an official competitor. Roberta Gibb had secretly run the race in 1966. Officials assumed K. V. Switzer was a man. Her iconic act is memorialized in the black-and-white pictures of Boston Athletic Association official Jock Semple—a man in a suit and tie—trying to tear the square of paper off the sweatshirt of a young woman. She has organized and promoted women's running for millions. Lest anyone think she was simply drawn to controversy and the limelight, Switzer went on to win the women's division of the New York Marathon in 1974.

Running with *Daily News* sportswriter Wayne Coffee,[6] I asked once, slightly embarrassed, "Is it hard to draw the line in the sand between god-given talent and effort?"

"Always," Wayne said.

"Impossible?" I asked.

"Impossible," he said.

After his first cross-country race, Amby Burfoot ducked under the bleachers to lose his lunch. His English teacher and cross-country coach, John Kelley, waited until this was over and then told him, "You've got real potential in this sport. If you stick with it, there's no telling how far you might go."

Amby reports that he had finished "ninth or something."

So I wrote and asked: "Was it your style that drew Kelley, or the fact that you'd run hard enough to lose the hot dogs and chocolate milk?"

"To answer your question about the first encounter," Amby wrote in reply, "I imagine that he went up to all my teammates after the race and said more or less the same. He doesn't play favorites; he adores those who are dismal failures. That's another of his wonderful attributes."

Amby won the Boston Marathon in 1968. In 2006, he ran his 44th consecutive Manchester Connecticut Road Race and took the over-60 age category by 20 seconds.

So whether Amby was born fast or not, we'll never know. Although he certainly got fast and has stayed that way. Amby Burfoot is a graceful writer. He's published several books and hundreds of articles and has been executive editor of *Runner's World* since 1985.

Kenny Moore's coverage of running in general and the Olympics in particular for *Sports Illustrated* was elegant and informed. He was there at the creation, training under Oregon's legendary coach Bill Bowerman, the man perhaps most famous for having made the first waffle trainers on his wife's waffle iron. The bottle of flat Coca-Cola with Kenny's number was taken and consumed by Frank Shorter during the Olympic Marathon in Munich. Another runner had taken Frank's. I've heard more than one person say that if life was a biathlon and the two events were prose and running, Kenny Moore would have the gold medal.

Jeff Galloway is known now as the inventor/promoter of the walk-run technique for the marathon. He helped turn the Peachtree Road Race into the biggest event of its kind. He helped John L. Parker sell early copies of his cult classic, *Once a Runner*. (Galloway injured my vanity at the Athens

Marathon, but that's not much of an accomplishment. A headwaiter can do that, and a complicated voice-mail menu throws me into a rage.) Jeff ran 10,000 meters in the 1972 Olympics. He also set an American record for 10 miles.

George Sheehan, the late, beloved *Runner's World* columnist, was a doctor. It meant the world to have a doctor, an actual doctor, in love with running. Many of us kept running against the advice of our doctors. Sheehan was a prose poet, so determined to root out and express the quidity of the human experience that when he was diagnosed with terminal cancer, he was excited about it. He wrote about the process right up to the mouth of the grave. He would have been a phenomenon if he'd been a mediocre runner. He had been a track star at Manhattan College. By the time he started running again, he was 45. He ran in his backyard (26 loops to a mile or eight, depending on your source).[7] Five years later, he ran a 4:47 mile, becoming the first man over 50 ever to break 5 minutes for that distance.

George Hirsch was publisher of *New York Magazine*, *New Times*, and then of *The Runner*. When that magazine merged with *Runner's World* in 1987, he became publisher. A founding sponsor of the New York City Marathon, he is now chairman of the board of the New York Road Runners Club. When he was 60, Hirsch broke 3 hours for the marathon. In 2006 at 70, he ran a 3:31 in Berlin, winning his age category.

When I interviewed Allan Steinfeld in 2004, he had taken Fred Lebow's place as CEO of the New York Road Runners Club and presided over one of the largest and slowest marathons in the history of the world. He was 5 foot 8 and weighed 124 pounds. He felt really good, he told me, at 117 pounds. "I was a sprinter," Steinfeld said. "I ran a quarter-mile leg at the Penn relays. Walking into Franklin Field that day was like going to heaven."

The first time I met Steinfeld was at a press conference, and I was shocked. Since nobody else seemed alarmed, I figured I'd stumbled on an open secret. "Is he sick?" I finally whispered to another member of the press corps. No answer.

First, he was small and light enough so that if he weren't a runner, I would have called him frail. Then his hand had been hurt in an accident. All of which I found disorienting. His eyes undid me. He wore glasses, and he had one eye, a regular eye—it's arctic blue—and then one eye that was all white.

I later learned that he'd lost an eye in an accident as a young man. For a while, he wore a patch, but then began to wear glasses for the good eye. And somebody told him that the patch was fine, and the glasses were fine, but not the patch and glasses together. So he got a glass eye. But, apparently, he's not always careful to make sure it's pointing in the right direction. What Steinfeld suffers from, it developed, is a complete absence of vanity.

Dr. Norbert Sander is the man behind the New Balance Running Center at the old Armory in New York at 168th Street. He took a ruin and turned it into an arena complete with a museum. He was in chinos, a Hermes tie, and dark blue button-down shirt the day he came out of a meeting to say hello. Dr. Sander still runs 40 to 45 miles a week. When I asked him if he ever missed a day, he got that shifty look compulsive runners have and said, "Yes, yes, I'll miss a day sometimes.... Don't like to." Dr. Sander won the New York City Marathon in 1974.

Mary Wittenberg is president and CEO of the New York Road Runners Club. This is her second career. She's a lawyer and had been a partner at her firm. You hear her voice now often at the races the club holds in Central Park. That's two—count them—two daunting careers. But she's also fast, and won the 1987 Marine Corps Marathon and competed in the 1988 US Olympic Team Trials—Women's Marathon.

I can't entirely shake the suspicion that these perpetually young athletes came out of Roswell, New Mexico, 60 years ago, bused in on the same UFO. They all know each other. "See how small a family, incestuous," Steinfeld said, "but a good one." And to a pleasing extent, they stick together.

Take the case of Gary Muhrcke. Muhrcke won the first-ever New York Marathon, which was in 1970, in 2:31:39. The course was run round and round Central Park. One hundred and twenty-seven runners paid a dollar, and 55 finished.

Muhrcke made the front pages in 1978, when he won the race up the 85 flights of the Empire State Building, and it was discovered that he was receiving a tax-free disability pension of $11,822 from the fire department. There were editorials and angry letters, but Muhrcke resurfaced in 1980 operating a running shoe store at 89th and Lexington. When I mentioned the pension to Fred Lebow, then the director of the New York City Marathon, Lebow said that Muhrcke had legitimate back trouble, and that running is not the same as coming down a ladder with a 200-pound man on your back.

The laurel given to the winners of the New York City Marathon is provided by Gary's wife.

These are men and women of national and international reputation. There are also local champions of the sport, cross-country coaches, of course, but others who freelance. It may be wrong to call Mike Barnow a local, but since I live in Westchester County, New York, he's local to me. Mike founded the Westchester Track Club in 1973 and is partners with Andy Kimerling in the Westchester Road Runner, a White Plains store operated by serious runners for serious runners. Mike's great good friend Adrienne Wald is editor of the club newsletter and directs the Westchester Marathon. Mike has coached nine Olympians, but he offers classes where, for a nominal fee—or no fee at all—anybody of any age can consult with an expert. Mike has a distinctive moustache, and I see him in the park on weekends and on Tuesday mornings, usually in a loosely knit group of young men and women who look as if they haven't eaten a good meal in a week. Mike was a star decades ago. He won a 10-mile race once in 55 minutes and clocked a 32-minute 10-K.

I had thought, of course, that I was a runner, never a jogger, mind you. I have finished 40-odd marathons, and I have run almost every day since 1978. But this is a much smaller club than the one I'm in. And even press credentialed, I'm not part of it. These are not my people. They're faster, slimmer, more self-directed and solitary than I will ever be.

My sons complain that when I'm in a bathing suit, they can count my vertebrae, but I don't have the runner's physique. I'm 5 foot 7, and even at 150, I'm more mesomorph (noisy and size medium) than ectomorph (quiet and size small).

At an Indian restaurant in White Plains not too long ago, my wife and I had a table next to three runners. I *couldn't* overhear the conversation— yes, I tried—but it was abundantly clear that they were runners. I don't know if it's the big lungs, or the lack of modulating fat and muscle, but the sound of the voice is often distinct, not higher, but with less bass. And, of course, they look different. Hungry. They look as if they've been hungry for a long time. "It's the lean wolf that leads the pack," says Quenton in *Once a Runner*. At dinner, these runners were as distinctive as Sikhs in blue turbans would have been.

Modesty must have been in the litany they all repeated, when rocketing here from Planet Fast. It's rare for these people to admit it when they win. And right away, they're looking for somebody to share it with.

In the second sentence of the introduction to the 50th anniversary edition of *The Four-Minute Mile*, Bannister writes, "On a windy and rain-sodden day in Oxford in May 1954 my friends Chris Chataway and Chris Brasher helped me to run the first sub-four-minute mile...."

Sure, they helped, but I think of an essay written for the *New York Times* on the 50th anniversary by George Hirsch. Hirsch reminds us that "for years, medical researchers had been saying that there were human limitations, and a sub-four-minute mile was one of them."

Chris Chataway and Chris Brasher paced their friend early, but that last lap was run alone. Bannister must have been in great pain. Nor was he a man who didn't know how it feels to lose. His performance at the 1952 Helsinki Olympics had been a grave disappointment. Now he was calling on his body for the "impossible." Every fiber of his young body must have been shouting, "Slow down! Back off!"

Bill Rodgers is beloved for having said he's in awe of slower runners since they have to spend so much more time on the course than he does. I would happily accept this compliment if I did not remember how long

2 minutes can take in a wrestling bout. Perception makes time elastic. The 1-mile race that climaxes the novel *Once a Runner* is a contest that played out in less than 4 minutes. It takes 17 minutes to read this section aloud.

"Boston Billy" won the Boston Marathon four times and took New York four times in a row. However gifted, he ran hard.

"The best pace," said Steve Prefontaine, "is the suicide pace, and today is a good day to die."

Salazar ran so hard at the Falmouth Road Race in 1978 that he passed out from heat exhaustion and dehydration.

"I was rushed to the medical tent," he wrote afterwards, "and put in an ice bath as my temperature soared. 'It's 104 and rising,' I remember hearing someone say. 'A hundred five ... now a hundred six ... it's a hundred eight, the thermometer doesn't go any higher.' "

The world is full of heartbreaking cases of injustice. Some women are beautiful, others are ugly. Some of us get all the breaks, others get no breaks at all.

Resistance is available to all of us. And pain.

No, I'm not a runner, not properly, nor do I long to be. I yam who I yam. But this difference only sharpens my admiration. Effort is effort. Heroism is heroism.

There is a moment—that may stretch for eternity—a moment when the runner should have backed off. He could have backed away. She could have pulled up and still had a respectable showing, maybe even victory. I can imagine the roar of desperate breathing, hear the thundering pulse. Color drains from the picture. Sounds are muffled.

He didn't let up. She didn't back off.

They ran right up to Death and touched his chin.

CHAPTER 11

Messengers and the Great Age of Pedestrianism

"MONEY WON IS TWICE AS
SWEET AS MONEY EARNED."
—FAST EDDIE FELSON, IN *THE COLOR OF MONEY* (1986)

It's risky betting on a creature that can be persuaded to lose, and few wagers are laid on track events today. Nonetheless, running—once a far more prominent spectator sport—also drew gamblers from every class.

The English have been staging races since the 15th century. In *Henry IV,* Falstaff tells Poins, "I would give a thousand pound. I could run as fast as thou canst."

The New Shorter Oxford English Dictionary defines footman as "1. An infantryman. 2. A pedestrian; a (good, fast, etc.) walker or runner."

One of the functions of this particular servant was to move smartly beside and in front of the carriage as security—and also to lift or push the contraption out of the mud when it got stuck. And to carry messages.

Fast men were employed throughout Europe for this job. "In France," writes Charles Russell, "this office was most frequently filled by Basques, which has given rise to the proverbial expression 'To run like a Basque.' In general mountaineers are swifter than inhabitants of level countries.

"Lower class people who wished to give themselves the airs of persons of quality, used to pretend to have a Basque in their service. It is to these that Henri Estienne alludes, when he says in his *Dialogues on the French Language*, 'And when you write in any place, even though it be but a little note, and you may not have an express porter, place the letter in the care of the first one you meet, and then you ought to say that you 'have dispatched your Basque, who runs like the wind.'"

"As England is an aristocratic country," Russell writes, "the services of these swift-footed officials were in great request. The qualities requisite were suppleness of the body and robustness of constitution; and the runners were, like jockeys, obliged to take every precaution to maintain them. Their mode of living was in accordance with a severe regimen. In traveling they always carried a staff five or six feet in length, terminated by a hollow ball of metal, generally of silver, which served at once as larder and cellar, for it contained their provender—hard boiled eggs and a little white wine."

Ah, the hard boiled egg and white wine diet. I remember it well.

"The ambition of the runners of the English aristocracy," Russell continues, "was to beat the horses in speed. Many instances might be cited of their having wagered that they would beat a team of horses, and however surprising it may seem, of their winning the bets. The Duke of Marlborough, in the eighteenth century, while driving a phaeton drawn by four horses, was beaten by a courier in the journey from London to Windsor; but the conqueror met the fate of some of his professional brethren of antiquity—he reached the goal, only to fall down never to rise again."

As the roads improved, the footmen got faster. The English noblemen fell into the habit of holding races between each other's servants.

Seventeenth-century diarist Samuel Pepys (pronounced "peeps") made this entry for July 30, 1663: "The town talk this day is of nothing but the great foot-race run this day on Banstead Downes, between Lee, the Duke of Richmond's footman, and Tyler, a famous runner. And Lee hath beat him; though the King and Duke of York and all men almost did bet three or four to one upon the Tyler's head."

With all this cash changing hands so long ago, it's hard not to wonder exactly which tradition the rulers of amateur athletics thought they were calling upon when they so restricted the athletes they oversaw. I think immediately of Jim Thorpe—an American Indian judged to be one of the greatest athletes in the 20th century—who had his Olympic medals taken away when officials learned that he'd been paid for playing minor league baseball. And of Steve Prefontaine, who wanted to maintain his eligibility for the Olympics, and therefore—although a great star—was poor enough to qualify for food stamps. And took them. One of the many incongruities of the attempt to keep athletics amateur was that during the Cold War, the Soviets had no compunctions about putting their stars on a salary.

On August 11, 1664, Pepys wrote of "a wager before the King, my Lords of Castlehaven and Arran (a son of my Lord of Ormond's) they two alone did run down and kill a stoute bucke in St. Jame's Parke." So the endurance hunt that Dr. Dennis Bramble and Dr. Daniel Lieberman wrote about in 2004 was still being practiced—at least for sport—in 17th-century England.

In the 18th century, according to Edward S. Sears, "Women had not yet been deemed biologically unsuited for running. In 1765 a young woman ran 72 miles from Bleneago Scotland to Newcastle in one day." Smock, or "she shirt," races "were common at festivals, weddings, and as additional attractions at cricket matches."[1]

The outfits were not prohibitively unbecoming and, in some cases, the male spectators were so enflamed by the display that they immediately made plans to marry the women they had cheered from the stands.

It seems unusual for a woman to have been an athlete, and yet in *Sporting Anecdotes, Original and Selected,* by Pierce Egan,[2] we come upon the "Sketch of a Distinguished Sportswoman."

"Lady Fearnought was the only child of a gentleman of large fortune, in Sussex, who was a perfect Nimrod in the chase; he was doatingly (cq) fond of her."

While races are not mentioned, it's clear that Lady Fearnought, nee Emma Beagle, was quite fast on her feet. "Her height was five feet eight; her person finely formed; she had a commanding and majestic appearance.... her hair a glossy chestnut, which flowed in luxuriant profusion upon her fine formed shoulders, in all its native graces, as she never would consent to its being tortured into the fantastic forms dictated by the ever-varying goddess, Fashion, to her votaries."

While the long run as hunt seems to have died out by then, 19th-century English schoolchildren ran in mock hunts. The once ubiquitous novel *Tom Brown's Schooldays,* first published in 1857, has a game of "Hares and Hounds" in which one group of students goes off cross-country spreading a trail of shredded newspapers and magazines and the other group, the hounds, must follow.

"Then the hounds clustered round Thorne, who explained shortly, 'They're to have six minute's law. We run into the Cock, and every one who comes in within a quarter of an hour of the hares'll be counted, if he has been round Barby church.' Then came a minute's pause or so, and then the watches are pocketed, and the pack is led through the gateway into the field which the hares had first crossed. Here they break into a trot, scattering over the field to find the first traces of the scent which the hares throw out as they go along."

Evolving from the racing footman, or perhaps starting separately on a parallel course, was the great sport of pedestrianism. The word once meant walking and/or running. And many of the feats performed in its era were go-as-you-will challenges, provided—of course—that you didn't will yourself a set of wheels or a team of horses.

The WordWeb Online dictionary defines pedestrianism as "The act, art, or practice of a pedestrian; walking or running; traveling or racing on foot." I make a fetish of the definition, because some contemporary references don't have the word at all, and others restrict it to race-walking.

In the 19th century, the word meant what the WordWeb Online dictionary says it means: racing on foot. Sometimes competitors walked, sometimes they ran.

Despite the sport's association with lowly footmen, one of England's most famous pedestrians sprang from the nobility. Captain Robert Barclay Allardyce (1779–1854) was a great popular star.

While the most famous exploit of the last Laird of Urie was to walk a thousand miles in a thousand hours, he was also known to cover a mile in 4:50. He performed his thousand-mile feat (which took more than 40 days) by repeatedly covering the same measured mile on Newmarket Heath.

The crowd swelled, of course, as time passed, and the fans grew so curious that Captain Barclay's route had to be roped off, or he wouldn't have had room to move. Beds for miles around were rented by spectators who had come from out of town to watch the spectacle. "The Dukes of Argyle and St. Albans, the Earls Grosvenor, Besborough and Jersey; Lords Foley and Somerville; Sr. John Lade and Sire Francis Standish were among the excited spectators on the final day," according to John Cumming in *Runners and Walkers: Nineteenth Century Sports Chronicle*.

Having covered the distance, Barclay collected his 16,000 pounds and went to sleep, giving orders that he be roused in exactly 8 hours. He was afraid that if he wasn't awakened at that time, he might never wake again.

The man's prodigious strength is documented in Francis Galton's *Memories of My Life*. "When upwards of seventy years old he was dining at my father's house in Leamington," Galton writes, "and on being asked, while sitting at dessert, whether he still performed any feats of strength, he asked my eldest brother, then a fully adult man of more than 12 stone in weight [168 pounds], to step on his hand, which he laid palm upwards on the floor by slightly bending his body. My brother was desired to steady himself by laying one finger on Captain Barclay's shoulder, who thereupon lifted and landed him on the table.... However, the Captain rather strained his shoulder by performing it, as he confessed to my father afterwards."

Walter Thom's *Pedestrianism*, which was published in 1813, put forth Captain Barclay's training regimen: "The young man who meant to be a fast runner and tireless walker was enjoined to go through a course of physic taking, between an ounce and a half and two ounces of Glauber salts every four days until three doses had been administered."

Glauber salts are named after Johann Glauber, the father of hydrochloric acid. In the 19th century, the salts were taken as a laxative. Their most common use today is as a filler for powdered laundry detergents.

Clean as a whistle, the would-be athlete was advised to walk "from twenty to twenty-four miles a day. He must rise at five in the morning, run half a mile at the top of his speed up-hill, and then walk six miles at a moderate pace, coming in about seven to breakfast, which should consist of beefsteaks or mutton-chops underdone, with stale bread and old beer. After breakfast, he must again walk six miles at a moderate pace, and at twelve lie down in bed without his clothes for half an hour. On getting up, he must walk four miles, and return by four to dinner, which should also be beefsteaks or mutton-chops, with bread and beer as at breakfast. Immediately after dinner, he must resume his exercise by running half a mile at the top of his speed, and walking six miles at a moderate pace. He takes no more exercise for that day, but retires to bed about eight and next morning proceeds in the same manner.

"Vegetables, such as turnips, carrots, or potatoes, are never given, as they are watery, and difficult of digestion," Thom continued. "On the same principle, fish must be avoided, and besides, they are not sufficiently nutritious. Neither butter nor cheese is allowed; the one being very indigestible, and the other apt to turn rancid on the stomach. Eggs are also forbidden, excepting the yoke taken raw in the morning...."

"With respect to liquors, they must be always taken cold; and home-brewed beer, old, but not bottled, is the best. A little red wine, however, may be given to those who are not fond of malt liquor; but never more than half a pint after dinner. Too much liquor swells the abdomen, and of course injures the breath.... Water is never given alone, and ardent spirits are strictly prohibited, however diluted. It is an established rule to avoid liquids as much as possible, and no more liquor of any kind is allowed to be taken than what is merely requisite to quench the thirst. Milk is never allowed, as it curdles the stomach. Soups are not used."

The caution against soups was amplified with a quotation from another health authority, Willich in *On Diet,* who wrote: "Broths and soups require little digestion; weaken the stomach, and are attended by all the pernicious effects of other warm and relaxing drink."

John L. Parker Jr. is famous in our time for having written that his hero, Quenton Cassidy, "did not live on nuts and berries; if the furnace was hot enough, anything would burn ..." Many champions of olden times professed highly individual diets. George Seward, the "American Wonder," took three 100-yard-dash races in 1841. The stakes were $50, then $250, then $500. After he defeated William Belden on Long Island's Centerville Course, nobody in America would run against him. So in 1843, he took a berth as a seaman on a ship to England and began a brilliant career overseas.[3] Seward favored boiled pig's head and cabbage, while Australian Charlie Samuels, "the prince of the black pedestrians," is reported to have trained on cigars and sherry.

All of which seems patently absurd to those of us living in the 21st century. That is until we think about it.

Consider Ian Fleming, the man who gave us James Bond. He had worked in English intelligence, planned raids during the Second World War, and presumably was aware of, if not responsible for, the training of crack special forces. In order to get to *Dr. No* in Fleming's 1958 novel, James Bond has to canoe to Crab Key, which is Dr. No's private island.

Others who had visited Crab Key had not come back. So Bond has his

Jamaican Jeeves, a man named Quarrel, whip him into shape.

"First of all," Bond tells Quarrel, "I want you to get me absolutely fit—
the way you trained me the last time I was here. Remember?"

"Sho, cap'n. Ah kin do dat ting."

"Bond unpacked his few things and changed into sandals and shorts.
Soon there was the delicious smell of coffee and frying bacon. They ate
their breakfast while Bond fixed his training routine—up at seven, swim a
quarter of mile, breakfast, and an hour's sunbathing, run a mile, swim
again, lunch, sleep, sunbathe, swim a mile, hot bath and ... Nothing
interrupted the grinding week ..."

I thought I must be missing something. I wondered how Quarrel had
trained Bond last time. This was in *Live and Let Die,* which was published
in 1954. Also in Jamaica, Bond had "started his training under the critical,
appraising eyes of Quarrel. Every morning he swam a mile up the beach
before breakfast and then ran back along the firm sand to the Bungalow.

"By the end of the week, Bond was sunburned and hard. He had cut his
cigarettes down to ten a day. . . ."

Be hard nowadays to find a runner who recommended smoking,
although I saw plenty of runners doing just that the night before
Bordeaux's Médoc Marathon in France.

Many of the early betting contests were "go-as-you-please," meaning that
the athletes could walk or run. Walking can ace out running over distance,
but it's hard to know at which point this happens. And of course, this
varies from one individual to the next.

For a time, the record speed for crossing the North American continent
was held by walkers, and the superiority of all-running over all-walking
seems to diminish over distance.

In the 1807 24-hour race between Captain Robert Barclay as a walker
and Abraham Wood as a runner, Barclay was given a 20-mile advantage.
This handicap, which both men accepted, seems to indicate the superiority
of running, and indeed Wood led at first. But then Barclay won the race.

Pedestrianism was a colorful sport of which Mensen Ernst was a colorful example. Ernst lived from 1795 to 1843. He'd promise to cover impossible distances in record time, and folks wagered for and against him.

Having worked in the English merchant marine, he ran for years—mostly in England—wearing his sailor suit. In 1832, he said that he could run from Paris to Moscow in 15 days. One hundred thousand francs were supposed to have been wagered for or against him. He made it in 14 days. In 1836, he ran from Constantinople to Calcutta in 4 weeks.

Today's long-distance stars can sleep for 12 hours a night and take a nap as well, Ernst was said to sleep just 4 hours a day, if possible, out of doors. While running, he cut this down to 15 minutes a day, leaning against a tree with a piece of cloth over his eyes. It was on a run across Africa, from Cairo to Cape Town, that he stopped to rest near the site of today's Aswan Dam. He leaned against a palm, put a handkerchief over his face, and went to sleep. He never woke again. He would have been about 48 years old.

So much for the idea that aerobic exercise guarantees longevity.

CHAPTER 12

Jeremy Morris and the Dawn of a New Age

"... STILL ALIVE."

—THE *NEW YORK TIMES*

I didn't believe it. I stopped reading. This is a big deal. I can count on the fingers of one hand the times during the past decade that the text of a newspaper has stopped me cold. This is partly my fault. I have a high stop-threshold. A tornado won't do it, unless it's local. Not a war either, unless it's local or threatens to be apocalyptic. I did pause, though, when I read that Jimmy Stewart wore a wig. The male rattlebox moth stopped me. His sperm packet protects Mrs. Moth from predators. It's also fully a tenth of his body weight. So I guess for the rattlebox moth, masturbation is out of the question.

Often as not, I flip right through the newspaper. Ten minutes later, I couldn't tell you—and not to save my own precious life—if 300 Liberians died in an earthquake, or if there were only 30 deaths, and they were librarians instead.

But this was about running: ". . . academic interest in nutrition is centuries old," wrote Bruce Weber in the *New York Times*,[1] "but physical activity epidemiology, a.k.a. exercise science, is youthful enough that the man who initiated it, a researcher from Liverpool, England, named Jeremy Morris, is still alive. (He'll turn 95 in May.)"[2]

Still alive!

I wondered if Weber had overstated the case outrageously, but a quick double-check indicated that he had not done so. Still uneasy, I wrote Dr. Steven Blair, then CEO of the Cooper Institute.

"Professor Morris is the scientist who invented the field of physical activity epidemiology and health," Dr. Blair wrote back.

So I went online and tried to track this scientist down. Several e-mails failed, but then one came back with a phone number. I called the London School of Hygiene and Tropical Medicine and reached Jennifer Richards. "I just sent you an e-mail, you know?" she told me. She had one of those delicious English accents. "Giving you Jerry Morris's home number. You should ring him in the evening. I think he's now on his way home."

"Is this the *actual* Jeremy Morris?" I asked.

"Yes."

"And coming to work?"

"Yes, still. At his age. Yes."

"Does he still walk every day?" I asked.

"I'm not sure. He does swim."

Morris's groundbreaking 1953 study found that the London drivers of double-decker buses—who remained in their seats throughout the workday—had significantly more heart attacks than did the conductors, who had to climb up and down stairs. Since the drivers and conductors were otherwise similar, this indicated that exercise reduced the risk of heart attack. Seems obvious now, but it was news at the time.

"Did you know what you were going to find?" I asked, when I reached the doctor at home. "Did you have a suspicion?"

"Not, really," he told me. "No."

"So it wasn't known that exercise was good for the health?"

"The whole connection between exercise and health was developed postwar. And when I say postwar, I mean post–Second World War," he said. "If you look at the textbooks from the 1930s, before the war, and look at today's textbooks—a few fundamentals are still there—but otherwise a whole new world has been created.

"We didn't know," Dr. Morris said. "Although I've always been a keen walker. My late father used to take me as a small boy for a walk outside of Glasgow, where we lived in Scotland, to a village 4 miles away, and our target was to do it in an hour. If we managed to do the walk, the 4 miles in an hour, I got a chocolate ice cream. If it took longer than an hour, I only got a vanilla ice cream. As you can imagine, the stimulus was quite strong."

"When you look around at all the joggers, and all the gyms, do you wonder if you've created a monster?" I asked.

Not at all, he said. His only regret is that there's not more exercise, that the doctors have not gotten the message out. The sight of runners cheers him. And he'd been delighted recently to find throngs of them on an island right off of Budapest, where he'd been on vacation with his children.

"So many bodily functions improve with exercise," he said. "The important thing is to carry it on into old age. My main concern now is physical activity in old age. There's such scope there. There's such potential there.

"It's very elementary physiology," Dr. Morris continued. "We start losing muscle and losing cardiorespiratory, heart, and lung capability, from our forties. Everybody does. Everybody. It's part of aging. Of course, if you're very fit, you start at a higher level, but the average person loses muscle at the rate of about 1 percent a year. And if you don't try to compensate for that—as you can to quite a large extent by exercise—by the time you get to be an old lady in the eighties, you may have lost half your muscle mass. And there's the basis for a lot of the frailty of old age. But it is possible to make good quite a bit of that loss of muscle by taking appropriate exercise. It has got to be exercise against some resistance, and most typically weight lifting."

He also recommends swimming for the heart and lungs. When Dr. Blair and his wife stopped to see Dr. Morris in London a couple of years ago, they met for tea at the hotel that Dr. Morris goes to for his swim. "He's 97,"

Dr. Blair said, "and publishing five papers a year. He's a remarkable man."

"I'm a habitual exerciser," Dr. Morris told me. "I feel it when I'm deprived, even for a short period. When I have a bad cold, I really miss it. You must know that. It's very striking. I feel deprived as much by my lack of exercise as by the running nose and the sneezing."

"There are people who call it an addiction," I said.

"Call it what you like," he said. "Habit's a more respectable term. There are many other habits which aren't so manifestly beneficial. And of course, with exercise you can always tell people they'll feel better. This is so common and so regular that you are entitled to tell people that if they take exercise, they will feel better.

"This is a great thing, because by comparison, when you tell them to stop smoking or change their diet, you can't say that so confidently."

I asked Dr. Morris if running, which was a sudden boom in my lifetime, might fade again. Then Dr. Morris made a statement so obvious that I was astonished that it hadn't occurred to me before. For weeks afterward, I kept coming back to it. Probably you've already figured this out, but for me it was news.

"We are the first generations in history, in the history of mankind, that have deliberately got to take exercise for health," he told me. "You see, there used to be a lot of activity in occupation in your work and in getting about. In transport. And in the home. And this has gone down so drastically that we've all got to think in terms of deliberately taking exercise."

As a new teacher in a master of fine arts program, I was asked if there was anything I'd like announced. And I said that I run 5 miles before breakfast and would welcome company. When, smiling, the woman leading orientation told the assembled staff and students that anyone who wanted to run 5 miles before breakfast could join Ben Cheever, it got a big laugh.

But slowly, achingly, the world is coming around. The USDA now recommends exercise of between 60 and 90 minutes a day for people who mean to sustain weight loss. Health and Human Services Secretary Mike Leavitt estimates that 66 million Americans need to lose weight.

Jeremy Morris changed the science of exercise epidemiology, but much of what he discovered had been intuited—at least in some circles—for centuries.

Walter Thom's *Pedestrianism* calls for a general move to fitness. This despite his having written the book with gamblers in mind. "To *Sporting Gentlemen* this work is particularly interesting," he wrote, "as they will find, concisely related, the performances of the most celebrated pedestrians of the present age. And from what has been already done, they may form some opinion of what is possible for others to accomplish; and thus regulate their bets according to the different circumstances of the cases under their review." [3]

Thom was concerned about the "indolent repose" of English soldiers. He compared the slackers in the British armed forces with the athletic warriors of Rome and Greece.

"Although the art of war be now different, in some respects, from that which was practiced among the ancients," he argued, "it is still not less requisite.... to perform long marches under the inclemency of the weather—and to preserve his spirit unbroken amidst the tumult of battle...." [4]

"And as exercise, particularly on foot, is attended by so many advantages to mankind," Thom continued, "the Author thinks he cannot conclude his work with any observation more apposite to the subject than those of the amiable Christopher Christian Sturm. 'Man, (says he) in a state of civilization, does not know how much strength he possesses; how much he loses by effeminacy, nor how much he can acquire by frequent exercise. We cannot but regard with pity those indolent beings who pass their lives in idleness and effeminacy; who never exert their strength, nor exercise their powers for fear of injuring their health, or shortening their lives.'" [5]

It has been clear for a long time—long before London had double-decker buses—that exercise in general, and running in particular, is good for the spirit and also for the body it inhabits. Nor is the lack of movement as safe as it may seem to be.

As Henry David Thoreau said, "A man sits as many risks as he runs."

CHAPTER 13

Running Is Transformative—
Even for Nonrunners

"I RAN ALL THE WAY ..."

—HARRY S TRUMAN, UPON RECEIVING A CALL ON APRIL 12, 1945,
TO COME TO THE WHITE HOUSE "QUICKLY AND QUIETLY"

I was once told by a grown woman that Reddi-wip had changed her life. And I suppose it had, but the hyperbole still knocked the wind out of me. People often say that a book or movie "changed my life."

"So what were you like before?" I need to ask. "How are you different now?"

The chameleons are apt to bristle and tell me that before consuming said book or movie, they "never *really* understood about the Paris Commune" or "why I should take molecularly distilled Icelandic fish oil. At least 2,000 milligrams a day."

These sweeping declarations of change are silly, but not nearly as troubling to me as is the belief that we don't change at all. G. K. Chesterton writes that "all conservatism is based upon the idea that if you leave things alone, you leave them as they are. But you do not. If you leave a thing alone, you leave it to a torrent of change. If you leave a white post alone, it will soon be a black post. If you particularly want it to be white, you must be always painting it again: that is you must be always having a revolution. Briefly, if you want the old white post, you must have a new white post. But this, which is true even of inanimate things, is in a quite special and terrible sense true of all human things."

Faith in a constant personality about which the world revolves, like planets around Ptolemy's earth, has done more to retard true understanding than has any other commonly accepted lie. The self is something we swim around. It's not something we are.

In a lecture recorded under the title "Your Body Is Your Unconscious Mind," the neuroscientist Candace Pert made an observation that I found both shocking and convincing. Science, she said, has advanced spectacularly by "slicing up in very fine cryostat-cut frozen sections hunks of dead meat. I mean, I've done that. I've spent years doing that. And I'm not knocking it. It's incredibly important, but you just have to know it's dead then.

"We're much more like flickering flames," said Pert, "than we are like hunks of meat, you know?"

"We are all patchwork," wrote essayist Michel de Montaigne. "And so shapeless and diverse in composition that each bit, each moment plays its own game. And there is as much difference between us and ourselves as between us and others."

I run about 1,500 miles a year, half of it in company. Take a long enough run, or go out in a heavy rain, or at dawn, and you're apt to hear and tell intimate stories. I've learned about sexual indiscretions, heard the details of sudden death. I've been taught to write with details, but much of what I've been told is so intimate that if I repeated any of these stories here, leaving out the names and places, I'd still be violating confidences. It was during a winter run over snow that I heard the first time ever about male impotence.

Runners can lie, of course. I was in a group once in which one member, tiresomely married and chronically chubby, suddenly dropped 8 pounds. He stoutly denied that he was having an affair. Nobody believed him. He seemed perpetually delighted.

Eduardo Castillo told me that he was a teenager and still in Cuba when Castro's revolutionaries were setting off bombs. Batista's police would try to catch those responsible and garnish the blast area with their dead bodies. If the police couldn't find the guerillas, they'd kill somebody else and leave the corpse at the scene in order to demonstrate control. He, Ed, was picked up immediately after a bomb had gone off. If Ed's uncle had not worked for Batista, Eduardo might easily have been shot.

My running buddy Rick Rennert traveled the world alone for a year or so after college, and his description of the beautiful women of Tel Aviv has significantly altered my understanding of Middle Eastern politics.

If there's truth in wine, there's also truth in high oxygenation. Trotting along at a decent pace, my son John has told me stories that would have caused my teeth to drop right out of my mouth if my dentist had not glued them in so securely.

For a decade, I ran with Ray Bowles, now 70. Ray grew up in Pocantico Hills and has a passion for history. He knows the best local stories, the ones that got into books and the ones that no one quite dared to write down. He's fascinated by the grandeur of the past.

Oddly, this interest has became the foundation for his family. As a college student, Ray was a tour guide at the Sunnyside, the restoration of Washington Irving's house. "I heard a lovely voice from the floor above and saw a girl descending the stairway in a period costume with a hoop skirt. It took 7 years for me to finally marry her 46 years ago."

Since I'm getting my exercise done, I'm happy to listen to anything a running buddy wants to say. Odd that I'm rarely bored. Although I'm afraid I do a lot of talking. Which, when I have spent the entire day alone writing, leaves me deeply remorseful. One of my rules—often broken—is to keep my own mouth shut at least half the time.

I brought my son John on a run once with Wayne Coffee. I was eager to have them talk to one another.

"Did you notice how quiet I was," I asked John after the run, after he'd said that he liked Wayne.

"Yeah," he said. "You looked blue with the effort."

Runners often tell me—sometimes boastfully, sometimes almost regretfully—how the sport found and altered them. Rick Rennert was in Manhattan, planning to write a novel, and feeling like a man on a desert island, waiting for a ship to appear. He was watching the New York Marathon with a friend, and the guy said something along the lines of "Who are these people?" And Rick looked at the faces of the men and women in the throes of extreme exertion, and he thought, "I want to do that. These are my people."

One of the most obvious demonstrations of change in the runner is the loss of weight. And—*join me in chorus here*—"they keep it off." Americans spend an estimated $30 billion a year on weight-loss books and products, and yet people who go on a diet to look good have a recidivism rate of 95 percent.

Weight loss is right up there with a full head of hair and a lottery fortune as the object most frequently sold for cash and most infrequently taken home.

It's not just weight, though, but the possibility of improvement. What I want is to be a better person, and running seems to be one clear way to move toward this goal. Moral advances are hard to measure. Without measurement, they're hard to believe in. But you can get faster. Or maybe just try. I hate it when people say, "All we want is for you to do your best." I never do my best. Maybe in the last 100 yards of a 10-K, but I have no kick, and so my best is nothing to write home about. But sometimes I do try. I try hard enough so that I'm gasping for air. And having tried that hard, then other qualities may fall into place.

Renee Askins states this brilliantly in her book *Shadow Mountain: A Memoir of Wolves, a Woman, and the Wild*.[1] The founder of the Wolf Fund, which saw the reintroduction of wolves into Yellowstone National Park,

Renee writes of the joy she finds in running. More surprisingly, she writes of the usefulness of losing.

A decent overall athlete, she was persuaded by her brother to go out for cross-country. Craig made her promise that she would not quit. No matter what. There was no girl's cross-country team, so she ran with the boys. She hated it.

"I didn't win. Ever. I thought the lesson was learning how to lose; instead, it was learning to relinquish control, how to not win and not quit."

Years later, she learned that she had exercise-induced asthma. She could perform decently during workouts, but then—infuriatingly—she ran less well at races. Neck and neck with a competitive boy, she'd run all out. "Bitch," he'd shout and then pass into the lead.

Renee writes that cross-country brought her to her knees, "and it was on my knees that I figured out promises often need to become prayers. Prayers teach patience and perspective, they teach mindfulness and attentiveness to the lessons at hand, they teach the humility needed to partition grandiose goals into pocket-size achievements."

Nor does the transformation need always to take place when the runner first begins. The long race is there always, as a sort of platform on which to evaluate, and sometimes alter your life.

George Hirsch's best marathon might have been one of his slowest.

"It was the New Jersey Waterfront Marathon in 1988," Hirsch said. He hadn't intended to run the marathon at all. "I went over for the Olympic Trials. I hadn't run a marathon in about 5 years. I went to the Expo. I was just standing around at the *Runner's World* booth, and this woman walks by me. We just looked at each other, and it was something. And she just kept walking. So I kind of went around the other way and bumped into her. And she said, 'Are you George Hirsch?' Even if I hadn't been George Hirsch, I would have said yes. And she said a friend of hers whom I knew had had me send a marathon training program to her months before. She wanted to thank me.

"She was running her first marathon the next day, and her goal was to finish. And then she said, 'But I would love to then run New York in the fall and just see if I could qualify for Boston.' And I said, 'What's your qualifying time?' And she said that would be 3:40. So I invited her to have dinner. She said no.

"I was 52 and I'd been long, long single. My friends thought I was a confirmed bachelor. I never thought I was. And I used to say, 'Find me a nonsmoking plumber who's a Democrat, and I'll marry her.'"

Hirsch had had no plans to run a marathon, but the next day, he went to the marathon start. "And I couldn't find her. And the gun goes off. I wait until every last person has crossed the start, and then I start jogging. And finally at 5 miles, there she is," he told me, his voice getting rich even today with the pleasure of the recollection.

"Three hours 37 minutes and 1 second later, we finished the New Jersey Waterfront Marathon, or she did, and I stepped aside."

That was Shay, George's wife, and they are still relishing the conversation started at mile five of the Jersey Waterfront Marathon all those years ago.

People often run at transitional periods in their lives, even if they've never run before and might not run again. Take Jim Dixon, the hero of Kingsley Amis's groundbreaking comic novel, *Lucky Jim* (1954). Dixon is the opposite of health conscious. The organ he puts most severely to the test is his liver—in metabolizing beer and excreting a bile so rich as to make literary history.

Dixon frets incessantly about his cigarettes. Nor has he restricted himself in order to save his life. It's money he's trying to save. He can't afford to smoke as many cigarettes as he wants.

And yet this least athletic of men finds himself running. He is running to catch the bus so that he can speak to the beautiful Christine before that object of desire gets onto the train.

"Dixon broke into a frenzied, lung-igniting sprint, while the conductor watched him immobile from the platform. When he was half-way to the bus, this official rang the bell, the driver let in the clutch, and the wheels began to turn. Dixon found he was even better at running than he'd thought...."

"'Well run, wacker,' the conductor finally says when Dixon mounts the bus."

Running is often there at critical junctions.

"I ran," thinks the Ed Norton character just before the climax of the movie *Fight Club*. "I ran until my muscles burned and my veins pumped battery acid. Then I ran some more."

Dustin Hoffman runs in *The Graduate*. And then for his life on the FDR Drive in *Marathon Man*. Forrest Gump runs until his leg braces fall off.

Running was tremendously dramatic when—before the sport took— grown men in suits did it. A movie director seeking to show great danger could have a dam break, a hillside burst into flame, or three grown men in suits and Florsheims running down the street. For an adult male to run was once a demonstration of wild abandon, a return to childhood almost as incongruous as sucking a binky or climbing a tree.

Harry S Truman, the 33rd president of the United States, is best remembered for the phrase "The Buck Stops Here" and for a 1948 victory so close that President-elect Truman appeared the day after waving a copy of the *Chicago Tribune* with the headline "Dewey Defeats Truman."

Truman's nomination to replace Henry Wallace as vice president to FDR was not popular.

"He was called 'the Missouri Compromise' and 'the Common Denominator' of the convention," according to David McCullough's *Truman*.[2] "The *Pittsburgh Post-Gazette* called him one of the weakest candidates ever nominated. *Time* magazine … portrayed him as 'the mousy little man from Missouri.'" Nevertheless, he was chosen and elected vice president for FDR's unprecedented and never replicated fourth term.

He had been in office for only 82 days and hadn't had a lot of face time with the president when he got the call on April 12, 1945. Truman was in Representative Sam Rayburn's private hideaway, according to McCullough, when Steve Early phoned and told him to come to the White House "quickly and quietly."

"He went out the door alone. Then he began to run, taking a different route," writes McCullough. "He kept to the ground floor this time, racing down a hall between a double line of bronze and marble Civil War generals and forgotten state governors, his shoes pounding on the marble floor." Truman ran first back to his office to get his coat and hat. Then out to his car. When researching the book, McCullough went to Washington and ran the course himself. Truman never acknowledged having thought that the president was dead. He said later that he assumed FDR had work for him to do.

"But if this was so," writes McCullough, "why had he run back to his office?" "I ran all the way," he wrote to his mother.

Truman's tenure in office was not untroubled, nor was he universally esteemed. He was elected to the presidency on his own ticket in that aforementioned 1948 squeaker but did not even win the nomination for a second term.

Today, however, this underdog is considered one of the 10 best presidents this nation has ever had. David McCullough's excellent history has something to do with this. Whatever the cause, we've come to look fondly on a man who spoke so plainly and acted after thorough, humble deliberation. Looking back, we can see the Marshall Plan and that Truman initiated broad-reaching civil rights legislation. He was the first president ever to address the NAACP and ordered the desegregation of the federal workforce and the armed services. He used to like to hold his press conferences at a brisk walk. Shortly after taking the oath of office for the presidency, he told reporters, "Boys, if you ever pray, pray for me now." How can you not esteem the man who—when the dread phone call came—ran to meet it?

But first he ran to get his coat and hat.

CHAPTER 14

American Running

"THE SKY WAS BLUE. IT SEEMED LIKE MUSIC.
I HAD JUST CUT THE GRASS, AND THE SMELL
OF IT WAS IN THE AIR. THIS REMINDED ME OF THOSE
OVERTURES AND PROMISES OF LOVE WE KNOW WHEN WE
ARE YOUNG. AT THE END OF A FOOT RACE YOU THROW
YOURSELF ONTO THE GRASS BY THE CINDER TRACK,
GASPING FOR BREATH, AND THE ARDOR WITH WHICH
YOU EMBRACE THE SCHOOLHOUSE LAWN IS A PROMISE
YOU WILL FOLLOW ALL THE DAYS OF YOUR LIFE."
—JOHN CHEEVER[1]

Charles C. Pyle's 1928 "Bunion Derby" from Los Angeles, California, to Madison Square Garden in New York was foot racing for cash and for the spectacle. Sports promoter "Cash and Carry" Pyle conceived of a contest modeled on the Tour de France. The multistage 3,422-mile race, which included a section on the spanking new Route 66, drew more newspaper coverage than any other sporting event in history. When it was run in reverse the following year, South African ultrastar Arthur Newton had his shoulder blade broken. He was hit by a car. But then the health of the athletes was not the purpose of this event. Nor did the spectacle prove to be good business. Pyle lost money. There was no easy way to extract an admission fee from the millions who lined up on the side of the road to watch the runners pass.

Marathoning—both indoors and out—was such a popular spectator sport in early 20th-century America that the *New York Times* warned readers against the distance. "There is reason for viewing with considerable apprehension the sudden popularity of the so-called Marathon race ..." began the article that ran on February 24, 1909. "It is only exceptional men who can safely undertake the running of twenty-six miles, and even for them the safety is comparative rather than absolute. The chances are that every one of them weakens his heart and shortens his life not only by the terrible strain of the race itself, but by the preliminary training which produces muscular and vascular developments that become perilous instead of advantageous the moment a return to ordinary pursuits and habits puts an end to the need for them."

When I was just starting to run, a Cassandra at the *Reader's Digest* made a point of telling me about this editorial. I didn't believe him. Despite their negative take on marathons, editorial writers of the time must have had deep lungs. Reading aloud, you're supposed to take a breath when you come to a period. Try reading this sentence in one breath: "The chances are that every one of them weakens his heart and shortens his life not only by the terrible strain of the race itself, but by the preliminary training which produces muscular and vascular developments that become perilous instead of advantageous the moment a return to ordinary pursuits and habits puts an end to the need for them."

Opinion as to what is or is not good for your health varies wildly not only across time but from culture to culture. Geronimo, an earlier American, was said to be running 25 miles in a day by the time he was 9. The great warrior lived to be 80, dying coincidentally on February 17, 1909, just 1 week before the *Times* article was printed.

Nor was Geronimo the first fast man on this continent. In *Indian Running: Native American History and Tradition,* Peter Nabokov writes that a successful revolt against colonial Spanish rule had been started in New Mexico in 1680 by Indian runners. Messengers, carrying deerskins detailing the plans, were dispatched to all the tribes. The runners went out for a second time "with knotted yucca-fiber cords" to use as countdown devices. Indians at the far-flung villages would untie a knot every day. When the last knot was untied, the uprising would begin.

Aztec messengers were said to have covered as much as 200 miles in a single day of running. Cortez wrote that within 24 hours of his landing in May 1519, runners had reached Montezuma, 260 miles away, and described the Spanish "ships, men, guns and horses."

In pre-Columbian Peru, Indians had cross-country relay teams to deliver fresh seafood to the city.

Nor were these systems unique. "In the East," writes Nabokov, "the Iroquois Confederacy was able to dominate upper New York State in part because of its organized runners."

Some Indian villages actually had tracks set up, and most games featured running, while running itself was the most popular sport after lacrosse. Since watches were not accurate, nor starts and finishes precise, we will never know how fast the natives were, but *Ripley's Giant Book of Believe It or Not!*[2] reports that in 1876, a Pawnee called Big Hawk Chief ran the mile in 3 minutes and 58 seconds.

American Indians who survived to compete often did extraordinarily well. In *Runners and Walkers: A Nineteenth Century Sports Chronicle,* John Cumming reports that Native Americans were presumed to be outstanding athletes. "So great was the impression of the Indian's native ability as a runner, sponsors of races in towns near Indian reservations set up separate races for Indians, excluding them from competition with white runners." A Seneca, Deerfoot, was a great champion in the 1850s and '60s, traveling to England to astound the crowds and defeat the local talent.

Born Lewis Bennet, Deerfoot was a public athlete of international note. He won a 5-mile race held in 1856 in Fredonia, New York, covering the distance in 25 minutes. For this, he got $50. The American Indian was 6 feet tall and weighed 160 pounds.

When Bennet arrived in England in 1861, the big runner attracted an enormous amount of attention. He sported a wolf skin blanket, and his headband displayed a single eagle feather. "In personal appearance, Deerfoot is majestic, with remarkably handsome features, and is mild and unobtrusive in his demeanor," reported the London *Sporting News*.

Deerfoot's first race in England was a 6-mile 41-lap contest, which he lost to Edward Mills. Despite this disappointing beginning, challenges from local champions poured in. The Seneca went on to run 15 races in 13 weeks, victorious in all but one, which he tied. Deerfoot was something of a ham, and although he spoke no English, he pleased the crowd with dramatic gestures and the occasional war whoop. He broke his competitors with super-fast surges.

Professional running was a draw in America in the 1830s with some horse tracks regularly hosting foot races. The first great public contest in this country was conceived when John C. Stevens bet Samuel L. Gouverneur that he could produce a man who would cover 10 miles in an hour. The two settled on the Union Race Course on Long Island for this demonstration. The purse was to be $1,300.

While no man was known to have covered 10 miles in under an hour in the United States, English runners had broken the barrier many times. The "Flying Butcher of Leeds" may have done so in 1690. Writer Walter Thom reports that "Reed, the noted pedestrian of Hampshire, in 1774, ran ten miles within an hour, at the Artillery Ground, London." But America was a new world, and new heroes were required.

The first American championship was held in the spring of 1835. Nine runners toed the line. Many wore pantaloons. Some ran barefoot, others in slippers. The crowd was estimated at 30,000.

A trumpet blast started the race. A 27-year-old basket-maker named Isaac Downes had already distinguished himself as a runner and was expected to win. Race sponsor John Stevens was backing a Connecticut farmer named Henry Stannard. Stevens had a stopwatch and called out splits to his favorite. Stannard won and also broke the magic barrier in 59.44.

Then, of course, promoters and competitors alike saw the possibility of pitting America's best against the English.

On October 14, 1844, a competition "between England and America" was staged at the Beacon Race Course in Hoboken, New Jersey. The Beacon was the first luxurious track built in America. This was to be a 1-hour race. Whoever covered the most ground in 1 hour would win.

Henry Stannard was up against a New Yorker named John Gildersleeve, an American Indian named John Steeprock, and three Englishmen—John Barlow, Tom Greenhalgh, and Ambrose Jackson. While the Americans dressed much as did the jockeys of the time, the Britishers were shockingly uncovered, wearing linen drawers that had been cut down for the occasion. The betting was heavy on the Englishmen. Gildersleeve won, covering 10 miles and 955 yards, although many suspected that the Englishmen had lost to keep their true speed in the dark so as improve their odds for later races. It was common for a professional runner to arrive in a new area and purposely lose his first races to the local champion. Then, when the stakes got high, he'd discover a second wind.

Tom McNab opens his novel *The Fast Men*[3] with an elaborate con in which a man says that using "the English Method," he can teach any drunk to beat the town champion. At random, he picks a drunk from the bar. The "perfect stranger" turns out to be a confederate and an extremely fast man.

The 1904 St. Louis Olympics certainly proved that hustling wasn't the only thing that could go wrong at athletic events. Held during the celebration of the 100th anniversary of the Louisiana Purchase, the confusion was of Olympic proportion.

Eleven countries were represented, but America seemed to have taken full advantage of its powers as host country, winning 77 medals. Cuba took second place with seven medals.[4]

It's hard not to suspect race organizers of favoring their countrymen. Johannes Runge of Germany had just won an 800-meter race when he was told that it hadn't been the *Olympic* 800-meter race. He'd run, he was told, in a handicap event. And now the Olympic 800-meter race was going to start immediately. Runge rushed gallantly to the second starting. He was tired, though, and finished fifth.

The marathon was the longest race and therefore susceptible to the most foul-ups. In those far-off times, many runners were still not entirely comfortable with the distance and inclined to go out too fast. It was a hot day in St. Louis, and the athletes were accompanied by trainers pedaling bicycles and shouting advice. This noisy throng was followed by a force of doctors and nurses in automobiles.

Fred Lorz of New York had a promising beginning, but then faded, and finally stopped running altogether. In dreadful shape, he accepted a ride in one of the motor vehicles that was now moving along the course.

In the meantime, Tom Hicks of St. Louis had also gone out too fast, and although he'd earned a lead of more than a mile, he felt terrible and begged his handlers to please let him lie down. Instead, they gave him a mixture of egg white and strychnine. (Although a deadly poison, strychnine's use was not yet barred.) Three miles later, Hicks was dosed again with the mixture to which French brandy had been added.

Meanwhile Lorz, having motored into the lead, was feeling much refreshed. He returned to the course and scooted past the drugged and discouraged Hicks. Lorz trotted on to apparent victory. Of course, the crowd thought he'd won, and Fred Lorz didn't see any reason to disabuse them of this. Hicks shuffled into the stadium now in truly wretched condition and assisted by a man running on each side.

By this time, Lorz had already had his picture taken with Alice Roosevelt, daughter of President Theodore Roosevelt. When Hicks finished, Lorz admitted that he, Lorz, had gotten a ride and should be disqualified. He didn't seem to think the confusion had been such a big deal. In this, he was quite alone. Lorz was immediately banned from amateur athletics, although the ban was later lifted, and he actually won the 1905 Boston Marathon, going the whole way on foot.

No protests were brought against Hicks for having been helped by others near the end of the race, although Italian Dorando Pietri's finish at the 1908 London Olympics raised a storm of protest.

But then Dorando Pietri got a *lot* of help. The picture of the mustachioed runner—clearly in extremity—but just about to fall through the tape, is one of the totemic images of running history.

Since the long run was still considered a possibly fatal ordeal, the crowd waiting in the stadium had been in considerable suspense. The English were praying that an American wouldn't win. The US team had enraged the British by refusing to dip their flag while parading by the Royal Box in the White City stadium. "This flag dips to no earthly king," a representative explained, adding insult to insult. The Americans themselves had been infuriated when, at the opening ceremony, the American flag had not been displayed along with those of other countries.

The British audience was therefore delighted when an Italian in a white shirt and red knickers was the first runner to appear at the entrance to the Olympic arena. The spectators thundered their approval. Pietri paused for a moment, and then staggered drunkenly off in the wrong direction, heading left, when the finish was to the right. Officials sprang onto the track, but when they tried to persuade the Italian to turn around, he seemed suspicious and continued to move away from the finish. Ultimately, Pietri did reverse course, but before he'd gone far, he fell down. And stayed down. The officials picked the runner up and got him going again. Again he fell. A second time, he was helped to his feet and started on the track. He fell again. The race officials gathered the hapless runner up, and Pietri was taken across the finish with an assistant on each side.

A Bloomingdale's department store employee named Johnny Hayes came in next, and the Americans asked that Pietri be disqualified. Their protest was honored.

"As Pietri lay recovering on a stretcher," writes Charlie Lovett in *Olympic Marathon*, "the Italian flag was lowered and replaced by the Stars and Stripes. The *New York Times* declared the show 'the most thrilling event that has occurred since that marathon race in ancient Greece where the victor fell at the goal and, with a wave of triumph, died.'"

So Hayes was the winner, but Pietri was the hero. A huge crowd turned out to see him leave London. A special golden cup, a replica of the one given to Hayes, was produced and engraved to Pietri "in Remembrance of the Marathon Race from Windsor to the Stadium July 24, 1908 from Queen Alexandra."

Dorando Pietri would later come to the States to race Johnny Hayes. He beat the American handily in two marathons held before standing-room-only crowds in Madison Square Garden.

The 1908 Olympics are also significant for having established the now-standard 26.2 miles. The course was laid out to start at Windsor Castle and finish in front of the Royal Box in the Olympic arena.

Running and walking over long distances on courses both indoors and out had been a popular spectator sport in the United States for some time, although it was widely believed that prolonged and intense exertion was ruinous to the health.

This was felt to be particularly true for the "weaker sex." This belief died hard. When Jock Semple tried to pull the numbers off Kathrine Switzer during the 1967 Boston Marathon, it was presumed to be for her own good. "Running," I once heard Switzer say, "was supposed to collapse my uterus."

This seems odd since Bertha Von Berg had won the first all-woman race held in Madison Square Garden in 1879, covering 372 miles in 6 days. The women were required to wear long dresses, keep their hair neat, and refrain from talking to the spectators. Apparently the outfits weren't terribly revealing, because a man in a dress was pulled from the course during one of the events. Fans routinely used to hand bouquets to their favorites as they walked or trotted past.

Whatever the doctors said, American children—both male and female—were primed to run. Paul Revere rode a horse, but most of us didn't have a horse. Disney's Davy Crockett ran in his fringed jacket. We had all heard tales of running the gauntlet. Daniel Boone was supposed to have outrun his Indian captors.

Nor did our forebears always run for the very best of motives. Take, just for instance, the infamous "Walking Purchase" of 1737.

William Penn had been esteemed by the Lenape Indians. He had been dead for almost 20 years when his scheming offspring produced a document indicating that the Lenape had promised the family some land. The Penns were entitled to as much territory as could be walked off in a day. When the Lenape said they'd honor the promise, the Penns cleared a trail and drafted three fast runners. One of these "walkers" ran 55 miles, and so the Penns of Pennsylvania claimed 1,200 square miles.

One of my favorite race descriptions is from Walter D. Edmonds's *Drums Along the Mohawk*. A band of Indians fighting for the English employ their chase strategy against a scout named Adam Helmer.

"There were forty Indians he judged. Mohawks too, coming up the trail at a dogtrot.... German Flats lay fourteen miles to the north and he [Adam] knew he had probably the pick of Brant's Indians on his trail, men who could run eighty miles through the woods between sunrise and noon....

"He eased up slightly, listening behind him.... He began to put on a little pressure to make the next bend; but just before he rounded it he heard the war whoop slide up its unhuman pitch and a wild shot cut the air high over his head."

There follows a long, but quick-moving passage in which Adam runs the 14 miles with the Indians sending one champion after another up in an attempt to break him.

Helmer accepts each challenge, keeping just out of range, but never going so fast as to break down. By the time the villages of German Flats see him, the last of his pursuers has given up.

"They saw the runner coming down the long hill, his body glistening with sweat and reflecting red from the low-lying ball of the sun. He was coming hard...

"Before dark they were thronging towards the forts by road and river. Those who had already reached Fort Herkimer stood in front of the church and stared at Helmer's naked chest. It was whipped with branches, the white skin welted and bloody. But Helmer was breathing easily again. He had never, he thought, felt finer in his life."

CHAPTER 15

Le Marathon le Plus Long du Monde

"I DRINK NOT FROM MERE JOY IN THE WINE NOR TO SCOFF
AT FAITH—NO, ONLY TO FORGET MYSELF FOR A MOMENT,
THAT ONLY DO I WANT OF INTOXICATION, THAT ALONE."
—OMAR KHAYYAM

After my son John and I had run on the grounds of Thomas Jefferson's
Monticello, we were scolded by a guard. But then we'd already done our
40 minutes. So I was able to keep from giggling later that morning when a
blushing tour guide said that despite Jefferson's many godlike qualities,
his slaves had had "difficult lifestyles."

When John and I travel, it is customary for us to run together as well.
We've run on tropical islands, and in Chicago. Most every runner I know
has had at least one exotic outing. Lieutenant Colonel Tom Graves has run
"in Iraq, Kuwait, Korea, Qatar, Panama, just about every country in

Europe, in Greece. My favorite is the first run out. You're not really sure where you're going. New city, new place, different world."

Graves goes into combat. Not me. But I did run through a terrific hangover one hot morning in antique Williamsburg in Virginia and got badly dehydrated. I've been lost on the streets of Sofia, Bulgaria. I once so infuriated my darling wife that she took a spoonful of sugar off the coffee cart in the Borghese Gardens and shot it at my chest.

But then we'd already been for a gorgeous run together and in the Borghese Gardens.

Running has thrown me into adventures that I would otherwise have missed. If I weren't a known runner, then Lettie Teague, my editor at *Food and Wine*, would never have sent me to France. This was in the fall of 2002, and I hadn't traveled without my family for a decade. But this was a marathon. Why would *Food and Wine* be interested in a marathon?

Because the Médoc Marathon serves wine at its water stops. First prize is the winner's weight in grand crus. When I heard this, I was astonished. *Sacre bleu!* Do they also smoke Gauloises? (In case you're wondering, they do smoke Gauloises, but mostly filtered cigarettes. I didn't see anyone lighting a cigarette while running, but the night before the race and at the celebratory lunch afterward, they all smoked. I wondered about this. Had the 1964 Surgeon General's Report on Smoking and Health not yet crossed the Atlantic? Had the job of translating it into French been given to somebody with my grasp of the language?)

The course reads like a wine list. Chateau Beychevelle, Chateau Gruaud-Larose, and Chateau Lafite Rothschild all ornament the route and all provide libations. The motto: "Médoc, le Marathon le Plus Long du Monde." The T-shirt pictures a drunken runner staggering through a vineyard.

If there's one quality you don't crave in a 26.2-mile foot race, it's additional distance. But then you can run the Médoc in a straight line. That's up to you. Le Marathon des Chateaux du Médoc passes 59 of the region's fabled properties, 18 of which broach their famous casks. Labeled

Degustation and indicated on the map with miniature red goblets, the wine stops also offer local delicacies—cheese, oysters, steak, and even sausage. That's right, sausage. I was more offended by the sausage than the wine.

Can this be healthy? The French die young, we think, forgetting Jeanne Louise Calment. She spent her life in Arles and remembered the painter Vincent van Gogh as "very ugly, ungracious, impolite. . . ." When Calment died in 1997, she was 122 years old. "I've only got one wrinkle," she liked to say, "and I'm sitting on it." When asked at her 120th birthday what kind of future she expected to have, she said, "A very short one."

Nor is this one lady the only French person to survive middle age. Americans have a life expectancy of 77.85. The French are expected to live for 79.73 years.

Calment took up fencing at 85 and rode a bicycle until she was 100. The old lady smoked until she was 117, only quitting because she couldn't see to light up and was ashamed to ask anyone else to do it for her. She never worked, which is part of the trick, but also she seems to have been unflappable. Me, I'm American. I'm highly flappable.

I'm the sort of flappable American who leaves everything until the last minute. Most of the competitors go to Pauillac—the town where the race begins and ends—a couple of days before the big event, but I'm an American. I couldn't do that. I was far too busy to go early to a beautiful region known for its fine wines. Actually, in my own defense, I would have missed my family. If they could have come along, I would certainly have gone early. But nevertheless, I am uptight.

Le marathon began at 9:30 in the morning of Saturday the 7th of September of 2002. I would leave New York on the night of the 5th. My travel agent phoned that afternoon to say that Air France was on strike. Fear not, she said. Travel off the continent was not affected, and my flight from Paris to Bordeaux would be replaced by a train. The railroad station was right at the airport. I'd be given the train tickets at JFK.

Friendly Air France personnel at Kennedy had *no idea* what I was talking about. They told me to get on the line to buy tickets. I got on the line. This was a long line. It was not moving. One of the women on the line was weeping.

Tempted to turn around and go home, I instead went back to the first clerk. She and her friend both peered at the computer. Then she came back. I should just go to France, she said, and hope for the best.

Like I said, I'm flappable. I was listening at the time to a recording of a biography of Winston Churchill. I credit this with my willingness to go on. It was just too incongruous to be defeated at an airline counter, while hearing about a man who had led a cavalry charge. "Never give in. Never, never, never ..."

So I got on the plane, which was only slightly delayed. Still, I arrived at de Gaulle jet-lagged, dehydrated, and having had 3 hours of sleep. Ordinarily, I won't run on the day before a marathon, but I sprinted across the terminal and to the place where the trains were. Not fast enough, though. The train was already full. *"C'est complet."* That's the sort of line the French like to deliver, especially if you're an American.

But then I was upset enough to melt even a Frenchman's heart. There were other trains to Bordeaux, I was told. All I had to do was take two different subways.

Harried and defeated, I lugged my bag and backpack down into the Paris Metro. I must have looked as hapless as I felt, because coming through the turnstile at Montparnasse, I sensed a hand on my wallet. Have you ever heard a dowager stub her toe? That's how I sounded. I let out such a squeal of outrage and dismay that the would-be thief vanished.

By the time I got to the right station, I was thoroughly disoriented. I found seats on two of the wrong trains, and was ejected from each, before finally settling in the right place on the right train. The trip to Bordeaux was uneventful, and a person less easily flapped—Jeanne Louise Calment, for instance—would have dozed, but I was far too worried about sleep to sleep. I had a paperback of *Consolation of Philosophy*, which—I'm ashamed to say—didn't hold my interest, even though it was written by Boethius, while he was in prison awaiting death.

I found this description of his execution on the Web:

"A cord was twisted round his head many times for a very long period so that his eyeballs started from their sockets; blows from a club finished off the shattered wreck."[1]

Marathon representative Florence Raffard met me at le Gare St. Jean and presented a Renault Scenic Automatic and a map, on which the trip to the pre-marathon dinner had been marked with a yellow highlighter. When she saw my face fall—I don't believe I actually wept—Florence agreed to guide me to the city limits. Unfortunately for both of us, we started just in time for the Friday-evening exodus. It took 2 hours to make what should have been a 15-minute drive.

By the time I reached Listrac and the Chateau Fourcas Hosten, which was hosting the marathon dinner, it was 9 p.m. I had been traveling for 24 hours. I'd been awake for 21 of those hours.

Fear not, Florence said, when I told her I wanted to skip the party and go straight to sleep. Another journalist, Dora Tuazin, was also staying at my destination, les Ormes de Pez. Dora would meet me at the "Diner des Mille Pates" and ride with me to the Chateau.

I met Dora at the party, and she said my race number and race shirt were waiting at les Ormes de Pez. "I have everything you need to run a beautiful marathon," she said.

"What I need to run a beautiful marathon," I said, "is to go to sleep right now."

"First," she said and twinkled, "you must enjoy yourself."

"All right," I said bitterly, "I'll enjoy myself. But only briefly."

And so I was led to a great white tent, which had been thrown up on the grounds of the Chateau. There were trestle tables, and a live band was sawing and banging away. And lots of people—runners presumably—were smoking cigarettes.

I took a piece of bread and an empty goblet. At home, I'll try to remember the name of a particular bottle of wine, or ask the store owner to help, or make my decision based largely on the price. *Does it feel like a $7.95 evening?*

Here all the wine was free, so I resorted to the "Oo la la" technique of wine selection. I'd lurk at the verges of the dining tent until a new wire basket full of bottles appeared and when I heard cries of *"C'est beau! C'est beau! Oo la la!"* I'd pop out of the shadows, glass in hand.

My French and my flapped demeanor identified me immediately as an American, and being American opened up two subjects: the World Trade Center tragedy, *"C'est dommage. C'est horrible."* And the New York Marathon, *"C'est magnifique."*

Among these celebrants, the New York Marathon seemed to be our nation's greatest achievement. Forget the Marshall Plan. Forget the beaches of Normandy. *Vive* Fred Lebow.

But then despite the wine, despite the heavy dinner, despite the cigarettes, these people were still runners. The Médoc Marathon was started in 1985 by a group of friends who had run New York in 1984. The New York Marathon celebrates New York. They wanted a marathon to celebrate le Médoc. New York is known for its size and diversity. Le Médoc is known for its wine. The event became as much a festival as a race. For reasons lost now in the mists of time, the competitors began to wear costumes and carry props.

Eight thousand five hundred entries were accepted for the 2002 race, with many others turned away. One hundred and forty-six Americans ran the race, but I didn't see one at the party the night before. When a group took the stage and belted out "New York, New York," it sounded like a French song to me.

A man dressed as a monk was waving a flag with a huge rooster on it in time to the song. The flagpole was a sponge mop. Yes, I'm sure, because I could see the mop head.

Quite drunk at this point, but far too tired and anxious to enjoy myself, I found Dora.

"I need to go to the hotel," I said.

"Chateau," she said.

"Chateau," I said. "I need to go to sleep." Dora's face fell. "But I am feeling fleet of foot," she said, "and I don't have to run tomorrow."

"What do you want to do?" I asked.

"I want to have fun," she said. "I want to dance. I want to eat dessert. Can't you go to the Chateau alone?"

"It's dark. I'm tired. I'll get lost."

"It's simple," she said.

"Can you have fun in an hour?" I asked.

"*Certainement,*" she said.

"All right," I said. "You have fun for an hour. Then we can go to the hotel."

"Chateau."

"Chateau," I agreed, took Dora's seat, and began disconsolately to eat her crème brûlée while she headed out onto the dance floor.

Winemaker Jean Claude Poisson plied me with a 1994 bottle from Chateau Fourcas Hosten. Many of the local vintners had contributed to the gala. I spoke with a young woman who said that when I smiled, I looked "just like my favver." Her "favver," not mine.

Dora didn't reappear until after 10 o'clock. "I want to go to the hotel now, please," I pleaded manfully.

Couldn't I find my own way to the Chateau? she asked gaily. I got up and stalked out of the tent. The car had one of those keys where the blade folds into the plastic that has the battery, and I couldn't figure out how to fold it back out again. So I stopped a reveler in the parking lot, and he did it for me.

The car started. Miracle of miracles, I found the place. I found a wall with les Ormes de Pez written on it, but I couldn't figure out how to get behind the wall. I had a cell phone, praise God, and called the number I had been given and asked for Isabelle, the woman who was to be my contact at the Chateau. Isabelle answered the phone, and she sent her husband, Jean Marc, out in a car to lead me onto the grounds. By midnight, I was in bed.

My eyes blinked twice drunkenly—and it was 7:30 a.m. I took a bath and joined a dozen French runners at breakfast. There were no vitamins at the table. No electrolyte replacement drinks. No aspirin, no ibuprofen. No Bengay. We ate bread and butter and jam. Also yogurt. This despite the fact that I've recently read that dairy products slow the long-distance runner.

Dora appeared. She seemed not to be furious at me, and so I thought I probably shouldn't be furious at her either.

"You look fine," I said in disbelief. "How can that be?"

"That's because you can't see my leever," she said.

Dora had my number and shirt. The shirt pictured a runner zigzagging drunkenly between vineyards, his nose bright red, a bottle in his hand. As we drove to the start, I asked nervously about the wine.

"You should drink it," Dora said. "It's good wine."

"What about finishing the race?" I asked.

Dora shrugged prettily. "Of course there are people here," she said, and her voice fell dramatically, "who come to run a fast race. But they are verrr-ry borrrring."

I'm a talker, and when I'm nervous, I make a lot of noise. But I remembered that in fifth grade, my French teacher had said that when I spoke the language, I sounded like a cow with a bellyache. *Une vache avec un mal de ventre.*

So I stood by myself and tried not to look lonely or nervous. Four great cranes had been set up on the road at the start, where Pauilliac nestles the Gironde. Each crane had a dragon's head. The dragon nearest to where I stood had a young woman inside the jaw and working the controls. The head reared back, and Roman candles began to shoot colored strips of paper down onto the crowd. This was not a marathon. This was a party.

And so the race began. It was slow at first, terribly slow. The course runs through many narrow streets, and I got stuck behind a wagon with a model of a champagne distillery on it.

Running along, I finally saw a couple who looked American. They were Canadian. I complained about the traffic jam. The man answered. "It's not about speed," he told me. "You add an hour and a half to your ordinary time."

"It's not the wine that slows you down?" I asked.

"No," he insisted. "I used to think that drinking was bad for running. It's not. There was a time," he said, and wagged his head sadly in disbelief, "when people thought that sex was bad for athletic performance."

I passed one wine stop, then another. I kept on running. Everybody else stopped.

Most of the competitors were in elaborate costume. One middle-aged man running as the devil—scarlet, with tail and horns—dragged a heavy chain at the other end of which jogged a woman of about his age and proportions. She was outfitted as a lost soul. Many were dressed as grandmothers, toting pocketbooks. I didn't appreciate it when they zipped by me. I suffered considerable humiliation in the courtyard of one Chateau, when I heard wheels on cobblestones and glanced back to see that I was being overtaken by a man pulling a wagon with several potted grapevines inside.

Then the landscape began to work on me. This region has been producing wine since Roman times. And yes, there were runners in Roman togas. All that claret encountered in English literature came from Bordeaux. The region still produces the greatest quantity of the finest wines in the world. Even if you didn't love the wine, you'd love the setting. There were stone walls on every side and beyond the stone walls, vineyards.

At the end of a row of grapevines, there is often a rosebush. Roses in the vineyards function like the canaries in the mine. Flowers are victim to many of the same blights that hit the grapevines. The roses get sick first. Despite their utilitarian purpose, they still look like roses, which is to say, beautiful. Set back behind the vineyards loom these great buildings in blond stone, les Chateaux.

So we ran through vineyards, heavy now with grapes—it was September, and every so often, we'd turn off the main road and jog up a graveled drive, past decorative pools and then into the courtyard of a vast stone building. There, we'd find a table with a white tablecloth and on the table, glasses of wine. Not plastic or cardboard cups of wine, but glasses. The men behind the table, often dressed formally, would refill the glasses of wine.

Some of the runners had enormous atomizers, like you'd shoot perfume out of, and they'd run up close to the crowd and squirt. Sometimes they squirted water, sometimes they squirted mustard.

I had a plan. I'd run an experiment. I'd wait until I was 10 miles into the race, and then I'd stop and drink some wine. Twenty minutes later, I'd see how I felt. So I stopped and had a glass of red wine. It was Bordeaux, of course, and hearty. You know I forgot to look again at my watch. I didn't, however, forget to stop at the next degustation. I wasn't going to skip Chateau Lafite Rothschild.

Now I was getting into the spirit of the event. Carriages had raced up these drives, with wicked, disdainful aristocrats riding inside, infuriating Charles Dickens. Hoofbeats had echoed through these very courtyards. There must have been damsels, right? And honor. I was part of something ancient and fine.

Marathon runners all know, of course, that marathon runners all need to go to the bathroom all the time. In the United States, it's the Gatorade. In France, it's the Bordeaux. But where do you go to the bathroom when you're running on a narrow road through some of the finest vineyards in the world? Answer: In some of the finest vineyards in the world.

At one point, I saw a young woman, looking slightly embarrassed, stepping out from behind a row of grapes, tucking her shirt back into her shorts. The best picture—and I had no camera—was three young men dressed as playing cards and peeing voluminously off of the road and into a field of famous grapes.

Yes, I did cross the finish line and had a medal draped over my neck, a bottle of Cuvee du Marathon 1997 pressed into my hands.

From the finish, I was led to a table, given another bottle of wine, this one opened, and served a steak with stewed tomatoes. I bummed a cigarette. When in Rome. The woman to my left was a doctor, Martine

Baspera. "Could all this wine be good for you?" I asked her, drinking my second post-marathon glass.

"*Mais oui,*" she said, and then ticked off six reasons why an adult male must drink at least two glasses of red wine a day. Even if wine tasted like cod liver oil, the sensible man would be advised to drink it. Red wine is a protection against heart disease, cancer, Alzheimer's. Anyone who didn't drink a glass of wine daily was toying with his health. Martine is a dermatologist, and wine, she said, is very good for the skin.

I wasn't the ugly American anymore, just one of a happy pack of revelers. Anyone who has run a marathon overseas will understand. The ordeal seems to melt away the iron framework of our differences.

Janet and I ran the Montreal Marathon twice. One year, we spent the night after and wandered around the old city the next day. We were wearing our medals under our civilian clothes. We ran into another couple. They had that same, I-might-look-fit-if-I-weren't-so-tired look. I pulled out my medal. Janet showed hers. There was a moment of embarrassed silence, and then they each produced a medal of their own.

In Montreal, I was still fast. In Bordeaux, I ran a 4-hour-and-36-minute race, my slowest ever, except on those occasions when I've run with friends who are first-timers. Or have been hurt.

Still, I'd do it again in a minute. Even with an airline strike, I'd do it again. Driving back to the Chateaux in a haze of endorphins and Bordeaux, I tried desperately to understand why wine and running now seemed such a good match and, conversely, why so recently, they'd seemed such a bad one. Wine may actually be good for your health, I thought. Running may actually be good for your health, too. I've been an obsessive runner since 1978. I don't run because it's good for my heart. Nor do I drink wine because it will give me beautiful skin.

CHAPTER 16

The Rebirth of the Olympics

"FASTER, HIGHER, STRONGER."
—OLYMPIC MOTTO

The first Olympic event was a foot race, and today's show is the greatest track and field competition in the world, but the man who resuscitated the Olympics was a boxer and a fencer, who took particular pleasure in rowing and rugby.

The Frenchman who had his heart buried in Olympia, Greece, was an ardent internationalist. "The Olympic movement," wrote Baron Pierre de Coubertin, "tends to bring together in radiant unison all the qualities which guide mankind to perfection."

An aristocrat and an idealist, he was also a scrapper, and if he hadn't been, the Olympics—dormant for more than 1,000 years—would not have been revived in 1896. Nor would the marathon exist at all.

Excited by archeological finds in Olympia and by his belief in the benefits of sport and the possibility of world peace, the baron hosted an International Congress of Amateurs at the Sorbonne in Paris in 1894. There, the International Olympic Committee was formed, and plans were made to stage the games in Athens, Greece, in 1896. Michel Breal, a French historian greatly taken with the story of Pheidippides, suggested a distance event to commemorate that run. (Incidentally, the longest race held in ancient Olympia is thought to have been just 24 stadia, or 4.6 kilometers. The ancient Greeks ran distance, of course, but just to get from one place to another, or—like Pheidippides—to carry messages.)

Coubertin liked the idea and scheduled a marathon as the final event. The Greek businessman Georgious Averoff, who backed the games, was also enthusiastic. Averoff had paid for the restoration of the ancient Panathenaic Stadium in which the Athens Marathon still ends today.

Eager to do well in a race so closely associated with their glorious past, the Greeks had two practice runs on the planned course, which mimicked the fabled trip from Marathon to Athens and covered 24.8 miles.

The Olympic trial held in March 1896 was the first marathon ever. The first Olympic Marathon was held on April 10th of that year. A field estimated at between 17 and 20 lined up near the Marathon Bridge, a speech was made, a pistol fired.

The Greeks were wild to win this particular event. A crowd of over 100,000 lined the road and filled the stadium. The contest began just before 2 p.m. Outside of the Greek team, only Gyula Kellner of Hungary had ever been in a race this long.

The runners were accompanied by coaches, doctors, and officials, some in horse-drawn wagons and others on bicycles.

Albin Lermusiaux of France—who had won the bronze medal in the 1,500-meter race—took the lead. He is said to have hit the half in an unbelievable 55 minutes. The spectators had already crowned him with a victory wreath when he was knocked over by another Frenchman on a bicycle. It may only be a legend, but I've read that that bicyclist was his coach. The racer rose and started off again, but quit with 8 miles still to go.

Australian Edwin Flack now moved to the front and sent a bicyclist off to the stadium to announce his victory, thus making the Greeks in the crowd extremely unhappy. At last a Greek, Spiridon Louis, took the lead. Apparently he, too, had been confident throughout and had eaten an Easter egg and stopped to drink a glass of wine.

The crowds in the streets of Athens were ecstatic to see Louis, and when he hit the stadium, Crown Prince Nicholas and Prince George jumped on the track and ran to the finish with him. Spiridon Louis won in 2:58:50. When the king offered a reward—anything the victor wanted— Louis asked for a horse and cart for his business, which was delivering water in the small village from which he came. To say *egine Louis* in Greek now means to become like Louis, and means to run fast.

There are many colorful and contrasting accounts of other rewards offered the winner of the 1896 race. He was supposed to have been promised free coffee for life, free haircuts for life, and even a bride.

The baron was pleased with the success of his brainchild, and so were the Greeks. "The most important thing in the Olympic Games," he wrote, "is not winning but taking part; the essential thing in life is not conquering but fighting well."

The Greeks treated the winners of the ancient games as if they had become a different species, half god, half human. The baron hoped that if athletes from all over the world could compete within rules, this would encourage international comity. Play within the rules, however unfair they may seem to be. The baron himself could not always see the struggle as essential and the score unimportant. He was bitterly disappointed in 1936, when the Nobel Peace Prize he felt he'd earned went to an Argentinian instead.[1]

And yet internationalism as embodied by the Olympics has often dramatized the brotherhood of man. One famous example being the experience of Jesse Owens in Berlin.

By 1936, Hitler was beginning to demonstrate the domestic and international ruthlessness that would blacken the history of the 20th century. He had persuaded a somewhat ambivalent world to let his Reich host the games. He had rebuilt the stadium, excluded Jews, and sponsored Leni Riefenstahl to make the film. The Germans won 33 gold medals to America's poor second of 24.

The man and state had moved beyond the constraints of ordinary morality. Whether or not Hitler snubbed Owens, a sprinter and long jumper, at the stadium is open to question, but Hitler said in private that he would never shake the hand of a black man. He also said that the Americans should be ashamed of themselves for letting blacks compete. And yet the leader of the 1,000-year Reich couldn't keep a black man from coming to Berlin and winning four—count them—four gold medals.

And in this historic case, the justice Owens's performance illustrated in a crooked country was garnished with a magnificent act of individual kindness and sportsmanship. The Führer couldn't even restrain his own champion Luz Long from helping Jesse.

Jesse had started to run the long-jump course for practice, as he always did, and was shocked when the official showed a red flag and called it a foul, as if the American had meant this exploratory trip as one of his three jumps. So thrown was Owens by the unfamiliar European rules that his second long jump was short.

At this moment, Luz Long, a German competitor, wearing a shirt with a swastika on it, suggested that Owens—now terrified of another foul— draw a line in back of the actual legal point for takeoff. Since the great jumper had more than enough power to go the required distance, the stratagem removed the one real obstacle—fear of a second fatal foul.

Owens took the German's advice and qualified for the event in which he would ultimately win a gold medal. Jesse would recall Long's act as one of the highlights of the games and of his life.

Luz Long was killed in the war.

In *All That Glitters* William Johnson reports that the Nazis tried to use the 1936 event to enrich their beloved master race. They arranged an Olympic love program. A beech forest was set aside within the Olympic village. Toothsome *Fräulein* were given special passes and told to select choice athletes. The girls were encouraged to mingle—in the most intimate sense of the word—with stars from abroad. Legend has it that after the maidens had given their all—not for England in this case, but for the Reich—they would ask for the man's Olympic badge. In case of pregnancy, the state would pay to rear the child.

I trust the baron would have been horrified.

CHAPTER 17

Let's Keep in Touch

"THE GOOD NEWS IS THAT THERE'S ONLY ONE HILL.
THE BAD NEWS IS THAT IT'S 8 MILES LONG."
—JEFF GALLOWAY, 1972 OLYMPIAN AND GROUP LEADER
AT THE ATHENS, GREECE, MARATHON

Getting on a plane to Athens, Greece, I found the aisle blocked by a pudgy woman fingering a backpack, which she seemed to have gotten at the marathon in Bordeaux. "You've run the Médoc?" I heard her ask a seated friend. I *had* run the Médoc Marathon. Now I wondered, and not without some bitterness, why I got no backpack.

This was in 2004, and I was in the awkward spot of a man starting to observe a sport he'd been participating in on an almost-daily basis since 1978. I felt a little like a trout who has taken up fly-fishing.

Ever the fearless correspondent, I'd begun my research with a package tour. *It's Athens,* I thought, *the course on which the Olympics was just held,*

and over ground on which the first marathon ever is said to have been run. I'll
have fun. These are my people. But were they?

I found my seat. "The man in front of me plays scrabble with his Irish
wife," I now wrote in my notes. Jay—that's his name—says he got the idea
of running marathons from the Arthritis Foundation at a "get-a-life
meeting." He answered an advertisement. He funds his marathon trips by
collecting for Joints in Motion, which raises money to fight arthritis.

"But doesn't running cause arthritis?" I asked.

"Could do," Jay said.

We didn't go into it at the moment, and I'm not a doctor, but many
doctors I know are distance runners. Nobody seems to know for sure what
causes the disease, which has many forms, and running may actually
protect against it.

Jay had run the Dublin Marathon twice. Paris, he told me, held a
terrific marathon. He is from Florida and has run Miami and Jacksonville.
He'd like to run Florence.

After our little chat, my new friend turned away and revealed what a
tall man he was by putting his seat back almost as far as it would go. "I like
him a good deal less," I wrote angrily in my notebook.

Before signing on, I'd phoned tour leader Jeff Galloway to ask if I was
too slow. "I can run a 7-minute-mile," I said, "but I often run eights."

Not too slow at all, he said. I said that I was more dogged than talented.
He liked that.

I also told Jeff that I was a writer. I also told him about my famous
father. If strangers don't know about my father, I tell them. I'm deeply
hurt, of course, when they almost inevitably become more interested in
my father's writing than in my own. This has been true for decades, and
yes, I have been in therapy, but there you go. I also have bad posture and
swallow my food without chewing.

Jeff seemed not to care terribly about my prose, or my father's prose
either. But he *was* interested in my slowness, and fed me several tortoise-
hare tales.

"In fact, I've found that most of those who've had a lot of talent from the time they were in high school did not achieve at the highest level," he said. "They got up to a certain point, got into the adversity and not winning, and they couldn't deal with it. And they dropped by the wayside. In fact, most of the people on any Olympic team are those who weren't the instant stars. They had to find the stuff inside them and also to find the stuff from other sources that helped them be the best that they could be."

A lifelong tortoise, I gushed back about the terrible handicaps of talent, wealth, intelligence. Beauty, of course, was a terrible curse. But after I got off the phone, sweaty with the intimacy of our exchange, I wondered if Jeff was implying that I might—now at 56—still be an Olympian? If so, then at least one of us was going to be gravely disappointed.

Once on the plane, I could see that I was not the only tortoise Jeff had charmed. Craning my neck to peer around, I saw many tortoises with shells size XXL. This might have been a tour for real estate salesmen, or Weight Watchers.

Then I thought I saw Galloway himself walk by. He had that Peter Pan look, a big black Nike Triax watch, and he was wearing jeans and no belt.

Now I've always insisted on a belt because a belt is designed to hold the pants up. People who see me wearing a belt, I figure, are forced to the conclusion that if I weren't wearing it, my pants could be down around my ankles. Therefore the belt says THIS GUY'S THIN. Whereas those who don't wear belts really are thin. Not wearing a belt is like being so rich you don't carry cash.

At least I wasn't wearing a money-belt, although I had ogled them at the TravelSmith Web site. Having been nearly robbed in the turnstile of the Paris Metro during my trip to run the Médoc, I had developed a yearning for secret pockets. My largest purchase had been the TravelSmith "Anything Goes" blazer in classic houndstooth. The day this arrived, I was so excited that I put it on over a lime-green polo shirt.

"How do you like my jacket with the secret pockets?" I asked, proudly, when Janet came home. "It goes with everything."

"You're going to Greece," she said.

"Yeah."

"You'll fit right in," she said.

So now I was on the plane and in my "Anything Goes" blazer and in my TravelSmith turtleneck and TravelSmith jeans, which had elastic in the fabric, a hidden inner zippered compartment in the right rear pocket. You could have murdered me, and it would still have taken an hour to find my money.

I liked the jacket, and it really does not wrinkle, but I found that I needed to travel with at least three pairs of eyeglasses, because I kept forgetting which secret pockets concealed them.

After we got to the hotel, which is on the coast of the Aegean in Vouliagmeni, "the jewel of the Greek Riviera," Jeff led a small group on a sort of run/walk, which he said would be 3 miles. Right away, I was disappointed. I like to go 5. I don't really feel that I've lived on a day when I haven't run at least 5 miles. But I also wanted to meet people, and all the people on the tour were following Jeff. We all seemed to be marathoners, relatively lean and fit. I guessed the 10-K contingent—and Athens does have a 10-K— were saving themselves for the race. We went up some stairs and then into the hills.

Galloway is the originator and chief proponent of the run/walk technique. In *Galloway's Book on Running*,[1] he tells of an unbelieving friend whom he, Jeff, had to coerce into taking a 1-minute walk/break for every mile of his marathon. Thinking that walking during a race was "sissy stuff," the guy nevertheless followed Jeff's advice and ran a 3:25 marathon, 15 minutes faster than he'd ever gone before. The time lost by walking, Jeff explained, was more than compensated for by the time he'd ordinarily lost by slowing down in the last 6 to 8 miles of the race.

I've heard people come out in favor of Jeff's technique, even for those who can run under 3 hours. Others disagree and think—as I do—that the technique is best for the beginner, or for ultras—races of more than 26 miles.

In *Racing the Antelope: What Animals Can Teach Us about Running and Life,*

Bernd Heinrich writes about the efficacy of alternating walk breaks with running in ultras, but concludes that even a 100-kilometer race "is still far too short a distance to permit any stopping if you are planning to win or set a record."

Now, on our first outing as a group, we were going to run, stop, walk, run, stop. So we ran along uneasily for a mile or so, all trying to keep a good view of Jeff so that we could see when he stopped. Then we'd all stop, too, in a sort of chain reaction, like a commuter train that's crashed into a wall. Then we'd walk for a minute and uneasily start up again.

Jeff led us up to a peak with a sweeping view. He said it had been a lookout in ancient times. There was a pit, off to one side of the summit, and Jeff said that this had probably been a shelter, and that messages were sent and received by runners. Just down from the summit, there was a molded white plastic chair. In the pit, there was an old but clearly not ancient plastic Coke bottle.

Jeff started up again and on we went with our game of red light/green light for adults. By now, there was considerable grumbling. The more fanatical of us wanted to just go full out for 5 miles, and take a shower and be done with it. When I asked the man beside me if he believed in the walk/run technique, he said he didn't know but that he had seen a marathon in Texas spoiled by it. You'd be running along, he said, and suddenly everyone in front of you would stop and walk for a minute. You'd crash into them, pass them. Then they'd run past you and stop again.

A young guy, a blond with a black Velcro brace on his ankle, jogged up beside me. "Want to just run?" he asked. I said, "Yes, I do," and we went off on our own.

Heading back to the hotel, I fell in with Jay, whose height was not a problem now that we were off the plane. He said that he'd taken to mixing yoga with his workouts. He told me also—and I've since heard this from others—that the only way to get hill training in Florida was to run the bridges.

Jeff was a little late for the next morning's run, and we were told that he was having difficulties with the alarm on his new Nike Triax. Again the gathering was relatively fit and fast. My plump Médoc colleague had not appeared, nor had others of her variety.

When Jeff exited the elevator, we poured out of the hotel and into a light fog, which made the curbing dangerous as we headed up along the shore of the Aegean. But it was a good group, and apparently we were going to get to run, run, run. Run, stop, walk in the fog would have been fatal. I fell in with a man of about my size, age, and speed.

Norm Heiser was traveling with his wife, Barb, also a runner. His son, Tim, and daughter-in-law, Dana, had come down from Naples to be with them. He was a Bush supporter, probably still is, and I had been heartbroken about Kerry's defeat. But I couldn't help but like, and even admire, this guy.

Norm, it developed, hadn't started running until he was 55. He was so out of shape at the time that there was some feeling that he was endangering his health. When I met him in Greece, he'd been running for 2 years and had lost 50 pounds. Five foot 10, he tries now to stay at about 155 pounds.

He was frankly gleeful about the pleasures of running. His wife ran with him, and sometimes one of the grown children. He'd run the Chicago Marathon every year, just because it was so close. He'd run the New York Marathon and had visited Ground Zero. Everywhere Norm and Barb had gone, they met these tremendous people. "Just the best people." There wasn't a touch of irony or sarcasm in the man.

Norm is the proprietor of Heiser's Garage and Autobody in Peoria, Illinois, and I know as much about his business as he knows about mine. We had running, though, and laughter.

I was invited to join his family, if I wanted. I wanted. After our meeting, I ate most of my dinners with the Heisers, and dinners—as married men forced to travel alone will tell you—are the hardest part.

Before the race, the tour took us on a trip to the Agora, which I knew meant public market place, since I knew agoraphobia means the fear of same.

Like the Forum in Rome, the Athens Agora is astonishingly rich in history. Both areas charge admission. In Greece, tour guides are licensed, highly educated government employees, and so following around behind a guide is thrilling.

Among the sights pointed out to us was a great flank of open rock. Significant speakers would hold forth there, we were told. Saint Paul spoke there.

I wondered what he'd looked like. Did Athens get the gentle, poetic man, or the stern one, the lawgiver? Was he thin, with a high, reedy voice? Was he a runner?

"I have run the great race," he wrote. "I have finished my course, I have kept the faith."

The Heisers hadn't joined the trip to the Agora, and so after the run, I wound up with Larry Whipple, a software engineer and recently bitten runner. We shopped for gifts to bring back home, talked about best marathon times, best runs. He had some concerns about his iliotibial band.

Back at the hotel, Jeff called a pre-race meeting and sold copies of his book. He warned against hyponatremia.

Even while Jeff lectured us, I thought the condition must be for very slow runners who doused their anxiety with gallons of water. But when the story finally hit the front page of the *New York Times* in April 2005, I was taken up short.

Gina Kolata's front-page article reported on a piece in the *New England Journal of Medicine* about runners in the Boston Marathon. You have to run fast in order to get into the Boston Marathon. And yet a sampling of 488 runners taken in that race in 2002 found 62 of them had hyponatremia, sodium levels driven dangerously low. One 28-year-old woman died.

Jeff talked about the Athens course. He said that he had good news about the race, and bad news. "The good news is that there's only one hill. The bad news is that it's 8 miles long."

The day of the race, we took a bus to the start, Jeff standing in the front drinking a Diet Coke and feeding us morsels of history.

He told us again how this had been a crucial juncture in the culture of the world, that we would pass the hill where 192 Greek heroes were buried. There was no mention of the 6,400 Persians who were supposed to have been killed that day. The Persian army outnumbered the Athenian army four to one. And then, of course, the great news was carried to Athens by Pheidippides.

"Rejoice! We conquer!" he said, and died.

Despite my smart-alecky talk, Norm and I caved on race day. We thought we'd give the Galloway technique a try and walk for 45 seconds every mile.

Norm and I expected to run at about the same pace, coming in somewhere near 4 hours. We had a problem. The course was marked in kilometers.

That's where Larry Whipple came in. He had the Timex Body Link System, which gets its information from satellites. The watch is small, supplemented with a GPS unit worn on the arm or at the waist. I liked the slogan: "Life is ticking." We were in far-away Greece, but at the start, the system worked.

So Norm and I figured we'd run with Larry, and he could tell us when we'd gone a mile. Now Larry was aiming for a slower race than we were, but we'd give it a try, with the idea that we could break up later, as our relative strengths became apparent.

I stayed with them both until about 8 miles, and then pulled ahead—I think it was ahead—but continued to walk for about 45 seconds every 8 to 10 minutes.

I was horrified to reach the half in 2 hours and 7 minutes. This put me on course for a 4-hour-and-14-minute marathon. This was slower than any of the other 40-plus marathons I'd ever run, excluding times with friends and the Médoc, of course. But that time I was drunk. So I forgot Galloway and ran all out for the second half, coming in at 3:55:28.

I've since been in touch with Jeff Galloway by e-mail, ever tantalized by the idea that if I stopped to walk each mile, I'd have a faster time. And I have sometimes stopped and walked during the first half of a marathon, but then I always hit the half so far behind time that I cave and run the rest of the way.

Dave Drucker, who's run a couple of marathons with me, recently exhibited the bad taste to get much faster than I am, partly due to the interval work he did with Mike Barnow and with a willingness to take days off. Dave ran part of the Westchester Marathon with me, stopping to walk several times early on. Dave's a lawyer, and if you tell him snow is white, he'll tell you it's black, or it might be black. But when I told him I didn't believe in the Galloway technique, "because it's never worked for me," he pointed out that I've never really given it a chance.

"What do you mean not given it a chance?" I said. I give it half the marathon, and by then I'm so far behind . . ."

"But you've never trained that way," he said. "If you trained that way, it might work. You don't know." And he's right, of course. Which gives him two strikes. He's also a faster marathoner than I am.

The Athens Marathon comes down into the city and ends in the magnificent marble Panathenaic Stadium. A stadium was first built on this site in 330 BC. The structure was rebuilt when the Olympics were reinstituted in 1896.

The post-race feeling that all men are brothers in paradise was heightened by the distinctly international flavor of the group. All men may not actually be brothers, but that's the way it feels after a marathon. You hear people speaking in tongues. This is not because they've been possessed, but only because they aren't American, or English. But you feel—you can't help but feel—that you all understand each other. There must have been music playing. I'm not sure now. Maybe it was in my head.

But when, while writing this, I phoned Norm to relive the race, neither of us focused on the thrill of the finish.

"Remember that guy who died?" Norm asked.

"As to the fellow who keeled over—I recall him vividly," Larry Whipple wrote in e-mail. "I'm not sure of the reality of it but heard the story that he had gone to the doctor just the day before complaining of indigestion. His doctor was concerned and suggested that he might not want to run the marathon, to which he reportedly replied, 'I'm going to run it even if it kills me.' Now, this sounds way too much like an urban legend to be his actual comment, but I suspect the doctor's visit did occur even if not exactly the day before. He was about my age as I recall (42 or 43) and apparently died on the way to the hospital."

He was on the left side of a divided road, both directions of which had been appropriated for the foot race. I was on the right side of the median but still close enough so that I could see beads of sweat glistening on his head and shoulders. The stranger looked younger than I and fit. His head was not shaved, but his hair had been buzzed so short that he might have been a Marine conscript. His eyes rolled up into his head. Another runner caught him and then sat on the road holding the fallen marathoner in his arms. A third man was on a cell phone, so there seemed to be nothing that our little party could add.

We kept going, and soon saw the ambulance.

There was a banquet on the night after the race. I sat with Norm and Barb and their son, Tim, and his wife, Dana. It was a catered event, and when I heard that guests would each get just two glasses of wine, I sped up to my hotel room and fetched the plastic liter of retsina I'd purchased the night before.

Janet had introduced me to retsina when we visited Greece early in the 1980s. I thought it tasted like the sap of a hemlock tree, but it was cheap and authentic. The bottle I'd purchased at the local grocery store cost about 2 euros. When I asked the clerk if he had anything better, he wagged his head disdainfully. "Retsina," he said. "There's only one grape."

But for the night after a marathon, this seemed just fine. Speeches were made, and the travel agents were thanked, and prizes given.

I felt great, and gloriously anonymous. Which I guess is how most people feel all the time. Or at least when they're drunk. I'd been gnawing off and on throughout the trip on the problem of Jeff not recognizing me.

And this made me sore about his own fame. Fame, which, incidentally, he earned himself. I inherited mine.

At one point Larry Whipple got somebody else in the group to take a picture of himself with Galloway, and I was sort of surprised. Larry just wanted the picture. It meant something to him, but not a huge lot. Whereas fame often means a huge lot to me. I take it personally.

Drunk or running, or otherwise fully engaged—or in the company of people I love and know, this means nothing, of course. And now I was drunk. And with friends.

At the evening's close, we were called up one by one, and every one of us was given a tiny replica of an amphora. And every one of us had his or her picture taken with Jeff. I staggered up to the podium. I was shocked to find Jeff looking deep into my eyes. I mean he was looking into my eyes in the way I rarely look into the eyes of my own beloved wife. I felt that he must be seeing right down to the empty bottom of my soul.

"It was great to get to know you," he said. "And let's keep in touch." I staggered back to the table feeling naked and unmasked. *Sure, he pretended not to know who I was,* I thought. *Any special treatment would have justly infuriated the other folks on the tour. But he knew, he knew.*

Great to get to know you, I figured, *he might say that to anyone. But keep in touch? That means he knows who I am. Ben Cheever. Sacker of Cities. Son of John Cheever. Been published in the* New Yorker *magazine.*

I was overcome with that mixture of pride and sorrow, the fruit of being known. Yes, you're special, maybe better. But also isolated, and held to a higher standard.

I sat there in the toils of my inflated ego and suddenly alone. Then Norm went up to get his amphora and have his picture taken. It wasn't until he'd stumbled into the chair beside me that the lightbulb in my head snapped on.

"What did Galloway say to you?" I asked.

"Well," said Norm, "he said it was great to get to know me."

"And," I asked. "What else did he say?"

"He said we should keep in touch."

CHAPTER 18

The Problem of Kenya:
Why Do They Insist
on Winning All Our Races?

"YOU'RE ALL KENYAN TODAY."

—SIGN SEEN ON THE COURSE OF THE NEW YORK CITY MARATHON

If the answer is "Oh, some Kenyan," then the question must be "Who won?" Running the New York Marathon last year, I passed a sign—I think on First Avenue—that read "You're all Kenyan today." This means: "You're all winners today."

Kenyan Paul Tergat holds the world record for the marathon, a 2:04:55 set in 2003 in Berlin, but the dominance is greater than this alone would indicate.

Boston hosts the most prestigious marathon in America, perhaps in the world. Kenyan men have taken Boston 15 out of the past 17 years. Bostonians call Catherine Ndereba—a Kenyan—Catherine the Great, because she's won their hometown marathon four times.

Kenyans are so fast that Qatar and Bahrain pay them to run under their flags. I'd be outraged, except that I'm delighted to have Bernard Lagat running as an American citizen. I saw him win the Wanamaker mile for us in 2006. He won again in 2007.

Fanatical American runners—and there are a few—talk of the Kenyan staple ugali as if it were a nectar of the gods. This cornmeal mush, boiled and stirred until it's solid, is a staple in East Africa. Because it's a staple in East Africa, and not eaten often in the United States except by East Africans, it's natural to make the connection. If A plus B equals C, when A is a runner, B is Ugali, and C winning.

Kenya is to distance runners what the Vatican is to devout Catholics. In 2003, in a world of 6.5 billion souls, only 100 were chosen to run a marathon in less than 2 hours, 10 minutes, and 40 seconds. Forty-eight came from Kenya. Forty-two belonged to a single tribe, the Kalenjin.

Oh, some Kenyan? Why are we so uninterested in the people who dominate the sport that 38 million of us enjoy? Don't we like a winner? Can't we learn from them? Is it because the top runners aren't American? Or is it simply because they aren't assholes?

Cosmas Ndeti is a Kenyan. He projected the outrageous confidence we often see in American icons. A born-again Christian, he won the Boston Marathon three times in a row. That was in 1993, '94, and '95.

He wasn't an outright asshole: He gave money to his church and paid school fees for poor children. And he was a shrewd competitor, always holding back and then taking the lead in the last miles. He said that because of Boston's downhill, many runners go too fast. "The marathon is about waiting, then attacking."

But he was outspoken. For an African, he was uncharacteristically outspoken. Asked after 1995 if he was ready to win in '96, he was supremely confident. "I'm ready for next year. My Jesus is the same yesterday, today, forever," he said.

"Ndeti was beloved of Western media," says John Manners, an expert on Kenyan runners. "He was a colorful guy. He was very brash. He behaved in a way that the Kalenjin regard as childish and unthinkable."

Ndeti is not a Kalenjin. But Moses Tanui, the 1991 world champion at 10,000 meters, is. He was also in the race in 1995, and Cosmas is supposed to have said something to Moses as he passed, about there being a difference between 10,000 meters and the marathon. Cosmas won, and Moses Tanui came in second. Congratulated on his victory, Ndeti said, "Oh, it was nothing. If I'd had some competition, I could have gone much faster."

"This is beneath contempt," says Manners. "To dishonor a defeated opponent violates every precept of Kalenjin manhood. You must be gracious in victory. So Tanui was enflamed. Next year, Tanui just murdered Ndeti. That was in 1996, which was the Centennial of the Boston Marathon with the most prize money and the most news coverage. Moses just blasted him."

So the American public, which had begun to relate to Ndeti, got somebody less loquacious. We got a new face to contend with, a new name, difficult to pronounce. We lost the one Kenyan who had reminded us of American sports heroes.

In December 2001, Tanui and Tergat went to Washington, DC, for a 10-K held to raise money for Operation Smile, a children's charity. President Bush, who once ran a 3:44 marathon himself, heard from Letsrun.com that the men were in town and invited them to the White House. A picture was taken in the Oval Office of the president sandwiched between the two Kenyans, the American flag in the background, all three men beaming.

Tanui's comments seem not to have been recorded, but Tergat displayed the sort of humility that is rare in America's top athletes and joked that he didn't want to wash the hand that had shaken the hand of the president of the United States.

"It was a great honor to meet President Bush," said Tergat. "It was totally unexpected and such a surprise. I could not believe it. It was like I was dreaming."

In contrast, Miami Dolphins coach, Nick Saban, and some of his players turned down an invitation to dine with President Bush at Joe's Stone Crab in Miami Beach. Politics had nothing to do with it, they said. They were just too busy. Craig Hodges was a backup guard for the Chicago Bulls in 1991, and so he was with that team when it met the first President Bush at the White House. Hodges wore a dashiki for the occasion and gave the president a letter asking him to be more vigilant in his support of African Americans.

Don't you love it? The American wears the dashiki, the Africans were both in suits.

Seated next to Tergat's biographer, Jürg Wirz, at dinner once, I asked if anything about Tergat surprised him. Wirz is a journalist after all, and we're apt to see flaws. Well, actually, yes, Wirz began, he had been surprised. I looked away, feigning interest in my dinner, waiting for the penny to drop into the slot.

Tergat, it turned out, was more humble than Jürg had expected. The great athlete was honest, considerate, hardworking. He was more loyal, more polite than his biographer had originally thought. He cared about his nation, about his family, the poor. I almost laughed out loud. In America, this would have been the setup for a comedy routine.

I figured Jürg was a great liar, or Tergat a truly great man. Either way, I had no story. Not a single salvageable anecdote.

The book *Paul Tergat: Running to the Limit* opens with this quote from the marathon champion: "Nothing is impossible if you try." There's a picture of the house he built for his mother with his first winnings. For his *mother*?

Prompted for a personal theme, Tergat said, "Ask yourself, 'Can I give more?' The answer is usually, 'Yes.'"

It all seems so simple. And so alien. And for scandal-hungry Americans, so, so boring.

Put off by these well-mannered stars, we turn our backs. We fail to learn how the winners train, what they think, eat, and how they stretch. Most tragically, we fail to broaden our understanding of this shrinking world.

Are we less interested in Kenyans because we are drawn to suffering, and they seem not to suffer? I think of Canadian Terry Fox, who ran an 11-minute mile. He didn't finish the coast-to-coast trek he started in 1980. He had a prosthetic leg and was dying of cancer. Twenty-five years later, he's still a great hero, and the money raised in his name is channeled into research. Highways and stadiums have been named after Terry Fox. Prime Minister Pierre Trudeau awarded him the Order of Canada.

Do we think the Kenyan's aren't trying? If so, we're profoundly mistaken. Tegla Loroupe was the first African woman to win the New York Marathon. That was in 1994. She fought a terrific battle just to get to the starting line. (There's a reason that African women are way behind African men to this day, and I don't think it's about ability.)

Tegla's father had four wives, and she had 24 siblings. At age 7, she had to beg her father to let her run 10 kilometers to school. When she began to compete, her gender and the region she came from were both held against her, as was her size. Tegla is 4 foot 11 and weighs 86 pounds.

Paul Tergat had 16 siblings. He champions the UN's World Food Program, which gives free lunches to Kenyan children. Without this program, Tergat says, he himself would have gone without lunch.

He's 6 feet tall and weighs 138 pounds. When he cuts back to light training, he skips lunch. Staying that thin and that fast may look easy, but it's not. An elite distance runner, I am told, should weigh 2 pounds per inch of height. So Tergat could legitimately weigh 144 pounds. By contrast, I'm 5 foot 7. This means I should weigh 134. I'm at 150 today and proud of it.

Weight matters. In horse races of a mile, one added pound is thought to slow the animal by a full length.

When Tergat came to Boston in 1992, he was a favorite for the World Cross-Country Championships. There was snow, and so he ran on asphalt, which he had done infrequently in the past. He felt a twitch in his calf. That evening, he couldn't walk.

"I was stressed. It was a terrible experience," said the normally stoic star. "I couldn't believe what happened to me. I thought this was the end of everything. To be there without being able to run made me cry."

You can call it confidence if you want, or desperation, but these runners have it. Lance Armstrong says that the cancer that nearly killed him has given him an advantage as a competitive bicycle rider. He cares more than other people. Kenyans have the same advantage Lance Armstrong has.

When Bill Orr was handling the elite athletes for the Los Angeles Marathon, he'd meet them at the airport. They'd come in, he told me, still smelling of charcoal fires and beat the best our grand civilization had to offer. Beat them hollow.

Nor was the marathon any more natural to Africans when they first began to run it than it has been for Europeans. Even after their brilliance on the track was known, Kenyans mostly restricted themselves to distances up to 10,000 meters.

In 1970, coach Bob Hancock, an Englishman, decided to break this pattern and train one of his Kenyan runners, Paul Mose, for the marathon. Mose finished his first 26-mile training run near collapse and said, *"Mbale sana, mbale sana,"* which translates roughly as "Too far, too far."

If it is an advantage being a Kenyan, that doesn't help at first, because you start your career running against other Kenyans. I've heard of young men who slept on the side of the road near one of the country's running camps, and then just appeared the next morning and tried to keep up.

The odds are dreadful. Most fall off the end of the pack, or get injured. But some survive. Richard Limo just showed up at a training camp one day. He went on to win a gold medal at 5,000 meters in the 2001 World Athletics Championships.

American star Steve Prefontaine is famous for saying that he wasn't a talented runner, just able to bear more pain than anybody else. The Kenyans are a nation of Prefontaines. They run without shoes. They run when they lose one shoe. Moses Tanui won a silver medal at 10,000 meters in the 1993 World Championships despite having to run the last lap with only one shoe.

Kenyans run when they're sick. Kip Keino went to the 1968 Olympics with a gallbladder infection. In an 8-day period, he was signed up for three events: 10,000 meters, 5,000 meters, and 1,500 meters. With three laps to go in the 10,000-meter race, he fell and lay momentarily on the infield clutching his gut. When the doctor approached, he sprang up and ran through, finishing last. He was advised to withdraw from the Olympics.

He found that if he ate no solid food, took only soft drinks and milk, he felt better. He ran the 5,000 and came in second.

In the big event, the 1,500, he was up against heavy favorite Jim Ryun, an American. Keino's teammate Ben Jipcho took the first lap in 56 seconds, which seemed a suicidal pace. At that point, Keino was back in third. Ryun, famous for his kick, was cruising at the rear of the pack. By the end of the third lap, Keino was in the lead, but the time, 2:53, seemed impossible. It looked as if Keino were going way too fast. *Track and Field News* reported: "He was expected to fall flat on his face at any moment." Ryun kicked. It was not enough. Instead of falling flat on his face, Keino won a gold medal. His 3:34.9 was a new Olympic record.

This toughness is often twinned with an innocence so dramatic as to be frequently misunderstood. Kenyan men who are friends will often hold hands in the way that only prepubescent boys would dare to do in this country. Bill Orr tells of two runners who came into Los Angeles for a race and walked up to the desk at their hotel holding hands.

When Bill asked them the next day how they'd slept, neither man complained, but they did say that they were unused to sharing a bed. Apparently the clerk had leapt to the wrong conclusion.

John Manners runs a project for the International Association of Athletics Federations, the world governing body for track and field. His aim is to make African stars more attractive to the Western press. He provides brief biographies and encourages the Africans to be more forthcoming in public. If this doesn't work, he says, "the sport is going to die in the West. It's already dying as a spectator sport, as a fan sport."

Why are these people so much faster than we are? There are roughly 300 million of us and 33 million Kenyans. The average per capita income in Kenya is $1,000, as compared to $40,000 in the United States. We have the comfy shoes, fabulous watches, the most nourishing food and vitamins. When our glycogen is depleted, we take Gu or Cliff Shot Bloks or

Sport Beans, the "energizing jelly beans." If speed and endurance could be bought, then we would certainly buy them.

What about their cultural and biological advantages? Such differences are often used to explain the success of whatever group is dominant at the time. During the 1920s, when Paavo Nurmi was winning his nine gold medals and leading a group of athletes called the Flying Finns, many thought Finns were the world's natural distance runners. Take this quote from a German writing in the 1930s: "Running is certainly in the blood of every Finn. When you see the clear, deep green forests, the wide open luxuriant plains with their typical red peasant homes, the heights covered by massive clusters of trees and the never-ending light blue of the horizon with lakes merging with the sky, one is overcome with an involuntary feeling of elation and because you don't have wings, you want to run."[1]

The assumption that Northern Europeans would rule distance races was buttressed by the environmental determinists who were supposed to have been debunked in the 1940s, but whose theories were still sloshing around in the schools I attended in the 1950s and 1960s.

They believed that geography and climate deeply influenced the individual, who in turn established a culture that reflected his or her climate-appropriate self. The tropics were expected to breed laziness and promiscuity, while more demanding climates produced more demanding culture and more productive people.

Americans, English, and Europeans—people like us—were clever, ethical, and resourceful—because we just *had* to be. In order to survive, we needed to hunt and kill fierce, shrewd beasts and build shelters against the unforgiving cold. We couldn't loll in the sun like natives of the tropics or stockbrokers on Grand Bahama Island, while naked, or nearly naked, women fed us bananas that had fallen, unbidden, from the trees.

American blacks were sometimes excluded from distance runs. Does this remind anyone of the history of Major League Baseball? In *First Marathons: Personal Encounters with the 26.2-Mile Monster*, Ted Corbitt tells of having been kept out of interstate meets because he was black. "Arthur

Newton, a Rhodesian who pioneered ultramarathoning in the twenties, said blacks would never run distance," Corbitt recalls. And then, in a gesture of forgiveness that I find Olympian, he goes on to say that Newton's books were of great use. "His comments about black runners are unfortunate, but he was a man of his times."

Clearly Corbitt is capable of gigantic amiability, but he was also tough and fast. The first president of the Road Runners Club of America, he is known in this country as the father of the ultra. He set national records at 25, 40, 50, and 100 miles, and in the 24-hour race.

He was in the habit of running 12 miles from his apartment in upper Manhattan to his job as a physical therapist at the Institute for Crippled and Disabled, which was at 23rd Street and First Avenue. He did this in chinos, a work shirt, and leather shoes. By commuting on foot, he was able to train for the sport that paid him nothing while fully employed as a physical therapist. One problem: He was often stopped and questioned by the police.

When interviewed for *First Marathons*,[2] he was 78 and still running. He estimated that he'd covered over 200,000 miles in his lifetime.

The theory that Caucasians would always rule distance events took a terrible blow in 1960, when Ethiopia's Abebe Bikila won the marathon at the Rome Olympics. Bikila set a world record of 2 hours, 15 minutes, and 16.2 seconds, running barefoot. Rumor has it that he would have won barefoot a second time at the Tokyo Olympiad in 1964, had Adidas not paid him to wear their shoes. (Some runners believe that shoes restrict the natural motion of the foot and inhibit running. Nike sells a line of shoes, called the Free, which are almost as flexible as no shoe at all. But then Nike warns customers not to run too far or fast in them. While there's very little restriction in the Free, there is also very little protection.)

Kipchoge Keino was the first African to win consistently in America and Europe, breaking through dramatically in 1968. Perhaps it was partly because of the novelty of his success, but Keino did get attention and was once on the cover of *Sports Illustrated*. A member of the Kalenjin, Kenya's fastest tribe, and a Nandi, the fastest tribe within the tribe, Keino had been through the grueling threshold into manhood, which included having his two bottom incisors knocked out and the ordeal of the circumcision ceremony. He's since put in false teeth, but the early pictures show the gap in his mouth.

Many other Kenyans followed Keino into the limelight. Like most conquerors, they have had their critics. There were so many charges that they were taking drugs that when Toby Tanser's book *Train Hard, Win Easy: The Kenyan Way* (1997) came out in a second edition in 2001, it had a second foreword written by John Manners to address the question.

"In the four years since the first edition of this book, Kenyans have steadily increased their dominance in worldwide distance running, especially on the roads. Yet for all their brilliance, what little coverage these athletes have been given in the US media has often focused on a single peripheral subject: performance enhancing drugs."

EPO (erythropoietin) is the drug most frequently brought up when distance runners are charged with cheating. Naturally produced by the kidney, it regulates the production of red blood cells. More EPO, and you manufacture more red blood cells; therefore your blood can carry more oxygen.

EPO was first synthesized in the 1980s and given as a treatment for a number of conditions, anemia and chronic renal failure among them.

But the healthy athlete who doses himself can increase the oxygen-carrying capacity of his blood, which could give cyclists and distance runners an edge. Too much EPO, and the blood becomes so thick it strains the heart. This can be fatal during sleep, when the heart rate is slowed down.

Wikipedia reports that "in retrospect, the deaths of a dozen or more elite cyclists in the early 1990s from heart failure while sleeping, were grim evidence of its (EPO's) overuse."

In 1998, Will Voet, a *soigneur,* or trainer, for the Festina bicycle team, was caught with a huge cache of doping materials, including EPO.

Manners denies the charges against the Kenyans, arguing that if they were willing to take pills, they'd start by taking anti-malaria pills. Wilson Kipketer, who at this writing holds world records at both 800 and 1,000 meters and who won a silver medal at the Sydney Olympics (2000) and a bronze at Athens (2004), came back to Kenya with his resistance low after several years living in Denmark and was nearly killed by the disease. Paul Tergat had a serious attack in 1997. Tourists visiting Kenya take pills to protect themselves, but most Kenyan athletes will not, according to Manners. If they won't even take "a benign, inexpensive, easily available, and perfectly legal medicine to prevent a potentially disastrous malaria attack," says Manners, "it's hardly likely that they'd risk a 2-year suspension by taking a dangerous, expensive, and illegal performance enhancer."

While I join the vast majority of the public in disapproving, I certainly understand why an elite athlete might be tempted to take a drug. In a poll described in *The Sports Medicine Book*,[3] Dr. Gabe Mirkin asked 100 top runners: "If I could give you a pill that would make you an Olympic champion—and kills you in a year—would you take it?" More that half said they would.

If Kenyans have been taking performance-enhancing drugs, that will certainly not make them unique. Therefore, the charge cannot be used to explain away their success. Unless, of course, they've found something rare in the West, but common to pharmacies in the highlands above the Rift Valley.

The secret of Kenyan speed is:

    a. Great-grandparents who were long-distance runners.

    b. Living and training in thin air.

    c. Ugali.

    d. Ambition sparked by poverty, but not dulled by malnutrition.

    e. Courage.

    f. All of the above.

CHAPTER 19

Going to Kenya

"UNIVERSITY OF CHAMPIONS"

—SIGN WELCOMING RUNNERS TO LORNAH KIPLAGAT'S
TRAINING CAMP IN ITEN, KENYA

The pigs who rule George Orwell's post-revolutionary *Animal Farm* have difficulty at first explaining who's a brother and who's an oppressor. Finally, they settle on a formula that even the sheep can remember: Four legs good. Two legs bad.

The schism need not be political, but it is significant. Like all evolutionary progress, standing up makes a lot of sense and no sense at all.

Orthopedic surgeons claim that if we didn't stand up, we wouldn't have back trouble, but then dachshunds have back trouble. If we didn't stand up, we wouldn't have orthopedic surgeons.

East Africa seems to be where all this standing up began.

A line of hominid fossil footprints found by Mary Leakey in Tanzania—
the country immediately south of Kenya—indicates that we were upright
3.7 million years ago.

We still stand for the Pledge of Allegiance today, and for "God Save the
Queen," and "La Marseillaise." Crawling is shameful. We want our leaders
to walk on their hind legs, and our robots to do the same.

We assume a brotherhood with animals that stand. The locals are said
to have believed that the orangutan (the Orange Man of Borneo) had
purposefully failed to learn to talk because he knew that once he did learn
to talk, he'd be forced to work.

It's gratifying to assume—as Orwell's pigs did at the end of his novel—
that whatever man does is best. The pig despot, Napoleon, is a hog for
power—put on clothes, got drunk, and walked with a cane. Then the post-
revolutionary farm changed its slogan: Four legs good. Two legs better.

Good or bad, standing up is central to what makes us human. And East
Africa is the cradle of our humanity, or at least the place where the earliest
evidence of our bipedal ancestors has been unearthed. It was in Hadar,
Ethiopia, in 1974, that a party led by paleoanthropologist Donald C.
Johanson found bones of a female who walked on her hind legs. The group
celebrated by drinking and singing the Beatles' song, "Lucy in the Sky with
Diamonds." That's how she got her name: Lucy. The creature, assumed to
be a distant ancestor, lived more than 3 million years ago, and her skeleton
shows evidence of a big toe. She traded one of her two pairs of hands for a
set of feet. Or, to put it in the words of one report, she had sacrificed
"manipulative abilities for efficiency in bipedal locomotion."

The skeleton of an 11-year-old believed to have died 1.6 million years
ago, and found in Kenya in 1984, indicates that this one didn't just walk,
he ran. Richard Leakey's find, Turkana boy, is thought to have been a
hunter, not a scavenger like the earlier ancestor, *Homo habilis*.

The boy seems to have had a narrow pelvis. Indications are that his
species had lost the potbelly of the early plant eaters. Had he lived to
adulthood, he might have weighed 150 pounds and stood about 6 feet tall.

And so we are exactly reversing the course of evolution, when in early adulthood, we give up our slender-runners' bodies and take on the pot-bellies of our more ancient ancestors.

The line that produced *Homo erectus* may have died off, but the land around the Rift Valley, the region so rich in fossils, has spawned some of the greatest distance runners of our age. It's almost as if they've been there all this time, and training.

Elite runners, and those who write about running, often make a pilgrimage to Kenya. Wayne Coffee, the *Daily News* reporter I run with in New York, thought I, too, should go to Africa.

"You should go with John Manners," Wayne told me, after we'd finished up our 5-mile run one day. Then Wayne went into his house and came out with a flyer that John had given him advertising a tour of Kenya for runners.

"Explore Kenya's scenic western highlands," the flyer said, "home of the world's greatest distance runners. Visit the picturesque villages, homes, and training camps of Kenya's running elite. Meet Olympians and World Champions. Talk with them, eat with them, run with them." "Run with them." I liked that. Not just because I wanted to run with Olympians—although I did—but because I wanted to run. I don't like to go anyplace where I can't run.

When I phoned the New York office of Micato Safaris, the travel company handling the tour's logistics, I spoke with a Patti Buffolano—I think this is right—who said that this was the first year ever for the tour and that her husband, a runner, would have liked to go himself. But he worked at the New Balance Track and Field Center, at the Armory at 168th Street in Manhattan, and February was right in the middle of the indoor running season.

I phoned John Manners. He told me that, yes, Kenyans were the best runners in the world. When I asked him if they had a secret, he laughed. "Yes, and no," he said.

I'd go to Kenya. I'd learn the secret. At the airport, with time to kill, I bought the January 2005 issue of *Track and Field News,* which had "Distance King" Kenenisa Bekele of Ethiopia on the cover as "2004 Man of the Year." Bekele had pushed "fellow Ethiopian Haile Gebrselassie aside." I wondered if I shouldn't be going to Ethiopia.

I flipped to the list of top men selected by *Track and Field*'s 39-member international panel. Bekele was number one. Number two was Hicham El Guerrouj of Morocco. Numbers three and four were Swedes. Five was Chinese. Six was Saif Saaeed Shaheen, a "Kenyan-turned-Qatari." I began to have warm feelings about Jeff Galloway. Athens—after all—was Athens, the home of the first-ever marathon. Was Kenya really Kenya? Should I be going to Ethiopia?

When we landed in Nairobi, members of the running tour clumped uneasily at the baggage carousel. I know that tours are frowned upon, but I like a tour, because starting out you feel that you are among friends, even if you all paid to be together. Turned out, I had spotted two fellow tourists between connections at Heathrow; but I hadn't known, because they weren't wearing running shoes.

I always travel in my New Balance running shoes, carry shorts and a T-shirt with my laptop in my carry-on backpack, and wear a running watch. In Athens, a woman told me how her husband—foolish man—once packed his running shoes in his suitcase, before flying out to Los Angeles to run the marathon. The suitcase was lost. The race was set to begin before the stores opened. The hotel staff located sneakers left by kitchen workers. He ran 26.2 miles in somebody else's shoes.

The group looked fast. I had mixed feelings about this. I like runners to be compulsive—if possible even more compulsive than I am. That way, I don't feel like an oddball. But I don't need them to be fast. What I like best, of course, is somebody more serious about the sport than I am, but also slower.

I didn't immediately identify myself. Around my neck, I was wearing something TravelSmith called a "Leather Pre-Board Organizer," but which looked just like a bib. I was relieved to see that there were other passport bibs in the group.

In fact, I phoned my wife at home to tell her that I'd landed safely and spotted the legendary Amby Burfoot, winner of the Boston marathon, an editor at *Runner's World*, who was standing on the other side of the baggage carousel.

"He's wearing a passport bib. So maybe passport bibs are cool now," I told her. I'd seen Amby once before, years ago, at a junket the *Reader's Digest* sent me to at a New York hotel. He's a tall man with red hair, a beard, the classic runner's build. Like fashion models, and those with a terminal illness, runners are apt to be thinner than the rest of us. Now he had an attractive young woman with him. She was making him laugh.

Riding from the airport to the hotel, I learned that she was his wife, Cristina Negron, an editor and writer. I was also relieved to learn that she was willing to make other people laugh as well.

I asked nervously about Kenya's status as the producer of the world's best runners. "Should we be visiting Ethiopia instead?" Nobody else seemed concerned.

At the hotel in Nairobi, there was a metal detector, operated by a man wearing a black sweater with scarlet epaulettes. I remembered that al-Qaeda had bombed the US Embassy in Nairobi. John Manners was in the lobby, a small man—about my size, with glasses and a beard. He had the learned, kindly demeanor of the chairman of an English department. From the brief snatches of conversation I overheard, he sounded eloquent, and I heard him laugh. This is always a good sign. When we shook hands, John looked me in the eye, but not down into the dustbin of my soul.

When I grilled John later about Ethiopians, he took the question but didn't sound at all disturbed. Having lived in the Kenyan highlands as a child and later as a Peace Corps volunteer, John's frank about his admiration for the nation in general and for Kalenjin in particular. But he's willing to talk about the competition.

"The Ethiopians have gotten a lot of press out of two athletes," he told me recently. "Haile Gebrselassie and Kenenisa Bekele. And a couple of women as well. But Ethiopia doesn't have anything like Kenya's depth. If you take the big prize-money road races around the world and if they don't restrict entries in any marked way—I mean they all restrict entry to a certain extent—and if there are, say, a dozen Kenyans in the race, then the chances are 12 of the top 15 places will be taken by Kenyans."

Before we went out to our vans that next morning, we learned that the first day's trip was going to take 6 hours instead of 4. Government regulations had recently changed, requiring that each vehicle carrying paying passengers be mechanically modified so that it couldn't travel more than 80 kilometers per hour.

I navigate the rutless asphalt of Pleasantville, New York, in an all-wheel-drive Lexus. We hit Kenya's fearsome roads in Micato's two-wheel-drive Nissan vans. Even at 80 kilometers per hour, our teeth rattled and our vision blurred.

The two rear seats of my van were occupied by Bill Orr and his wife, Susan. He owns an insurance company. She's a pharmacist at Wal-Mart and part of that rare and dwindling tribe, a reader. They seemed to know a great deal about running and also about Kenya. In addition to his insurance business, Bill has been the elite athlete coordinator for the Los Angeles Marathon and the Cherry Blossom 10-Mile Race in Washington, DC, among others. Kenyan John Kagwe, who won the New York Marathon in 1997 and 1998, stayed with Bill and Susan in Florida for a while and honored the streets of their neighborhood by training there.

"In Kenya, if you drive straight, it means you're drunk," said Bill, "since any sober person would swerve to avoid the potholes."

Shortly after we left Nairobi, the road began to climb. We stopped at our first high-altitude viewpoint to gaze down at the Great Rift Valley. I was beginning to smell the earth and to notice the light.

We were headed for the legendary highlands. I didn't know much about the Rift Valley at the time, but whenever it was mentioned, there was a sort of hush in the van as if the place were freighted with significance, like the Empire State Building, or the Little Big Horn.

Hours out of the city and beginning to labor uphill, we overtook a girl of about 12 and a much younger child whose age and sex were unclear. Barefoot, but dressed in bright clothes, they were running, not walking, on the side of the road. Probably going home from school for lunch, said our Micato guide, Philip Rono. "You see how we get our runners."

The highlands, when we reached them, were breathtaking. The roads were of red earth. In places, they were clogged with bicycles that looked like the English three-speed bicycles of my youth, but which were made in China and had just one speed.

The cement buildings on the side of the road were basic in structure, and not always in good repair. In front of these buildings, there were large, open-air bazaars selling, among other things, American T-shirts with slogans and the names of teams. But out behind the thin band of human-ity lay sweeping hills and mountains, with nothing to jar the eye. Director Sydney Pollack, who filmed *Out of Africa* in the Kenyan highlands, has said, "If there was a Garden of Eden, this is where it would be."

Pollack shows Africa to great advantage but does not give an unrealistic picture. The countryside is breathtaking. And nearly as foreign to a New Yorker as I would have expected.

Out of Africa features the rare scene in which somebody is told—as I have often been told by doctors—not to run. Denys Finch Hatten, played by Robert Redford, tells Karen Dinesen Blixen (pen name: Isak Dinesen), played by Meryl Streep, not to run. He's not worried about her knees or tendons. He's worried about the lion that's been eyeing her.

"I wouldn't run," Finch Hatten said. "If you do, she'll think you're something good to eat."

The weather in Kenya in February was out of Camelot. "In the daytime you felt that you had got high up, near the sun," writes Isak Dinesen in

Out of Africa, "but the early mornings and evenings were limpid and restful, and the nights were cold."

We were headed up into the hills that hang above the Rift Valley in Western Kenya, higher than Dinesen's farm. She was at 6,000 feet. We went up to 8,000. The air was fresh, but flavored with the smoke of wood or charcoal fires.

We had lunch at the Eldoret Club. We would stay there for several nights. Picture an English colonial outpost, one that's been there for a long time, with a golf course, a wall, a gate. The staff are attentive, and there are rules, times and places where a jacket must be worn.

The public rooms are large and airy, the tablecloths are white. The buildings surround a courtyard with a swimming pool and a barbecue pit. The membership—largely African now—is staid, prosperous, and seemed slightly censorious. It's not the sort of place you'd want to giggle in.

After eating, we drove into Eldoret proper. The roads were paved, and there were some tallish buildings. If it hadn't been for the charm of novelty, Eldoret would have had no charm at all. There were newsstands and cell phone stands, and there was a cyber café, where the connection was glacial. But Eldoret is so close to the sources of human speed and endurance that Nike once manufactured a shoe called the Eldoret. It's no longer for sale, and I know, because when we got home, I tried to order a pair.

We went first to Kip Keino's bookstore. Then we met the great runner himself, who seemed genuinely pleased to ask our names, shake hands, and look us in the face.

Later that afternoon, John took a van-full out for our first run ever in Africa. We were all clamoring—as runners will—for a chance to put in an hour, but John insisted that we were expected that evening for cocktails and begged us to go out for just 20 minutes, and then come back. "Fifteen minutes would be better," he said.

Daniel Komen, who holds the world record for 3,000 meters (indoors and out), joined us with two other international competitors that first afternoon. The Kenyans jogged easily with us, chatting politely. We passed a tide of Africans on foot and bicycle going the other way. Most waved and called out greetings. Couples often traveled together on a bicycle, the man pedaling, the woman in a dress sitting sidesaddle on the luggage rack. Not a bicycle helmet to be seen. We finished our too-short run and pulled up to the van, just as the sun was setting, giving a gold-leaf edge to a giant cloud. If this is the high point of the trip, I thought, it will have been enough.

Back at the club, we showered and met at the bar. There assembled, we found a clutch of great runners past and present. Kip Keino presided. He wanted everybody to have a drink, and not water. Yes, Kipchoge Keino is the "uncoached" policeman who smoked Jim Ryun over 1,500 meters in the 1968 Olympics in Mexico. Once the best-known athlete in the world, after Muhammad Ali, Keino has now retired into the status of living legend. He operates a training camp. His wife runs an orphanage. Three stadiums bear his name.

Meet a star in America, and maybe he'll be kind. And maybe he'll be nasty. What he won't be—what he can't be—is entirely present. These men were present.

I know, I know, the circumstances were unusual. We'd traveled to Africa to honor these runners. We were foreigners and came in the company of John Manners, a man these men knew well. Still, it was extremely pleasant to be so close to an excellence that seemed free of narcissism. I stood with Yobes Ondieki at the bar. He had on a white sweater. Yes, it was a little cold at night. Just like Camelot. Yobes recalled how it felt to be the first man to run 10,000 meters in under 27 minutes. He told me he had no idea how fast he was going in that 1993 race in Oslo, but said the memory was still precious today. "God is good."

Within the select pool that is Kenya, the smaller, and even more talented group is a tribe, the Kalenjin, and within the Kalenjin, the subtribe that has produced the most star athletes is the Nandi. Kip Keino is a Nandi and a hero among his people.

In a paper titled "Raiders from the Rift Valley" first presented at an academic conference in Glasgow in 2004 and since published in the book *East African Running: Towards a Cross-Disciplinary Perspective*, Manners discusses the Kalenjin. This tribe or linguistic group, he says, has "collected about 75 percent of [Kenya's] top athletic honors, and an even more disproportionate share of the world's biggest prizes."

Since the 1968 Mexico Olympics, when Kenyans took eight medals on a track that was 2,200 meters above sea level, altitude has been given much credit for their success, according to Manners. "It makes sense. The thin air at 2000-meter altitudes causes the body to increase its supply of oxygen-carrying red blood cells and promotes the development of sturdy hearts and lungs." But he points out that altitude isn't enough. "Witness the dearth of Nepalese and Peruvians among the world's elite."

Manners goes on to examine other environmental, historical, and cultural factors that may have contributed to the success of the Kalenjin and then speculates on the possibility of genetic factors. Most of the paper is devoted to an intriguing discussion of how certain ancient practices common to the Kalenjin and other herding peoples in East Africa—in particular, cattle raiding and circumcision—might have functioned indirectly as genetic selection mechanisms, giving strong runners a significant reproductive advantage.

Manners may have been the first to write about this pocket of talent, although not even John could have guessed how important it would prove to be. As a boy, he had loved sports and was attracted to the superlatives that still pepper his conversation. A baseball fan, given an early subscription of *Sports Illustrated* by his grandmother, he particularly liked speed. The great Yankee batter Mickey Mantle was a personal hero.

Fifty years later, eating lunch outside at a roadside stand in Kenya, he remembered why.

"I liked Mickey Mantle because he was the fastest down to first, at least when batting left handed. Willie Mays, I'm sure, would have been faster over 100 meters, but Mays was a righty. And Mantle, hitting lefty, could get to first base faster."

"You don't remember the time, do you?" I asked.

"I'm pretty sure 3.1 seconds."

John's family lived in Africa for a year in 1957 while his father, an anthropologist, did field work. During that time, John did not go to school. He explains in the introduction to his book-in-progress about Kenyan runners: "The only institutions open to me as a white child would have been all-white boarding schools, the nearest of which was 35 miles away in the district capital, Kericho. My father never considered enrolling me in any case, lest my tender mind be polluted by what he presumed would be the racist attitudes of the other students."

So John stayed home and played soccer with the local boys: "To my eyes, innocent of any real knowledge of the game, these barefoot kids were marvelous soccer players, and what was perhaps more noteworthy, they were also tireless runners.

"In June, as our time in Sotik was running out, I had what I suppose was a kind of epiphany. What I saw then has come to shape much of my enduring preoccupation with Kenya and the Kalenjin. The occasion was the annual Buret Division track meet, one of a series of regional competitions culminating each year in the Colony Championships."

First prize for the 6-mile race was a kerosene lamp. Manners was astonished at how fast the barefoot runners went.

Two weeks later at the Nyanza Province Championships, the tribe that he had been living among produced many of the winners. "In race after race, Kalenjin runners outlasted, outkicked, or simply ran away from the best of the other tribes," John has written.

"They cleaned up," he told me years later. "I wanted some justification for my, you know, utterly groundless, root-for-the-home-team prejudice. And I got it."

Returning to the highlands above the Rift Valley with the Peace Corps in 1969, Manners taught English and coached track for 3 years.

Now he lives in New Jersey and after working for 20 years as a writer and editor for Time Inc., he writes freelance and runs a few pro bono projects all having to do with Kenya.

While in Africa, he was scrambling to resolve last-minute glitches in one of his projects, a scholarship program. He has helped get nearly 30 Kenyans into top American colleges. In this effort, he has been helped by 800-meter Olympic medalist Mike Boit. He has gotten some funding for the scholarship drive from marathon world record holder Paul Tergat.

Our second morning in Africa brought us to Saint Patrick's High School, an unprepossessing collection of brick buildings. The sign for Saint Patrick's doesn't just need to be repainted, it needs to be rebuilt. "Under Brother Colm O'Connell," Manners told us, "this high school has produced more world-class runners than any other single educational institution in the world—at least in the last 30 years." In one night in Zurich in August 1997, three world records were broken by students or former students from Saint Patrick's. By 1997, the pupils at this small school (420 students) had won 22 medals in worldwide track championships, four in the Olympics, two of which were gold.

Brother Colm led us into the school's court and to a stand of trees, each planted to commemorate an athlete. There were many trees. Ibrahim Hussein's tree—just for instance—had a sign in front of it that read: Boston 3. New York 1. Honolulu 3.

The boys wash their own clothes. For a long time, students and faculty went without running water or electricity. An athlete gets one pair of shoes a year.

We visited the dining hall and saw the "wall of fame," a very ordinary wall and badly in need of a coat of paint. But it's plastered with pictures of runners. Some are reclining in groups, others running—one at a time— through this ribbon or that one.

And as for the magic diet, lunch was just being set out in aluminum bowls, which looked just like the one with which I used to feed my Labrador retriever. The contents—corn and beans—looked just like my Labrador's kibble.

After Saint Patrick's, we climbed back into our vans and drove to Kamariny Stadium, which is set into a bowl high above the Rift Valley. I could not entirely shake the notion that the worn stands and outbuildings were fakes thrown up by a movie crew to give a contrasting ramshackle background to the excellence of the runners practicing there. One of these was a white man, doubtless a pilgrim from our slower culture. Goats grazed the infield, and there was evidence that cows with plenty of fiber in their diet had been there not long ago.

Schools were closed that day, and so groups of children dressed in impossibly bright sweaters of blue or green had come down to ogle the *wazungu* (European).

We were invited to join the workout. I watched for a while, embarrassed, and finally fell in behind some young men who were running intervals on a zigzag course laid out on the grass inside the track. I tried desperately, and unsuccessfully, to ape their speed and grace. I could smell them. It was a healthy, gamey scent, not the musk of anxiety that I produce between frequent showers.

One upstart schoolboy of 4 or 5, lugging a full book bag, had the indecency to keep abreast of me and then passed. Going by, he looked me right in the eye, intensely curious about this huge, slow creature.

Our lunch had been scheduled at a local restaurant, but Lornah Kiplagat ("Kiplagat" means "born at sunset") insisted that we come instead to her High Altitude Training Centre in Iten, which was within walking distance of the track.

I hadn't thought of the word for years, but when I stepped onto the centre's campus, Shangri-la was the name that popped unbidden into my mind. Others reported that they'd had the same impression. The sign on the gate reads: "Welcome to High Altitude Training Centre Iten (Kenya)," and then there's a line drawing of a runner in hills. Below this: "University of Champions."

Kiplagat, a small woman with the grace and poise of a natural athlete, ladled out pumpkin soup and pressed seconds of fresh bread, sliced cheese, meat, and salad on her guests. (No ugali this time.)

I sat across from John Manners, who was explaining the Kalenjin advantage. "As horseless cowboys, they have always run, often great distances to steal the stock of other tribes," he said. "The fastest, bravest men collected the most cattle, and since cattle were the currency used for bride wealth, the fastest, bravest men were able to marry the most wives and father the most children."

"I wish it was all genetics," said Brother Colm, who has been coaching for 20 years. "Then I could rest. You have no idea the amount of work that goes into this."

Having paused in her efforts to render her fat guests fatter, Kiplagat listened quietly. When she spoke, it was almost a whisper. She seemed not to mean to challenge either of the other two theories. "We *are* tougher than anybody else," she said. "And smarter."

After lunch, we took another too-brief run on the now-familiar blood-red trails above the Rift Valley. Lornah Kiplagat wanted to show us the new house she is building and came along, moving freely in the group so that we could each marvel at the economy of her stride and the ease with which she engaged us all in conversation. Children in uniform—skirts or shorts, and sweaters—called out to the *wazungu* in their musical voices. "How are you? How are you?" And if we didn't answer promptly enough, they'd answer for us. "I am fine. I am fine."

The day after lunch with Lornah, Manners brought us to the North Rift Provincial Cross-Country Championships, one of many feeders for the nationals. The fastest local men and women run there, and in the case of the junior division, the fastest girls and boys. Those of us who had no shame could join in and run in the 4-K or the 12-K. Nine signed up for one race or another.

The race was deep in the country, off a road even more rutted than those to which we had grown accustomed. This was at Kishaunet in West Pokot District.

NikeRunning.com appeared in black letters on the orange plastic start and finish banners, and there were recognizable shorts and singlets among the competitors. But every other sight was strange and new. There were men in uniforms with rifles, but also men in blankets with spears. We were engulfed in oceans of children. I was shocked to find myself looking into the face—faces—of a boy of 5, or 6. I thought he had two heads, until I realized that a much younger sister was strapped to his back.

The course was a 2-K oblong laid out on a seldom-used airstrip with one bog and one hurdle. The crowd—mostly children—was held back with tape strung between sticks. It wasn't difficult to find a vantage point. The first race was the junior girls.

When it began, I saw one little girl pull out into the lead and go haring down the hill in front of me. She was wearing a pink dress with a wide skirt. She was barefoot. It made me want to cry.

Times were taken at the finish by two men with running watches and a third who held a dedicated stopwatch and a mechanical counter, the sort I haven't seen for decades.

Brother Colm O'Connell was there, and a handful of professional runners' agents. But our group was far and away the largest gathering of white people at the North Rift Cross-Country Championships.

Nine of us lined up before the 4-K. Several emissaries were sent out by officials to make certain the *wazungu* had everything they needed.

We were the best equipped runners on the field. Just for instance, we all had shoes. Amby Burfoot had taken his off. But Amby owned shoes; he just wasn't wearing them. We all had watches.

When the whistle blew for our first event, we, the *wazungu*, began to run along with everyone else. I guess the people in the crowd looked at our faces, saw that we were trying, and then compared our speed to the speed of the Kenyans who were also running.

A ripple of laughter ran through the spectators. No malice. We'd surprised them. None of the crowd response for which America is justly notorious. No booing. No tossing of beer bottles. They cheered us on. "How are you? How are you?" they called out—and then: "I am fine. I am fine." I also heard *Pole, Pole,* which is Swahili for "slowly, slowly," but can also mean "take it easy." Which must have been their response to our straining faces.

When I was 200 yards from the finish, a Kenyan who had finished long before came back and ran beside me. He was in blue Adidas shorts and a blue Adidas singlet. He was tall, slender, with his hair so short it showed only as a light change in color and texture. The cool, quiet efficiency with which he motored along was heartbreaking in its beauty.

I got carried away and tried to match his stride. I could feel something going in my left leg. We held hands and crossed the finish line together. Two men. Two nations. One athlete.

Amby had hurt his feet quite badly, but six of us were ready for the 12-K, which was six loops around the course. Mark Fine lost a shoe in the bog during the 4-K. First lap of the 12-K, and he lost both shoes. A picture of the *mzungu* (singular of *wazungu*) deep in mud with a shoe in each hand ran the next day in the *Daily Nation*.

I didn't lose my shoes, but this was not because I was going so fast. Having spent all that time in the equatorial sun and at high elevation, I was terrified that I'd lose count and finish the race before I'd run the full distance. I was equally terrified that I'd lose count the other way and circle the course forever like Charlie on the MTA. The Timex I was wearing had a lap counter, and I got that working, but then—of course—I forgot to count a lap.

Amby came out at the fourth lap and asked if I was okay. I said I was okay. "If you suddenly feel cold, or dizzy," he said gently, "then you should stop."

When I indicated an unwillingness to stop, he asked if I wanted water. Did I ever. The Kenyans don't generally drink in races short of marathons. They rarely drink on training runs either, unless they're going for 2 hours.

When I came around on the next lap, Amby appeared with water. Since it was clear that I intended to finish, he did his best to encourage me. "I want a picture of you in the mud," he said. "I've got money riding on it."

I had to run the next-to-last lap with my finger in the air, saying, "I have one more lap to go." At this point, I'd been passed so many times that the officials were understandably confused.

They were taking up the tapes that marked the course when I ran the last lap, and a herd of cows came on the field before I was quite done. I soldiered on, although I considerately let the cows go first. When it comes to animals who weigh hundreds of pounds, I'm always exquisitely polite. There was some laughter from the crowd. Turned out that the impossibly old, impossibly slow *mzungu* was also afraid of cows.

On our next-to-last night, we ate dinner at the home of Micato owners Felix and Jane Pinto. Paul Tergat was there. He's 6 feet tall and weighs 138 pounds, but in a suit, he looks like a big man.

On our last, precious day, we went to another picture-postcard setting, the Ngong Race Course in Nairobi, to see the Kenya National Cross-Country Championships. Because of the depth of talent, the event has been called the greatest distance race in the world. (And no T-shirt!)

I've never seen so much excellence and so little pretension in the same spot. Many of the runners were children. Many ran without shoes. The course looped around the grassy colonial horse track. Golfers waited for gaps in the flood of elite runners, and then pulled their bags across the track in order to get at a driving range, which was in the center of the field.

Tape strung between stakes was all that separated us from the athletes. When I run with a handful of friends in the park near my house, we sound like a locomotive working a grade. But here masses of men and women flew past, making no more noise than a light wind in an alley of trees. I was shocked again by the grace of these competitors. Catherine Ndereba. In Boston, they call her Catherine the Great, because she's won their marathon four times.

She finished 13th.

CHAPTER 20

Not an Army of One,
but an Army of Run

"THE COWARD DIES A THOUSAND DEATHS,
THE HERO ONLY ONE."
—PROVERB

The cheerful, humorous conversational style of Travis Patriquin lives on
my digital recorder. He has a warm, rich voice and a tendency to explode
into laughter. We talked when I was visiting with the army in Germany in
the winter of 2005. Patriquin was not a bitten runner. Or if he had been
bitten, he'd gotten over it. He said he liked to march, because when you
marched, you got somewhere, whereas "When you run...." And yet he was
eloquent in praise of the sport. He'd been in the army a decade, and he'd
done his share of running.

"There was an exercise physiologist when I was going to the lieutenant's course," he told me. "We called it the infantry officer, basic course. And he ran the army physical fitness unit. They write all the physical fitness manuals, they write all the new exercises, and if exercises are being done improperly, they redo it and teach everyone how to do it the right way. And he was showing us a bunch of alternative training techniques, like Indian war clubs, for upper-body strength and biometrics for sprinting, and somebody got up and said, 'Hey, you have one to replace running?' And he said, 'Son, there will never be anything to replace running.'

"I bet if you came here 1,500 years ago when this was a Roman camp," Patriquin said, "there would be Roman Joes running around the outside of the camp."

I was shocked to learn that even the top generals ran. I had been under the impression that the higher the rank, the slower the man. Ulysses S. Grant filled every nook and cranny of his double-breasted getup. As did Bismarck. Churchill favored a roomy one-piece jumpsuit that disguised his bulk. Even Napoleon, the little corporal, seems to have been 3 months pregnant.

Peter Boyer, who worked as a correspondent in Iraq, told me they have a place for running on the deck of aircraft carriers. Soldiers everywhere strip their body armor and head out for a trot in the morning. Himself a chronic runner, recently forced by injury onto an elliptical trainer, Boyer would pump his arms and beam, so that I could see the joy in it.

I was put in touch with General Mark Hertling. "Running has always been a part of military fitness and readiness," Hertling wrote me in e-mail. "I have completed runs, marathons, and triathlons (the most recent was 3 weeks ago here in Germany), and I have a masters in exercise physiology, and I taught PE at West Point. My wife is a fitness instructor, a jazzercise franchisee, and an avid runner. (We have a great story for you as to how military wives used training for a marathon to deal with the stress of their soldiers being deployed.) Our oldest son—who ran track and X-country for Wake Forest—is currently in Iraq on his second tour, and our youngest son—who swam at West Point—is just starting his career and is also an emerging triathlete."

So first, I went to Camp Ray in Friedberg, Germany, the base where Elvis once served.

I hope I don't lose you here, but I must say at the outset that to run with soldiers there was to take all my assumptions about the US Army and have them turned upside down. I had mourned the loss of the democratizing draft. As much as I'd feared the draft during Vietnam, I thought it appropriate that an army protecting a democracy include everybody. My father had forged lasting friendships during World War II. After training with a heavy-weapons battalion in Georgia, he had been plucked from the regular army and reassigned to the Signal Corps in New York, where he made—I think—movies about how to brush your teeth. The group in Astoria had many notable writers. Dr. Seuss was there. William Saroyan is supposed to have rattled the egalitarian atmosphere when he and Irwin Shaw showed up at morning drill in a chauffeur-driven Rolls-Royce.

Late in his life and signing books, I saw my father approached by a man who had known him in Georgia. It was immediately clear that he liked this guy, that the bond formed in the infantry had not been shattered—as many bonds are in this country—by differences in status and economics. The stranger called my father "Joey." The name I knew was John.

People go into the army now because they have to, I had thought, and yet my guide in Germany, First Lieutenant Will Bardenwerper, was a Princeton grad who had been working in midtown Manhattan. He was a financial analyst who decided to join up when the World Trade Towers were destroyed. My guide's provenance was unusual enough so that I heard him teased about it, but there were also two Rhodes Scholars in the First Brigade Combat Team of the First Armored Division, as well as a great many West Point graduates.

Nor did Bardenwerper's commitment to service seem all that unusual. "It was a chance to serve my country, a chance to give back, a chance to defend," I heard over and over again as I ran with soldiers through the darkened German countryside. This was late in the year: so the PT (physical training) runs I was invited on—all of about 6 miles—started and ended before the sun came up.

On my first morning in Germany, I ran with First Lieutenant Brian Braithwaite, who expected to leave soon for Iraq, where he would lead a platoon. The trails in and around Friedberg are exquisitely maintained, which is a lucky thing, because we barreled along in zero visibility. A stray root would have been problematic in the extreme. When we hit puddles that had frozen, we skated and splashed right through.

Racing along at my side, Braithwaite explained his responsibilities as the commander of a Bradley Fighting Vehicle. When the gunner was about to shoot, he, Braithwaite, would also look through the sights and make certain that the target was justified. This raised the terrible question of a commander's responsibility for the misdeeds of others, and I asked if there weren't some men in the platoon who made Braithwaite uneasy. "I love my men," he said.

We were running beside a river then, on a mud path, but it was still a black night. The lieutenant and I were setting the pace, although I think this had more do with Braithwaite's rank and good manners than my speed. The soldiers ran in PT uniform—shorts, running shoes, a gray T under a gray windbreaker and a striped glow-in-the-dark strap that could be worn around the waist, or across the shoulder bandolier-style. It was much like the many morning runs I've made in groups in the States. Except when we had to cross a particularly dangerous stretch of road, one man would step out into traffic, raise his arm, and stop the cars. This was not a group of individuals. This was a team and with authority.

After the run and showers, we all met for breakfast. One man's favorite PT run (maybe *favorite* is the wrong word here) had involved carrying metal road wheels taken from Bradleys or tanks. These weigh 30 pounds apiece. Apparently, it is not uncommon for the men to run carrying something. In one case, they carried jugs of water, but there were fewer jugs than men, so they had to pass off as they moved together as a group, learning each other's strengths and tolerances.

In the infantry, the air of respectfulness was present, but not forced. Everybody saluted, and I remembered that this gesture had started when knights wore helmets and used to open their visors to each other in passing. This was always done with the right hand, while the left held the reins.

At one point, an extremely high-ranking officer came through a crowd I was in, and all the men stood at attention and saluted. This left me feeling embarrassed and out of step. I didn't want to seem disrespectful. "I shouldn't salute?" I asked Bardenwerper. "No," he said. "You shouldn't salute." "So what should I do?" I thought of bowing.

"You're a civilian," said Bardenwerper. "We're a democracy. You outrank everybody here."

I had met Tom Graves in his office in Germany, which had a T-shirt drying on the closet door and three—count them—three pairs of identical Nike running shoes on the floor. Now 42 and a lieutenant colonel, Graves was in the ninth grade living in Germany when he got a copy of Joe Henderson's *Walk, Jog, Run.* Henderson, an early editor of *Runner's World,* wrote in an author's note: "Like most runners who've been at running a long time and enjoying it, I want others to see the same light and to share this activity from which so many blessings seem to flow." Graves recalled the book fondly. "It had the hard-easy days, the long runs," he said. "It went through my whole family. My dad was in the military. My mom started running; I started running."

We took a run with Graves and his men, also before dawn, also across the German countryside. We stopped once to let the slower soldiers catch up, and the lieutenant colonel's Garmin Forerunner lit up in the dark. Graves likes to go fast, and when we ran together, he waited until we were half a mile from the base and then said that those who were feeling their oats could race in. And so we all did. The lieutenant colonel had a lot more oats that morning than I did.

He has a reputation for toughness, but belies this in conversation. "I find that if you make running painful, people won't want to run," he said. "So I try not to make it painful."

He holds his staff meeting on Wednesday. This is called the commanders' run and is convened at 8 minutes per mile.

I got the distinct impression that the soldiers, like my fanatical friends at home, have sometimes run even when it wasn't exactly good for their health. Lieutenant Colonel Pete Lee, who owns every issue of *Runner's World* back to 1991, told me his favorite marathon was the one he ran in Zurich, shortly after eye surgery, and expressly against doctor's orders.

Like their civilian counterparts, they often want to stretch a workout. Six feet tall and weighing about 210 pounds, Will Bardenwerper was always disappointed when we settled on 6-plus miles for the morning outings. "Ten," he kept saying. "We *could* go ten."

Bardenwerper had run when he worked in New York, and also when he worked and lived in Boston. Working as the brigade public affairs officer, a posting that should last no more than a year, he told me that he eagerly awaited reassignment to what he hopes will be combat duty.

I was particularly cheered to learn that in the no-nonsense infantry, running was considered essential. All other things being equal, a fitter soldier is a better soldier, and will recover more quickly if wounded. Not to mention—although several people did—how much easier it is to carry a disabled marathoner than a disabled left guard. Every soldier has to pass the Army Physical Fitness Test at least once, but characteristically twice a year. This requires sit-ups, push-ups, and the 2-mile run. In order to get 100 points out of 100, the army wants men ages 17 to 26 to run 2 miles in 13 minutes. There's a sliding scale for age and sex, with women of that age wanting the same score expected to cover the distance in 15 minutes and 36 seconds.

The soldiers used to run in boots. Now everyone gets running shoes, and the larger PXs have specialists who will match a shoe to the soldier's foot and stride.

While the military running world and the civilian one are quite separate cultures, they do support one another's shared passion. Therefore, many prominent races in the States sponsor simultaneous, or satellite, races overseas in Baghdad and Afghanistan. The Honolulu Marathon does so, as does Boston. The mother race will send T-shirts, numbers, and sometimes even timing equipment.

After Germany, I had hoped to go to Iraq for the marathon that the Honolulu race sponsored in December of last year. When the date was changed, I was told the race might be cancelled and so gave up the plan. It wasn't cancelled, and I wondered if I hadn't simply chickened out. When I tried to reconnect, to get myself papers for a different race, I kept going down cul-de-sacs.

I couldn't find a race to get into, but even if I could find a race, it seemed possible that I might fly to Jordan or Kuwait, be denied a visa, and have to fly back. At one point, I called the US Embassy Annex and got a message that said if I "knew the whereabouts of Abu Musab al-Zarqawi," I should call this other number, which was then given. Then I tried the second number for the US Embassy Annex and got the same message. Since that time, the former leader of al-Qaeda in Iraq, al-Zarqawi has been killed. I wonder if voice mail had anything to do with it.

I wrote everyone I knew, including Lieutenant Colonel Tom Graves. Did he know of a satellite race I could get into?

"Dear Ben," he wrote back. "I'm sorry it has taken so long to get back with you. We've been pretty busy here recently. Last week, we had four wounded Spartans. Three were returned to duty (a military term to mean that they were treated by a doctor and given a couple of days of rest and are now back in the fight), two from IEDs (improvised explosive devices) and one from getting shot in the head (sniper round went through his helmet and was deflected up over his head leaving a deep cut, but no serious damage). The fourth Spartan was a squad leader who was shot in the stomach, and the bullet clipped his colon on Saturday. He is now in Landstuhl, and I think he'll be fine as long as there is no infection. His interpreter was also shot in the knee, which is a big loss. The good news is that the two Specialist Team Leaders took charge of the squad and worked the radio/medevac to get their boss to safety. It always amazes me to see a 19-year-old step up to the plate when the chips are down.

"Concerning local races, I'm in an info void out here in Western Iraq (I'm in al Anbar province in the town of Hit about 50 miles west of Ramadi). I have heard rumors about a marathon in Camp Speicher but don't know when. Right now, the temps are starting to rise, with highs in the low 100s. If you are looking at running this summer, you might want to find a way to get acclimatized?? (I would suggest running on a treadmill in a sauna with a hair dryer blowing in your face??)"

After multiple frustrations, I was excited (is excited the right word here?) when I learned that the Atlanta Peachtree sponsors a satellite event in Baghdad. I wrote organizer Julia Emmons. The 110-pound dynamo who had turned her event into the largest 10-K in the world told me the story was an old one and sent clips. The articles read like this: "We're at the start of the Peachtree in Atlanta, and they're also holding a race in Baghdad. Now we're going to phone Baghdad. Baghdad can you hear me?"

I e-mailed Emmons. I wanted to *run* in Baghdad. She wrote back: "The Atlanta Track Club cannot endorse anyone going into a war zone, thus potentially in harm's way."

I could see her point, but think of it this way. At the time, we had 130,000 military personnel in Iraq. That's a mighty risk. How dramatically is this changed by the introduction of one more journalist, however frightened?

I played erratic e-mail ping-pong with my army contacts. The race was just weeks away when Major Todd Breasseale gave me the green light. Suddenly, I could see Emmons's point. Sure, there were 130,000 military personnel in Iraq, but none of them were me. I'd been trying to do this for months, but now it seemed hasty, ill-considered.

My wife—and bless her heart for this—didn't want me to go. Because of the irregularity of military flights into Baghdad, it would take almost a week to get there, and I was going to have to spend a full week in Iraq. The last days at home passed in a welter of anxiety and ill feeling. There were forms I didn't understand, shots I needed. And why did the army want to know my blood type? Janet walked by my office and found me standing at my desk holding a piece of string that went from the top of my belt buckle to the second button on my polo shirt.

> Janet: "What are you doing?"
> Me: "Measuring myself for a bullet-proof vest."

"I'm writing a book about running," I'd say, when the subject of my trip came up. "This will be the biggest race ever held in Iraq," I explained. "July 4th."

"Oh, that's very brave," everybody said, which sounded like code for "Are you out of your mind?" The runners were more direct. "How hot does it get? Is there a T-shirt?"

I took a C-130 from Amman, Jordan, and landed on the military side of Baghdad International Airport, which is mostly outdoors, mostly sandbags and cement abutments. A cheerful Major Breasseale met me there. I was in chinos, a black polo shirt, and my black TravelSmith blazer. The temperature was likely around 120 degrees. He told me afterward, "I could tell you weren't from around here." We drove down the Irish Highway, once the most dangerous stretch of road in the world, but apparently now quite safe.

Still, I was glad to pass through the towers and enter Camp Victory. It's set in what had been a vacation complex for Saddam Hussein, his family, and Baath party loyalists. The palaces—and there are many palaces—are surrounded by lakes, the water brought in from the Tigris River.

The vast complex—more than 60 acres—looks like a health spa, or a sanatorium with all the colors washed out. The buildings and Humvees are brown. The dust—and there's a lot of dust—is brown also. The roads are gray. The water is gray, as are the giant carp that swim in it. The helicopters are black. Apparently, there was no budget for color. I saw leaves on a couple of puny date palms, but aside from the scum in the lakes, almost nothing is the green of life.

One morning after a run, I heard machine-gun fire. "The range?" I asked with false bravado.

"No," said the soldier I was with. "It's one of the towers." As he spoke, the high chatter was replaced with the deeper percussion of a much-heavier caliber.

"The tower shooting back?" I asked.

He nodded. "Or another tower," he said, and explained that sometimes the insurgents drive a car toward the towers, firing as they go.

"They can't have much luck," I said.

"Nope," he said. "They don't have much luck."

There's a small dirigible moored over camp, which, with other unmanned aircraft, is constantly spying down on the surroundings. For this reason, the insurgents are afraid to expose themselves long enough to aim their mortars. And so the fire, when it comes at all, is wildly inaccurate. This was told to me repeatedly and seemed a great comfort to the soldiers, although I couldn't quite shake the knowledge that a person could be killed by a mortar, however badly aimed.

I never tasted the panic that must be a big part of this war for soldiers, but I was frightened once. Major Patrick Stich and translator Alex Kurd brought me to the Blackhawk Bazaar, a collection of small shops behind razor wire. Here "fine" watches are sold, pirated editions of movies, old pictures of Saddam, and hookahs as big as cellos.

Coffee being brewed in the traditional manner can be purchased by the cup. Major Stich and Alex Kurd had been given drinks by an extremely welcoming local store owner, a Somali, who had refused to let them pay. They were returning to bring this man a goody bag, including candy and cans of Starbucks coffee. But now the shop was closed. Kurd was told that the proprietor had been murdered by the insurgents for doing business with Americans.

I was frantic to get back to Camp Victory. The camp felt safe, although it never felt cozy. Saddam had money, but he did not have taste. The acres of marble may not actually be marble, but some sort of composite. The glass beads for the many chandeliers are not glass, but plastic. The hand-painted tiles seem to have been hand-painted in a frightful hurry.

The main palace is called Al Faw and is named after the place where the Iraqis had a great and bloody victory over Iran. The halls are decorated with sayings from the wise men of history including, of course, Saddam himself. Major Breasseale, whose office was inside, describes the building as "the love child of Elvis Presley and Tony Soprano."

The roads around the lakes are often thronged with armed Humvees with signs in English and Arabic warning everybody to stay back 100 meters. Early in the morning and at dusk, the automotive traffic is light, and the running traffic quite heavy. While I was there, the temperature reached 129 degrees. For this reason, much of the running is done at dawn, or after sunset.

Navy Commander Matt Simms organized the Peachtree satellite race and won it handily in 34:50. He also had won the marathon sponsored by Boston and held at Camp Adder near Ur in April. He didn't mention this, of course, and I wouldn't otherwise have known had the Boston results magazine not arrived at home the day I returned from Iraq.

While the stress of military life makes a run especially delicious, holding a race in a war zone presents its own problems. Just for instance, there's incidental fire. "We have an overhead announcement system called 'the Big Voice,'" Simms told me. "It'll say 'Uruh, uruh, uruh, uruh,' like that, and you'll say, 'What's it saying?' There's a marathon at an air base at Taj, just north of Baghdad, that they run every year called the Midnight Marathon, because it starts at like 10 o'clock at night. I know that in the middle of that race either last year or 2 years ago, they had to stop because the Big Voice came out. You'd better stop and ditch somewhere. Doesn't matter if you're doing a PB [personal best].

"We just had a little fun run on a base that's adjacent to this one," Simms continued. "There was activity in the neighborhood adjacent to the base. It sounded like people were discharging weapons. And you never know if they're shooting each other, or if they're shooting in the air, or if the soccer team won, or what they were talking about. They just about stopped that race, but they let us finish."

The army ran another marathon in Tikrit, Simms told me. "They'd evidently measured the course with a Humvee odometer," he said. Simms was running with another man with a GPS. "And we get to the 1-mile mark and his GPS is like 1.3. It's like 'This is not going to be good.' We get to 6 miles and it's 7½. At the half-marathon, it was 15.5. Back in the old days, people would have just said, 'You know, that felt *long*.' But now, every other guy's got a GPS. So they figured out that the marathon was going to be 31 miles. And so they rerouted the course in midstream. It wound up at 28.8."

Major Stich also ran that race but without a GPS and had been dismayed when he hit the half at 2 hours, since he'd previously run a full marathon in 3 hours and 7 minutes. The course was an out-and-back, and he remembers being told to make a new turn. As he ran along, he waved his arms in the air, so that the other soldiers would know to make the turn. "Everybody was throwing their hands up. They're like 'Thank you! Thank you!'"

It's tough enough to run a marathon, without adding another 2.6 miles. Tougher still to live in a country where the explosions you hear are not trucks backfiring. And yet the soldiers I ran with seemed to be facing their predicament with grace and—more surprisingly—with humor. I felt honored to be among them.

Not everybody in the army loves running. "You can't outrun a bullet," one soldier told me, "so why die tired?" But many are passionate runners. Come out onto the streets of Camp Victory at dawn as I did for a week, and you'll see hundreds of soldiers in gray PT T-shirts and black shorts. They wear striped reflective belts. This, the short hair, and lack of earphones all distinguish them immediately from their civilian counter-parts.

Running is so well thought of in the military that I was told on more than one occasion that even "a blockhead" can do well, if he or she just runs fast enough. The sport's esteem cuts both ways. Master Sergeant Paul Stevenson was a track star at the University of Tennessee, and also a star in the German club he joined while posted there. When stationed in Kuwait, his commander singled the sergeant major out as a running buddy. "And then a transfer came up," Stevenson told me. "And the commander said he'd make some phone calls. He said I didn't have to go."

"So what did you do?"

Stevenson laughed quietly. "I guess that was when I got one of my phantom injuries."

Sergeant First Class Gene D. Worthy, of Titusville, Florida, had "been running for about 20 years, because I've been in the army for 20 years, but I ran because I had to. I started running for fun in Baghdad."

"On the days that I don't run, it's because I've been reading *Runner's World* and learned about the need for recovery. So I do take a day off, and it bugs me.

"Sergeant Banister is the one who got me into doing this," Worthy said, pointing to a friend we'd run with. "He encouraged me to run the first 5-K about 5 months ago, which we held on Camp Stryker. And we ran what we call down the wall. It's a dirt road down the perimeter wall. Dirty and dusty and sweaty, and I loved it.

"I used to run 14 minutes and change [for 2 miles], which is respectable. I'm over here in Iraq, running on a dirty, dusty road where crazy things happen, and my goal now is to hit 12 or under. I'm running high 12s now.

"One of the appeals of running is it's the one place I can be alone over here," Worthy continued, "alone with my thoughts, reflect on my day, think about the family. I spend most of my personal mental time with my kids when I run."

A run is crucial when a fellow soldier has been killed, Captain Nicole E.

Ussery said. The officer must metabolize the horror and sorrow, without letting it demoralize the troops, she explained. "Running allows you to remember who you are."

The soldiers spoke cheerfully about their own risks and mortality, about a friend who had been shot while running—a stray bullet—and who had been shot five or six times altogether. They couldn't decide if they wanted to be with him, because if there were bullets, he'd collect them in his own body, or if they wanted to avoid him, because he was bad luck.

Captain Ussery kept up easily with the men. "I never ran before coming into the army," she told me. "Being a female in the army, they either think you're squared away or not worth anyone's time. Running is a way to get in shape. When it's time for physical fitness tests, or best-lieutenant competitions, I can hold my own.

"Running lets me work out the frustration of fighting a nameless, faceless enemy that doesn't wear a uniform. It's a chance to be alone, to reflect on the day."

If running alone is an opportunity to get away from an individual's troubles, then the races held in Baghdad are a sharing in that escape. Even in civilian life, there's something apparently absurd about waking in the middle of the night in order to do something devilishly hard, in order to run a race you won't win and for no money and very little glory.

Talking with Simms on the evening before the race, I heard that General George William Casey Jr., then the US commander in Iraq, is a huge supporter of the sport. Simms said that at the last 10-K, "Casey ran just over an hour." Bernard Creque, director of Morale Welfare and Recreation, was working in the background while this discussion was going on.

"General Casey," he said, "No, no. He ran it in 30 minutes."

There was laughter, and somebody said, "Promote that man."

So at 4:30 a.m. on July 2nd, I climbed into a crowded SUV. (The date was as close to July 4th as they could manage and still catch a Sunday, which is the day they have off, although in the military, days off are always conditional.) The boss was there, Lieutenant Colonel Michelle (Shelly) Martin-Hing. I'd never seen her pull rank at the office, but now any trace of hierarchal preference was absent. Major Breasseale was wise-cracking cheerfully about how slow he'd be. A former marathon-a-year man, he had broken an ankle (rugby) followed by a leg, wrist, and thumb (skiing). Knee trouble was slowing his recovery.

I saw men coming into the start on bicycles with headlights and with guns. Apparently, if the race is a duty assignment, you have to bring your weapon. These were stacked and guarded.

There were lights, and there was music, and there were Portosans. Written in magic marker above the toilet I used was "There is no such thing as friedly fire. Think of that 101st." A second toilet poet had drawn an arrow from the word "friedly," and suggested that the first toilet poet learn to spell.

We'd begun to move toward the start, when a truck came in from outside the wire and parted the crowd of runners, as if it were a boat and we the sea. This was full of stern men in combat gear. Their getups and expressions contrasted sharply with the cheerful, lightly dressed men and women around me.

In the gray light of dawn, Simmo and a chaplain got up on a platform. We heard a letter from Julia Emmons in support of the troops this day and every day. Then we heard a prayer thanking the Almighty for the tremendous good fortune our nation had already experienced, and wishing humbly for more of the same. Then we turned back away from the starting line, stood at attention, and a live band played the national anthem. Some of the men stood as ballplayers do, with one hand over the heart, others with their arms down at their sides, fists clenched.

I can't remember now if the race was started with a gun, or a whistle. There were plenty of guns around, of course, but somehow a gun doesn't seem right.

General Casey didn't run that day, but his habit of turning up at these contests was good for me. After Casey, then over 55, had come in ninth in the 50 to 60 age category, race organizers had introduced 5-year increments. This also gave me—at 58—a much better chance of placing.

We ran on pavement around Saddam's ornamental lakes. The event looked and sounded like a lot of 10-Ks held in the States, with runners joking, "I've peaked" or "Is it over yet?" after the first mile.

No crowds, though, along the curb. No dogs, no husbands with strollers. There were no children holding their hands out to be slapped.

Soldiers, like other runners, are able to channel their competitiveness during a race so that brotherhood comes easily. So when somebody passed me, I said, "Looking good," which is what they said to me, when I passed them. "Looking good." Or "Way to go."

When I got to the finish table for the 55- to 60-year-olds, the man who gave me the pen said, "You're my first customer," and I was delighted. Turned out nobody had yet finished in the over-50 category either.

First in my age category, I thought, *this is how it feels to be happy. This! Now!* "First in my age category," I told everybody. I was a little disappointed by the reaction of my friends. Major Patrick Stich, Sergeant Major Paul Stevenson, and Royal Navy Petty Officer Sarah Turner acknowledged my accomplishment, but they didn't exactly jump up and down.

"First in my age category," I said again and again, as if I might not have been heard or fully understood. When the awards were given, it turned out that Stich had not only won his age category but was also in the top 10 overall, as was the sergeant major, who was running through a bad Achilles. Sarah Turner was the fastest woman, not just in her age category either.

Breasseale had the tact to agree that I'd been robbed when I was only given the award for the first over 50, and not a second award for the 55 to 60 age category. The prize was an Ultimate Direction water bottle with a crimson nipple and a mesh bag to carry a key in. It's on my desk this moment.

We all agreed that in our little group, the hero of the day was Lieutenant Colonel Martin-Hing, who took minutes off of her personal best and seemed to be teetering on that fulcrum between the regular health-conscious runner, and the joyous fanatic. I had heard her say the day before that she'd reached her weight goal.

Of course my success is partly attributable to my age, and the dearth of old soldiers. I ran 44:21, which is just a shade faster than a 7:10 mile, and finished 47th out of 760 soldiers. It was the largest race so far in Iraq. I ran to write about it and also for the T-shirt, which is the Peachtree shirt exactly, only with "Baghdad Division" on the sleeve.

When I was running with Major Stich the next morning, Simms appeared, and slowed to pace us and give details of the race. I said I'd noticed that there are Iraqi troops in camp, and wondered if any had run. Simms said not yet, but that he's hoping to get some in the next event. Now that does sounds like a victory.

Casey's legendary enthusiasm for the sport is echoed all up and down the chain of command. Lieutenant General Pete Chiarelli, who headed the multinational force in Iraq until 2007, didn't run in Iraq. But then he didn't sleep in Iraq either. Or rather, he was said to sleep for 3 hours a night. At home, he runs nearly every day. "How long has this been going on?" I asked. "About 35 years," he told me.

Reflecting after the race, Sergeant First Class Gene Worthy said, "I think the reason behind the festive atmosphere at the Peachtree is that we had almost 800 people together in one place, in Baghdad. And it had nothing to do with Iraq. It didn't have anything to do with the bad guys, the good guys. It was 800 people together to go run. I think that's why you saw a smile on every face you saw."

Back in Germany, I'd been with the First Brigade Combat Team 1st Armored Division. The "Ready First" Combat Team. Since my visit, they have been to Iraq and had unusual success. Commander Colonel Sean B. MacFarland had been reluctant to talk with a reporter, because he wanted his men to get the credit. At the end of my stay, though, I cornered him.

A runner and a student of running, he told me about Dave Wottle, the man who ran the 1,500 and the 800 in the '72 Olympics and set a world record for the 800. He's also one of the few who ever outran Steve Prefontaine. I liked the Wottle story so much that I asked MacFarland to tell it again in e-mail. He wrote, "Wottle went from last place to first place for the win mostly in the last 200 meters. The famous 'kick' that won the race for him was an illusion, though. His 200-meter split times were amazingly consistent: 26.4, 26.9, 26.4, and 26.2. It was a phenomenal display of energy conservation. In the army we call that 'tactical patience.' It means waiting for the right conditions to commit your reserves. I ran the 880 in high school track in the mid-'70s and we all knew about Dave Wottle's even splits.... I sometimes use Dave's race as a metaphor to coach junior officers who want everything right away and worry when they see others advancing ahead of them, or who are too quick to commit their tactical reserves in battle. Energy conservation, even splits, or tactical patience all amount to the same principle and its one of the things running taught me about life."

When I was in Iraq, I sent e-mail to the addresses I still had from Germany, but nobody responded. When I returned to the states, though, Lieutenant Colonel Tom Graves wrote that he had lost a man the day before to sniper fire. "I don't know if you have ever read *Heart of Darkness* by Joseph Conrad, but the trip over here always reminds me of that book.... The key is to never lose the belief in the sanctity of human life." He hadn't been able to run much, but was planning to run the Athens Marathon with his wife, Karen.

Truth—it seems to me—lies in contradiction. The joy of running—and most regular runners know this joy—is balanced with a knowledge of death. Runners didn't invent death anymore than soldiers invented it. For some of us, it has offered up a chance to be heroic.

The more time I spent with the men and women in the army, the more I respected them, the more impressed I was with their dedication, intelligence, courage. My early suspicion that the army was a dead end for people who might not triumph in civilian life had been shattered beyond repair by Captain Travis Patriquin. I met Captain Patriquin in Germany. He was dazzling in conversation. He was also an example of an enlisted man who'd been in the army for years before he decided to go to college and then officers' school. He had learned to speak several languages and was the civil military officer for his brigade.

Searching the Web, I found a picture of Patriquin's desk. He'd put up some lines written by George Orwell: "We sleep safely in our beds because rough men stand ready in the night to visit violence upon those who would do us harm."

I applaud the sentiment and am thankful to those who take the job. From what I saw of Patriquin, though, he was no more eager to visit violence than I am. He was a man of intellect and humor, who knew how to talk to reporters, and keep them amused, without damage to his dignity or their own. He knew how to make men laugh.

In December 2006, Travis Patriquin was killed in Iraq by an improvised explosive device.

CHAPTER 21

But Will It Kill Me, Doc?

"THE MAN OF KNOWLEDGE IN OUR TIME IS BOWED
DOWN UNDER A BURDEN HE NEVER IMAGINED:
THE OVERPRODUCTION OF TRUTH. FOR CENTURIES
MAN LIVED IN THE BELIEF THAT TRUTH WAS SLIM
AND ELUSIVE AND THAT ONCE HE FOUND IT
THE TROUBLES OF MANKIND WOULD BE OVER.
AND HERE WE ARE IN THE CLOSING DECADES
OF THE 20TH CENTURY, CHOKING ON TRUTH."
—ERNEST BECKER, *THE DENIAL OF DEATH*

My question is simple: Will running kill me? I've been asking this question
for 30 years. I asked Fred Lebow, must have been 20 years ago, when I
interviewed him for *Newsday*. "I love to run, but is it really good for me?"

Fred thought it was good for me. That's what all the studies show, he
said. Since then, Fred Lebow has died of a brain tumor. He was 62.

I didn't ask Jim Fixx, but longevity was certainly in the air the first time I met him. His big red book, *The Complete Book of Running*, had just come out and rocketed to the top of the bestseller list. He wrote repeatedly and explicitly that running prolonged life. Fixx died while running. He was 52.

I ran my second marathon with Eduardo Castillo, and he ended up in a medical tent. Ed was dehydrated and couldn't keep anything down. The man in the cot next to him was taken away. "A heart episode," Ed told me.

Robert Maxwell, the former track star and cofounder of the PowerBar Company, died of a heart attack in March 2004. Maxwell was 51.

I wasn't there, but running buddies said a man died here in Westchester County at a race last summer. "They put the paddles on him," I was told.

In October 2004, the *Wall Street Journal* ran an article titled "Can Exercise Kill? The answer: Yes, and probably more often than you think."

I read it when it was published. It still gives me the chills.

The story reports that, within 7 months, two doctors at Johns Hopkins in Baltimore had died of heart attacks while running. A third physician keeled over at the fitness center. "The oldest was 51."

The writer, Kevin Helliker, went on to report that "vigorous exercise is triggering tens of thousands of US deaths a year."

Harvard University professor Arthur Siegel, who is also the chief of internal medicine at McLean Hospital in Belmont, Massachusetts, was frequently cited. "During long-distance runs," writes Helliker in remarks attributed to Dr. Siegel, "the body sustains muscle injury, and it can react to this injury as if it were bleeding, by rendering blood more clottable. In people with hidden blockage in their coronary arteries, this thickened blood can result in sudden cardiac death."

"Half a million Americans a year are going out to run marathons," says Dr. Siegel. "They incur a dose of exercise that is enough to cause muscle injury that could, under certain circumstances, have grave consequences."

In December 2006, the *New York Times* ran an article titled "Is Marathoning Too Much of a Good Thing for Your Health?" by Gretchen Reynolds. Dr. Siegel was a star witness again. The hearts of Boston Marathon finishers "appear to have been stunned," Dr. Siegel said. He recommended a full medical screening including tests that I know my medical insurance will not cover. Those with any history of heart trouble, he said, should "train for the race, getting the cardiac benefits of endurance exercise," and then watch the event on television.

Articles of this ilk are padded with disclaimers, but I forget them. The shocking images and phrases lodge in the brain. What if I told you I had tea and blueberry scones at my Aunt Sarah's house in Texas, and that there was a rattlesnake in the bread basket? You'd forget that there were blueberries in the scones. You might even forget that my aunt is named Sarah. The rattlesnake you'd remember.

Dr. Kenneth Cooper, the father of aerobics, also appeared in the *Wall Street Journal* article and said: "Exercising to excess can harm our health."

When Dr. Cooper came to lunch at the *Reader's Digest* decades ago, he told the group of editors—mostly runners—of a young man he'd known, remarkably fit, who'd died of cancer. Dr. Cooper postulated that excessive exercise had damaged the young man's immune system.

We'd had a pre-lunch jog, and I expect that most of us were sipping the one alcoholic drink the magazine's Guest House provided. I don't believe Dr. Cooper had a drink. I'm certain that he didn't finish his dessert. I noticed, because I always finish my dessert.

In his 1994 book, *Dr. Kenneth H. Cooper's Antioxidant Revolution*, Dr. Cooper lays out case after case of ultra-fit friends of his who died of cancer. "Perhaps the most interesting, and I am sure the most controversial, topic in this book is the idea that too much exercise—sometimes referred to as 'distress' exercise—may actually increase the risk of developing medical problems."

One response to all this is to get angry, to quote William Blake, at these doctors: "Prudence is a rich, ugly old maid courted by incapacity." Or I could draw from the closing of my father's first novel. "Fear tastes like a rusty knife and do not let her into your house. Courage tastes of blood."

Besides which, these scary articles and statements are grotesquely anomalous. On November 3, 2006, the same *Wall Street Journal* that had been a platform for the censorious Dr. Siegel published a bemused but not alarming article about adventure marathons. Bored, I suppose with stunning their hearts at home, some runners were going to China for a marathon on the Great Wall. Marathon Tours offers exotic destinations and a "Seven Continents Club." By March 5, 2007, the Antarctica Marathon, scheduled for 2008, was already sold out. There's a package for "running among the wildlife" in Kenya.

Nor does it always go well for the distance runner intent on startling surroundings. Bad stomachs spoiled a marathon that Americans traveled to Africa to run. Pollution delayed the Hong Kong Marathon: "4,000 runners required treatment, 22 required hospitalization, and one runner died."

These mishaps are reported cheerfully, while the Boston Marathon has been presented as an event for lemmings. All the jogging doctors in Baltimore have died. And there's a rattlesnake in Aunt Sarah's bread basket.

This is what makes me thankful for science writers like Gina Kolata of the *New York Times,* who wrote *Ultimate Fitness: The Quest for Truth about Exercise and Health.*[1] Kolata is not a doctor, or an Olympic athlete. But then, she doesn't have an axe to grind, a product to sell, or even a public persona to maintain. She's a careful, thorough researcher. It's astonishing what this can deliver.

I'm known to be a chronic runner, so people drew my attention to an article that ran in *New York Magazine* in 1991. Dr. Irving Dardik had a system, whereby you exercised for 10 to 11 minutes at a shot. People who had put in less than 40 minutes in a month were showing astonishing results.

I was embarrassed. Why should I insist on treating myself to 5 miles a day on the trails behind our house? Dr. Dardik's method wasn't supposed to be as good as mine. Dardik's Heart Wave method was supposed to be better. It took no time away from more useful pursuits. It was low impact. How could I defend myself? Dardik was a doctor and had been on a committee associated with the Olympics.

Kolata got an "exclusive" press kit about Dr. Dardik's discovery, maybe the same one that hooked *New York Magazine*. In her book, she followed the story carefully and with growing wonder. She detailed the evidence brought to support Dardik's claims, and the many credentials he displayed. She watched the story long enough to report that Dr. Dardik lost his license to practice medicine in New York State. He was charged with having told five people that he could cure their MS. His bills ran as high as $100,000.

Reading Kolata's book, I learned surprising facts. Just for instance, that the fat-burning zone is a nonstarter and that the heart-rate zones have little scientific basis.

If you're not paying careful attention, health news as presented by the media will make you into a silver-plated cynic. "If it's fun, I shouldn't do it. If it tastes good, I shouldn't eat it." Many's the health recommendation that will be exactly contradicted. Thin people live the longest. No, actually, you should be slightly chubby. Eat more salmon. Salmon is full of deadly mercury.

The facts about running have been batted around like a Girl Scout in the ring with a heavyweight champ. I'm not even going to touch on the hysteria, and there's been plenty of that. Mainstream opinions have repeatedly contradicted each other. In the 1960s, it was felt that water might give marathoners cramps, and competitors were advised to mini-mize their drinking. When I started running marathons in the late '70s, we were urged to drink before we were thirsty—to drink like Democrats are supposed to vote in Chicago—early and often. Now it turns out that marathoners can ingest so much that they die of hyponatremia, a water intoxication caused by plummeting sodium levels in the blood.

Lactic acid, which appears in quantity during intense exercise, was long thought to slow the athlete down and lead to soreness afterward. Lactic acid was bad. Now some experts say that lactic acid is good.

Long-distance running was once judged foolish and dangerous. Then a minority got hooked, and they saw it as a cure-all. If you were persistent enough, you might give Death the slip. I mean how fast could the old guy be, wearing that hooded cape and hauling a scythe?

The more you exercised, the better off you were. Now the pendulum is swinging back.

Studies indicate that the greatest health benefits are shown in the gap between those who don't exercise at all and those who exercise a little. Early reports of this came from Dr. Steven Blair, then director of research at the Cooper Institute in Dallas, which was founded by Dr. Kenneth Cooper. The greatest and most easily measured gains in fitness and longevity were shown for those who exercised moderately. Walk 20 minutes a day, five times a week.

But the much-decorated and hugely prolific writer Joyce Carol Oates would rather run. "Running! If there's any activity happier, more exhilarating, more nourishing to the imagination, I can't think what it might be," she writes.[2] "On days when I can't run, I don't feel 'myself' and whoever the 'self' is I do feel, I don't like nearly so much as the other."

Oates finds walking is a poor second to running, no matter how slowly you run.

Novelist and Pulitzer prize–winning columnist Anna Quindlen is a walker as is mystery/comedy/crime writer Lawrence Block.[3]

Both would run instead if they could do so without serious injury. "I would imagine a lot of fast walkers are people like me," Quindlen explained. "Onetime runners who can't any more because of injuries. It's a little frustrating. Every once in a while, I push my pace so hard that suddenly I'm not walking anymore but running. And then my back and my knees remind me of why I can't do that, and I ratchet back a bit."

Many of today's writers are runners. But walking has a deeper tradition. Even writers who didn't walk, paced. Churchill moved around while dictating, while C. S. Forster would get up and walk between—or even during—bouts at the desk. So important was moving to his process that he did it even while suffering from angina. Wordsworth, Dickens, Thoreau, and Walt Whitman were all notorious for their expeditions on foot.

My father often walked from his house in Ossining up the aqueduct to the Croton Dam and then back. He delighted in saying that excepting the great pyramids of Egypt, the dam was the largest mortised stone edifice in the world.[4]

Walking is safe. Running is more satisfying. This is a vast oversimplification, but I would argue that I get from running what my father got from walking *and* gin. But now some doctors would warn us off running, funnel that energy into walking, because of a condition we might have, an illness not yet diagnosed?[5]

"To me this sounds like exercise as medicine," Kolata writes, and I couldn't agree more. I want my fun. I want to eat my dessert and Dr. Cooper's, too, if I can get my hands on it. How much fun can I have, though, before I kill myself?

If a little exercise goes a long way, then does a lot of exercise do harm? And if so, how serious might that damage be?

Dr. David Nieman, a professor of health and exercise science and director of the Human Performance Lab at Appalachian State University in North Carolina, is studying this question. "By far, the most important finding that has emerged from exercise immunological studies during the past 2 decades," he wrote, "is that positive immune changes take place during each bout of moderate physical activity. . . .

"The future of exercise immunology is determining whether or not exercise-induced perturbations in immunity help explain improvements in other clinical outcomes such as cancer, heart disease, type 2 diabetes, arthritis, and aging."

In his 1998 book, *The Exercise-Health Connection: How to Reduce Your Risk of Disease and Other Illnesses by Making Exercise Your Medication*, Dr. Nieman noted that fewer than 4 in 10 Americans exercise enough.

That said, he's quite frank about the stress that marathons and ultramarathons put on the body. His studies have shown the rate of upper respiratory tract infection (URTI) goes up when people run a marathon. One in seven marathon runners reported an episode of URTI during the week following the March 1987 Los Angeles Marathon, compared to 2 in 100 who did not compete.

"Right around 90 minutes when your glycogen is definitely getting low, everything starts to turn," Dr. Nieman said. "There's a sharp increase in stress hormones, blood glucose.... It's beyond that threshold where you start seeing the immune system reflect stress."

Some people are not built to take this stress, Dr. Nieman said. "I just received an e-mail yesterday or 2 days ago from a lady who, every time she runs a marathon, gets sick and stays sick for weeks. She e-mailed me wanting to know what she can do. Well, my counsel to her was just leave marathon running alone.

"I'm more impressed, though, with how the majority of people, even when they get into that zone, snap back usually in a pretty good fashion, without any apparent harm. Even after the Los Angeles Marathon, we showed a six-fold increase in the odds of getting sick compared to controls. But only one out of seven got sick. That means that six out of seven ran the race and didn't get sick."

Dr. Nieman has done research on the Western States 100 for five summers in a row. This contest takes 26 to 27 hours to complete.

"They first called me there because they noticed what they considered to be some cancer cases occurring among some of their repeat runners. That was worrisome. So they wanted me to come in and take a look at the immune changes that occurred during the running of the Western States 100."

"There is as of yet," he told me, "no epidemiological data to verify that exercise stress can lead to cancer."

So how much is too much? The Badwater Ultra is 135 miles long, and the course (it starts in Death Valley, California) and the season (summer) are both selected for maximum discomfort. Nor does the excellent documentary *Running on the Sun* make it look at all wholesome. There's more vomiting than at a frat party. There are vivid shots of the bleeding stubs of the amputee racers. One participant shows the camera how he's had his toenails removed to prevent them getting hurt and slowing him down.

"I don't think there's a thing about this that's good for the human body," says race organizer, Dr. Ben Jones.

Dean Karnazes won Badwater in 2004, and then in 2006, he ran 50 marathons in 50 states in 50 consecutive days finishing at the New York City Marathon in 3 hours and 30 seconds. And Dean is reported to be in excellent health.

But most of us would be as unwise to try to replicate Dean's ultras as we would be to try to replicate Paul Tergat's marathon. The chances of illness after a race can be reduced by drinking a quart of Gatorade per hour or by taking quercetin, a plant pigment that is available on the Web, according to Dr. Nieman. Appalachian State has a $1.1 million grant from the Department of Defense to study the effectiveness of quercetin as a supplement.

When asked how to know if you've gone too far, Dr. Nieman told me that many researchers agree that when your exercise isn't fun anymore, that's a signal. The marker, he said, is the absence of joy.

Even the professionals talk about the joy.

"I just love to run," said "King of the Roads" Bill Rodgers.

Dick Beardsley, famous for his duel with Alberto Salazar during the 1982 Boston Marathon, wrote in his autobiography that he'd "never been the slightest bit bored with running." "I don't consider hard work and great fun mutually exclusive," he continues. "Who decided that anyway?"

Marathon world record holder Paula Radcliffe suspects that some day she might withdraw from competition. "However, I can never see myself hanging up my running shoes because I can't imagine a time when I would not want to run; it is too much a part of me."

My friends from the 1980s are still working out, many still running, and all recall their early days with pleasure and satisfaction. When I spoke with Peter Canning, whom I used to run with at the *Reader's Digest* 25 years ago, he'd just signed up for a century, a bicycle race of 100 miles.

Peter rides the century every year and expects to do it for another decade. He was up over 200 pounds when he started running. "If it weren't for running," he says and laughs, "I'd probably be dead by now."

Eduardo Castillo's father had died at 38. Eduardo was 11 at the time. Janet and I took Eduardo out to dinner on his 38th birthday. He'll be 65 this fall and is hoping to run the New York Marathon this year.

Jerry Dole, the one who accused me of being late for one of my first runs, is 74 and still goes out most days.

"There are people up here in Dorset [Vermont] who sort of set their watches by my plodding run," said Jerry, always famous for self-deprecation. "They go, 'Ah, ya. We seen you running.' Actually, I got stopped speeding by a cop not too long ago. And he was about to write up a ticket, and he said, 'Heah, haven't I seen you running around here?'"

"And I said, 'Yeah. I go running every day.'"

"And he said, 'Well, I'll give you a warning this time.' And I figured he must have been a runner, too. He recognized a fellow idiot."

This sample's very small, but it echoes out in the way that the more dramatic stories do not. If long-distance running is a blight, it's been very cleverly disguised.

Nor is the trail always smooth and unobstructed. I ran with Ray Bowles for at least a decade. During a Turkey Trot 10-K in Chappaqua years ago, he was hit twice from behind by an impatient motorist who came onto the course near the finish. Organizers had closed off one lane of traffic, and one driver—reported to be mild mannered and even considerate on foot—just couldn't tolerate the wait. He pulled out of the lane of cars, and hit Ray from behind, which threw him up in the air, and then—since the car was still going, it hit Ray again, when he came down.

The worst part of it, Ray tells me now, was lying there in the cold, waiting for an ambulance. In 2006, Ray set a new state record in Florida for over-70 swimmers in the 200-meter individual medley.

"I'm a lot better swimmer than I was a runner," Ray says, but adds that it was running that got him back into serious athletics as an adult.

I was gleeful making contact with these old friends. Interesting how we talk around the pleasure. The joy is the elephant in the room. Runners often say that they do it so that they can eat what they want and not get fat. They expect that the gratification of the coarser appetite will be more readily understood. Often as not, they eat that big breakfast so they will have to run at lunch.

Nor do I think any of these people would be surprised to learn that exercise is not a cure-all, that running—like anything else—can be overdone. And that tolerances vary from individual to individual.

Unable to reach Dr. Kenneth Cooper himself, I phoned Dr. Stephen Blair. Now at the University of South Carolina's Arnold School of Public Health, Dr. Blair worked for 22 years at the Cooper Institute. When he left, he was president and CEO.

I didn't flat-out ask him my original question: but will it kill me, Doc? Still, that's what I was driving at. I told him I ran most every day. "About 35 miles a week." He told me not to worry.

"You can commit suicide by drinking too much water and throw your electrolytes out of balance," he said. "So sure, it's possible to do too much. But I assure you, that's not a public health problem."

In other interviews, he has said, "... physical inactivity is one of the biggest public health problems we have. Inactivity and low fitness are powerful predictors of morbidity and mortality for millions of Americans."

I asked Dr. Blair directly about Cooper's public warnings. I said it was alarming to hear from the father of aerobics that exercise might damage the immune system, might lead to cancer.

"He's entitled to his opinion," Dr. Blair said, "but I don't agree. I mean I've been following the patients from that clinic for 27 years, and we do *not* see higher cancer rates, even in the most fit 5 percent of the population.

"You have to remember that a certain dose of physical activity improves the immune function. So, in my opinion, the doomsayers have overstated the case."

"I've run nearly every day for 40 years," he said. "Twenty-five miles a week isn't bad for a 58-year-old fat man. And I can hardly remember anytime over all those thousands of miles when I felt worse at the end than I did at the beginning. You just nearly always—99.9 percent of the time—you feel better at the end. It's good for you."

Nor does he think you need to get thin before you run. "In our research," Dr. Blair told the *New York Times,* "people who are obese but fit, according to cardiovascular measurement, actually have death rates half of normal-weight people who are unfit."

"One of the ironies of the creative process," wrote Ernest Becker, "is that it partly cripples itself in order to function. I mean that, usually in order to turn out a piece of work the author has to exaggerate the emphasis of it, to oppose it in a forcefully competitive way to other versions of the truth; and he gets carried away by his own exaggeration.... The problem is to find the truth underneath the exaggeration, to cut away the excess elaboration or distortion and include that truth where it fits."

Yes, there *is* a snake in Aunt Sarah's bread basket. We *are* going to die. All of us. Running doesn't need to kill us.

Death will do that.

CHAPTER 22

Too Much of a Good Thing

"OVERTRAINING IS THE BIGGEST PROBLEM INCURRED
BY RUNNERS WHO LACK THE EXPERIENCE OR DISCIPLINE
TO COPE WITH THEIR OWN ENTHUSIASM."
—MARTY LIQUORI

Dr. George Sheehan called it the dark night of the soul. The bitten runner's nightmare is not death. I'm afraid that someday—maybe tomorrow—I'll wake up injured and never run another step. Scares the wits out of me. This is absurd, I tell myself. Millions of people—I've known some of them intimately—don't run. They haven't skipped a day because there seemed to be something floating around in the right knee. They haven't taken the week off because of a sore Achilles tendon. They've taken the decade off. They've skipped a life.

It's not possible to plumb the depths of another's psyche, but when I look into the eyes of these others, *los otros*, these nonrunners, I don't always see misery. Many are not even immensely fat. Some are. But look at it this way—if living contentedly without running is an achievement, then doing so when your clothes don't fit and the world pities you, well, that looks like conquering Everest to me. These cheerful folks mustn't be condemned. They should be congratulated.

Nothing about fitness guarantees kindness, or even judgment. Nor is there anything about being slow that rules out excellence. FDR wasn't much of a runner. The great Christian apologist G. K. Chesterton was fat. Churchill probably wasn't impressive over 10 kilometers either. Buddha looks an easy man to beat.

Taking a life off seems to work. It's taking the day off I have trouble with.

Asked if he was addicted, my cousin William Winternitz Jr , an orthopedic surgeon, now in San Diego, said he didn't think so. "I don't think I'm there yet." Bill's in his fifties and been running since he was 16. "With a couple of years off in college for smoking," he said.

Those who should but can't take a day off probably make up less than 1 percent, according to Bart Yasso of *Runner's World*. "They find this running thing, and they think 'Okay, well this is really good for me.' It's certainly better than taking cocaine.

"It's not that the compulsives run every day," Bart explained. "It's that they run the days they shouldn't run. The number one injury word is not 'chondromalacia' or 'plantar fasciitis.' The word is 'compensation.' Because people will run with an injury and compensate for that injury and then really get injured. They think they're going to die if they don't go out and run."

Cousin Billy treats people for running injuries. "I haven't seen anyone acting the way I assume I would act if I had to give up running, " he told me, then corrected himself. "I actually just recently took care of a doctor who was hurt, and he couldn't run for 2 months. And I could see it in his eyes. He looked scared."

Kenny Moore opens his biography of Bill Bowerman with a scene in which the great Oregon coach restricts his athlete, making him promise never to run "except in my sight."

"I did not suffer this gladly," Moore writes. "I was tempted to do secret, defiant runs, but he had enlisted the rest of the team and half the town; every friend a possible traitor."

"The word 'cross-training' started about 20 years ago," Yasso said. "I like the word 'balance training.' You know that pounding the pavement every day is going to beat you up, so why not do something else sometime? And then when you come back to the running, you feel so much better about it. You go, 'Wow, I missed that.'

"There's a guy who did Leadville [The Leadville Trail Marathon] every year," Yasso continued. "Like he did the race right out of hernia surgery. And like he had to run with his hand over the stitches to get by. He had to take a crap in the race, and he knew he couldn't squat down, so he just had to crap standing up. He knew that if he squatted down because he was pushing himself, his stitches would burst. That's crazy. To me, that's not right."

Some streaks get stopped. Marty Linksy, a writer and lecturer at Harvard University's Kennedy School of Government, broke his streak after 9½ years. When he came out for a run years later, we stretched and he told me, "Now if I'd done this, I would have been okay." He's coming back now, but the man who couldn't take the day off, the guy who used to bounce in my kitchen, when the other runners were late, he's taken off months at a time. And—surprise! surprise!—he didn't revert to the fat boy he still thinks he is. Marty stayed thin and channeled his energies elsewhere, writing, and taking acting classes, going to Italy, spending time with his wife and son.

While it lasted, he was deadly serious about that streak. He traveled often, and so worked out routes at several international airports. His worst run at an airport was in Los Angeles. Even in those pre-9/11 days, they wouldn't let him off the grounds, "so I just went back and forth on the sidewalk for 40 minutes."

But then the streak also provided unexpected pleasures. His best airport run was in England out of Heathrow with his wife, Lynn. They headed into the countryside, "and it was beautiful, just gorgeous."

Lynn had forgotten her shirt. Marty lent her his. She didn't want to run with a bra on, and so, standing out in the open, she removed it from under the borrowed shirt. Marty reports that the polite English cabbies parked nearby watched entranced and in silence. "When the gyrations were complete, they broke into applause."

But then there are streakers who don't get hurt. My friend Gerry Krovatin, a lawyer working out of Newark, New Jersey, is one such. Out on a small boat, he had to row to shore and get in his essential run, despite a storm that was brewing.

"The streak will celebrate its 15th anniversary about 5 days after the New York Marathon this year," Gerry said. "I started it after the 1992 Marathon, one of the two you coached me through."

Gerry said that the dinghy trip to shore was one of the "high (or low) points of the streak. Keeping it alive by running with two broken ribs was another milestone. Come to think of it, there are a few hangovers in there that deserve honorable mention."

When in Washington for an important trial, he will often run on the Mall, touching the Washington Monument for luck. "I've done it a bunch of places—running out to touch the arch in St. Louis, the Eiffel Tower in Paris. Before Anna and I got married and we lived in SoHo, I used to run south to the World Trade Center, touch both the towers and run back. Can't do that anymore."

Ron Hill was an Olympian, one of the fastest streakers of all time. He is said to have run twice a day every day for 30 years, except on Sunday, when he ran just once. I suspect that this is not an accurate characterization of the man so many people admire, but Ron Hill's 1972 journal illustrates what it can look like to an outsider when you live for fitness. Hill was a strong favorite to win the Olympic gold medal for the marathon, but I've seen the same myopic obsession in weekend warriors. I've come damn close to displaying it myself.

While Hill was concentrating on his diet and race preparations, Palestinian terrorists took Israeli athletes hostage in the Olympic Village. Seventeen people died.

Tuesday, September 5th. Got up at 8:00 a.m. felt bog-eyed ... ran 7 miles in the heat, knackered, just putting one leg in front of the other, arms felt very tired too ... scrambled egg and pepper and ham with tea for breakfast ... there was a story of some shooting ... Arab guerillas had shot two Israelis and had about 20 hostages ... rumours flying of the Games being postponed 24 hours ... that would affect the diet ... tried out my silver shorts ... ran 7 miles ... of the course ... had to climb over a gate to the Nymphenburg Park ... dinner at 6 p.m., fish, sprouts, roast beef and salad, four different cheeses, tea, coffee and orange ... Craig Sharp, a canoeing coach, advised me to come off the "diet" tomorrow, so I got my chocolate ready, Mars bars and things I had been hoarding....

Wednesday, September 6th. 12:01 a.m. It was now Wednesday, I couldn't wait any longer, had a box of muesli and can of pears all mixed up with fructose and milk ... had three pieces of chocolate ... went to sleep at 12:30 a.m.... woke again at 5:30 a.m.... had a Mars bar, slept again until 6:30 a.m.... got up to go for a run, there were two notices on the bulletin board, the first said, "The Competitions would start again at 1 p.m. or 2 p.m."[1]

Do remember that this was his training diary. And many of the athletes—including Ron Hill—were badly shaken by the bloodshed. Stopping the games would have given the killers even more attention, which was—after all—what they wanted. And besides which—the man was hungry. He was in the starvation, or carb depletion, part of the carb-loading diet, which was common for decades. The theory was that if you starved your body of carbs, when you finally did eat right before the race, your famished muscles would grab up extra glycogen and water. The diet became less popular as the public arrived at the conclusion that any advantages accrued during the carb-loading phase were more than cancelled by the stress of the starvation phase, which invited pre-race illness.

The advantages to never taking a day off are substantial. I ran the morning of the first day I woke up in London, and so first saw the Thames on a run. I ran the day my father died. I've run when it was so dark in the woods, I kept plunging off the trail and into trees. (Yes, this was before they sold those terrific little headlamps, first used in specialty sports but now widely available.)

I have a friend who once surprised a herd of kangaroos during a run. I once ran onto a field and thought I'd surprised two huge, beige-colored bears. Then I saw that they weren't bears at all, but people, big naked people, who'd been entangled on the field. I'm sure it was much more fun than it looked like.

When my neighbor, the journalist Herb Hadad, heard that his first son was born, he went for a run.

"For days afterwards," he wrote, "well-wishers wanted to know why I was limping. The reason was my excessive celebration of fatherhood. I had seen Evelyn as a mother for the first time and my new son. I had kissed them, left the hospital and broken into a run, running uphill all the way to our street two miles away. And then, instead of returning to our empty house, I had continued to run, through the woods until it was dark, until I was in a state of exhausted bliss."

I, too, took celebratory runs when my sons were born. I also run when I'm in despair. I once ran 6:30s when I was crying. My first novel had been rejected by the very editors who had been primed to snap it up. I felt that I'd cut out my heart with a pair of cuticle scissors. My agent Andrew Wylie had wrapped the organ in a towel and sent it to three editors, one after the other. They'd all had the same response: "This doesn't look like a heart. More like a tennis ball that somebody's run over with the lawn mower and covered with ketchup."

I'd "transitioned" from a fully employed magazine editor to a member of the willfully unemployed, the son of a famous writer struggling with a book that might have been titled "Whither Me?" I ran 3 miles to the highest point in the park near our house, sobbing all the way, and I passed some hikers, who looked a little bit surprised to see this grown man blubbering as he went by. After some more crying, and I don't cry easily, I ran back home. Then I was okay. Not cheerful, mind you, not good company, but I was okay. The world could keep me from getting published, I thought, but it couldn't keep me from writing. Nor from running either.

The only times I wish I hadn't run, the only days I wish I'd taken off, are the days when my running hurt my running. And this has happened.

I've been there, laying out 9-minute miles, with all the style of something that Dr. Frankenstein might have come up with on a bad day.

I've seen it in others doing the same joyless shuffle on the trails or roads. They're not the fat, slow ones. They aren't running because they want to fit into pants, or because they fear the lash of ridicule. These people are lean, they're weather-beaten, but Lord are they ever slow.

At least I wasn't a speed addict. If you try—just for instance—to run three 7-minute miles every day, then you'll probably get badly hurt. I think that's why President Bush, the first runner, is riding a bicycle. I'm envious at first when somebody tells me they never run for more than half an hour, but they never go slower than 7:30. Seems perfect, but it doesn't seem to be sustainable. Nor is it really sensible to fall into the more common routine of running the same route every day at the same speed, but getting slower and slower. Much wiser to mix it up. Hard and then easy. Take that dreaded day off.

It hurts me to recognize this, but there are people who have reached the point where they really can't run anymore. When I see old buddies who have been knocked off the road, I have trouble looking them in the eye. From where I sit, it looks like tragedy, and one for which I have no tendency to rubberneck. If we become reacquainted through some other means, it always turns out that the train wreck didn't happen.

Sometimes there's a terrible passage, but all the men and women I know have come out the other end, bounced back, and found that ecstasy they'd come to expect in some other passion, swimming, acting, poetry. It may take years to find the path through painful exertion and to learn to trust it, to know that the impossible ends in a bang of joy. Take running away, and your ex-runner, your former runner, will still be throwing herself into work, some sort of work, and coming out the other side exhausted and happily spent.

Running all the time, running without joy, is bad for you. More important, it can be bad for your running. It can—and often does—lead to the niggling injury that throws you off balance. One hurt leads to another. The athlete is slowed and finally stopped.

It's not the death that lands you in a coffin I fear so much, as the other one, the living death of compulsion.

CHAPTER 23

Who Are We?

"MY FEELING IS THAT ANY DAY I AM TOO BUSY
TO RUN IS A DAY THAT I AM TOO BUSY."
—JOHN BRYANT, DEPUTY EDITOR OF THE *TIMES* (LONDON)

If I had to die, or even if I had to—God forbid—stop running, I'd still look back on all those miles and on that Creamsicle-colored bicycle with gratitude.

The life I've lived since that first adult mile would not just have been beyond my old, sedentary self: It would have been inconceivable.

Peter Canning says that his own life was as significantly transformed. He came back from Paris at 200 pounds and looked at himself in the mirror. "I was just married (not happily), and I was a bit of a gourmand." This was in the late '60s, and he'd heard about jogging. So he tried it.

He went at his jogging as he had gone at his gormandizing. Soon he was running 5 miles from his house to his office at the *Reader's Digest*. "It was an adventure. In the winter, it wasn't yet light, and I'd go down through the dark streets and across the golf course, get to work before everybody else, and take a sponge bath. It was a great way to start the day. And when you look at your face in the mirror, and you weigh 200 pounds, and when you look at 167, that's a big difference."

Then as now, people talked about health, but Jerry Dole says he started because "Peter seemed to be enjoying himself."

Having seen his favorite editors all besweated up on the corporate campus, DeWitt Wallace had a shower installed in the basement. This was during the late 1960s, and the runners would go out at lunch, often passing through the elegant Rotunda that was sometimes thronged with visitors come to see the building and admire the masterpieces then on display.

Andy Jones was another early runner. "He would come around," Jerry Dole remembers, "and no matter how many tourists there were in the hallway, he'd say, 'Well, fellas, let's do the ball buster, today.' The 'ball buster' meant we went across the street, and up the hill."

"I don't know how the *Digest* ever put up with us," Dole says now. The runs got longer, and the crew swelled to include, just for instance, Patricia Nell Warren, who has gone on to write several successful books, many involving same-sex love and often built around runners.

I was in the second or third generation of jogging junkies. When Peter, Eduardo, my wife, Janet, and I went to races, Peter's girlfriend, Galen—a teacher—used to sit in the bleachers, smoking cigarettes and correcting papers. There must have been some interval of training, but the way I recall it now, she put out that last cigarette, ran her first race, and won her category.

Galen is an attractive woman, and mannerly in the extreme. But when you get her interested in something—Peter, running, education, conservation, horses, Peter—it's like dropping a lighted match into a crumpled pile of newspapers that has been soaked with gasoline. She quit smoking and got fit in a hurry. I have a picture of myself—in great shape and finishing a triathlon. I'm smiling, but the shadow in my eyes is there because Galen beat me.

Men and women give up smoking, change body type, escape bad marriages and bad jobs, get promoted and/or quit as a result of the clarity they find out on the trails or roads. Like Jeremy Morris, I'm always gratified to see a runner, especially when traveling.

Way back in 1979, my father wrote an essay about running, which was rejected by the *New York Times* but purchased by the *Reader's Digest*. In the past, he wrote, he'd been heartened when he traveled, by the sight of lovers. Now he was encouraged by the runners. This was at the height of the Cold War. He saw "five runners crossing in front of the Kremlin in Red Square."[1]

There's a joke that men and women of a certain age, demeanor, and dedication should run in a shirt that has "Bad Marriage" or "Busted Relationship" on the front and back. Certainly it happens. Happened to me. But running can also be useful for the family as it is for the individual. Janet got out her shoes and ran again as a present to me on my 59th birthday. My best present.

Running provides an intimacy with strangers, but also a place to be candid with your intimates. The time I've spent running with my oldest son, now 21, has been precious in the extreme. It's difficult for a father to speak frankly with his son. It's difficult for a son to speak frankly with his father. John was the firstborn and therefore point man in the jungle of his father's psyche. Sometimes we had to stop running to bellow at one another.

"I used to think you were the best son in the world, until this!"

"And I used to think you were the best father in the world, until this!"

It's a family axiom that while running, the brain doesn't get enough oxygen to sustain a falsehood. Other times, I've enjoyed myself so much that I tried to conceal my pleasure so as not to embarrass him.

My younger son, Andrew, now 18, used often to spend the intervals between academics and athletics running around the campus of his high school. Three years ago, I cajoled him into "a 20" in the park near our house. I was wearing a Nike Triax with a shoe pod, and so we'd have some idea of the distance covered. Andrew kept sprinting ahead, jogging in place at the intersections until I plodded up and nodded in the direction we should take. At about 17 miles, neither of us was having much fun anymore, so we headed home. Then I dug deep and passed my teenage son. Then he dug deeper and beat me home.

Running has also increased my intimacy with prose and with poetry. I've listened to thousands of books while running, first on cassette and now in MP3 files. I've listened to the classics, poetry, and also quantities of genre fiction. Twenty years ago, near our house in Pound Ridge, I had a run which included a series of cruel little hills on Upper Shad Road. I was so enthralled by a book written by Lawrence Block that I reached the summit of the last hill without noticing that I'd come to the first one. I listened to *Lear*. And then again. And I listened to *Lear* again. I listened repeatedly to Oscar Wilde's *The Importance of Being Earnest*. My knees wobbled with suppressed mirth.

I'm not a quick study, but I have listened to some splendid books and had—not often, but sometimes—glorious and ecstatic moments, sucked into a thrilling narrative, or into the presence of a towering intellect. And yet, I'd almost always prefer a live human being. I never know what a person might say. Or what I might say myself.

I went long once with a Russian émigré I'd never laid eyes on before and who joined the group I run with weekends in the Rockefeller State Park Preserve. He was fast and kept pushing the pace. My Nike Triax with shoe pod credited us with some sub-7-minute miles. When we finally pulled up together at the parking lot after an hour and 38 minutes, I caught my breath and then said, admiringly, "Man, but you're fast."

"Thanks," he said. "Actually, I was just trying to see if I could get you to stop talking."

Hard to communicate the power of the connection made on a run. I've learned not to take strangers at their word. You shake a hand, look somebody in the eye, exchange pleasantries. But you've learned nothing. Is he faking? Does he despise you? Do you despise him? Run 5 miles with that person, and you are friends. You might sleep at his house, lend him a car. Maybe she has much more status than you do, maybe it's the other way around—after 3 miles, it doesn't matter.

Just as top editors at the *Reader's Digest* ran with a rank beginner, lieutenants, majors, even generals in the army make a point of running with their troops. A bond is formed on the road that could win a battle and actually does save lives.

At the 2006 Millrose Games, I found a man in the stands I used to run with 20 years ago, out of the 47th Street YMCA. He's at least 10 years my senior.

"Still running?" I asked.

He nodded and smiled. "Celebrex," he said. Ordinarily, I'll encounter somebody like that, walk off and picture him turning to his companion of the hour and tossing a biting observation at my retreating form. I'm not famous, but I'm well enough known to be despised. And possibly my running buddy was wickedly funny behind my back. And yet I was certain that at base, we were friends. We'd seen each other in shorts, we'd heard one another gasping for air.

We'd had fun together, adult-onset fun. You can toil for a decade in the same office with another human being without ever getting as close as you do in the course of a single 5-mile trot up the East River in a heavy sleet.

If we're a club, we're a big one and growing. There were nearly 38 million runners in the United States in 2005 according to Running USA. More than 11 million of them ran on at least 100 days during the year.

What the early Christians said about their faith can aptly be said about our sport. Runners are not always the best. But if you take X person—however good or bad—and add running, then X plus running will always be better than X alone.

When I went to Oregon in 2005 to run the Hood to Coast Relay with the *Runner's World* team, editor-in-chief David Willey took the first segment of the race, which was a thigh-busting downhill that began on the shoulder of Mount Hood. He approached the end of his section just ahead of an older man, but instead of beating the stranger out, he pulled up so that they could cross the line together. Not certain whether to believe my own eyes, I wrote David about it later.

He wrote back: "Ha! It did seem a touch, well, asshole-ish, to nip somebody at the tape after running down a mountain for 6 miles on the first leg of a 197-mile race. Must be my Midwestern upbringing."

But why should I be surprised? Dick Beardsley crossed the finish line of the inaugural London Marathon (1981) holding hands, sharing the victory, with Norwegian Inge Simonsen.

I've heard that at one point, the AAU threatened to disqualify winners who insisted on crossing the finish line holding hands, or even with apparently identical times. It was happening too often.

The generous impulse radiates out from the field of competition. Kenya hand John Manners has put off finishing his own book for years so that he could negotiate scholarships at Ivy League colleges for Kenyan boys and girls. The patterns of understated generosity are replicated and replicated again.

One coarse and limited measure of this impulse is that races raised $656 million for charity in 2005, up from $520 million in 2002, according to USA Track and Field.

What I most treasure, though, is the genuine affection the sport stirs up, despite a competitive core. For me, this is the supreme virtue of running. I remember when I first stumbled on this truth, must have been nearly 30 years ago. I was 6 to 7 miles into a 10-mile race, and I realized that I liked the man I was beating, and that I also liked the man who was beating me. This was then an unprecedented experience for me, this was competition, ruthless competition, but without bitterness. In life, in tennis—hell, in backgammon—the loser doesn't like the winner. Sure he may come to like him. Grinding his teeth, he'll say all the right things. In running—at least at my level—we like each other. We're not polite, we're not good sportsmen, we like each other.

"If this race can turn one more person into a runner, then it's worth it," said Navy Commander Matt Simms in Baghdad, as he staged a 10-K race for the troops. "Because it makes the world a better place."

There's a lot of evidence for this. First, if you measure better one runner at a time, it certainly feels that way. Having persuaded my older son to do 5 with me recently, and pulling my shorts out of the wastepaper basket in my bathroom through which I cycle my running clothes, I thought, *when have I felt like this? And the answer was: On Christmas Eve when I was 6, and I'd already heard—from behind a locked door—my father and sister playing with the Lionel train set I knew would be mine.*

Proofs that regular aerobic exercise is good for the mind and body continue to drift up at a fantastic rate in scientific journals. I've heard running linked with longevity, of course. I've read that it can stave off heart disease, cancer. It reduces blood pressure. I've read that it protects against Alzheimer's disease. Perhaps most important, I've read that parents who exercise are twice as likely to have children who exercise. I've read that running can reduce stress and increase reasoning power.

"Centuries ago, it was commonly thought that the heart was limited to a certain number of beats and that those who used them up too fast would die young," wrote Jane Brody, in the *New York Times* on June 20, 2006. "Now we know better. The heart is a muscle, and like any other muscle in the body, exercising it makes it stronger. Over all, each hour spent exercising (up to 30 hours a week) adds about two hours to a person's life expectancy, according to the Harvard Alumni Study, which has tracked deaths among 17,000 men for more than two decades."

Another *New York Times* article run on November 1, 2005, said studies indicate that exercise reduced the risk of colon and breast cancer. "Exercise is like a seat belt," says Dr. Ann McTiernan of the Fred Hutchinson Cancer Research Center in Seattle. "It's not a guarantee, but it can reduce your risk."

"Researchers in Norway followed 53,242 men for an average of 16 years and found that the risk of prostate cancer was reduced by more than half in those who walked during their work hours and also engaged in leisure time exercise," writes Dr. David Nieman in *The Exercise-Health Connection*.[2]

Which does not mean that some of what we believe now won't later be discounted, or contradicted. Even the best minds are mistaken. Remember that Aristotle, while a great genius, thought the brain was an organ designed to cool the blood, a primitive neck-mounted radiator with hair.

I'd run, even if it was bad for me. Adam Bean of *Runner's World* expressed sentiments I've heard from scads of others over the years. He'd been playing tag with an injury, and so I was happy to see him suited up for a run I was joining, but also afraid that if I was wrong, I'd be putting salt in a wound.

"You can run?" I asked tentatively.

"I can run," he said. "I don't know about you, but when I can run, everything else is okay."

Despite recent studies now trumpeting the health benefits of moderate exercise, my favorite event is immoderate—the marathon. This race is an ordeal designed to break the men and women who attempt it. The distance killed Pheidippides. The human body seems to be designed to run 20 miles. After that, the glycogen stores are exhausted. Even the elite know the wall. Frank Shorter caught the attention of the world when he won the Munich Marathon in 1972. He had known he was fast since the sixth grade, when he'd won his school's overall field day championship—the prize, a copy of *Famous American Athletes of Today*. But Frank started out as a track and cross-country man. Running beside Kenny Moore during his first marathon, Shorter hit the dreaded wall, turned to his friend, and asked a question that has troubled tens of thousands of others: "Why couldn't Pheidippides have died at 20 miles?"

Life forms are almost endlessly adaptable, but for most of us, a marathon is a red-letter day. For most of those who undertake the distance each year, the trial goes beyond health, beyond self-improvement, beyond the self. Effort over that distance requires surrender.

I'm more and more inclined to think that this planet is not going to fall into rubble, or explode like a 5-inch salute. The dreadful future I had picked out for myself never materialized. I had it figured right down to the burnt coffee, overflowing ashtrays, condescending neighbors, and a waistband that bit me savagely in the middle. Instead, I'm fit at nearly 60.

If I was so gravely mistaken about my own life, is it possible that I'm wrong about the world as well? Maybe this is not a tragedy we've all been scripted into. Now don't get me wrong. I'm still a melancholic. I'm still in a constant state of outrage and disappointment. That's my style. I just wonder how much of a prophet I'll turn out to have been.

Humans are capable of exceeding their own wildest expectations. We can go around corners, beyond what we can see or even imagine.

Roger Bannister wrote of this in his book *The Four-Minute Mile*. "John Landy, my great Australian rival, who had run three four-minute 2 second miles, said, 'Two little seconds are not much, but when you're on the track those fifteen yards seem solid and impenetrable, like a cement wall.'"

In a book about the early barnstormers, I read of a father who with his young son approached the pilot of an airplane that had landed in a field. The man asked the pilot what kept him and his heavier-than-air machine from plummeting to earth. "Air," the pilot said, and the father, crestfallen, turned sadly to his son. "Ask a silly question, and you'll get a silly answer."

Liked manned flight, the changes I have seen in my own life and in the lives of other runners I have known are often so dramatic as to beggar belief.

Tragedy is easy to picture—the fatal or crippling car crash, the black spot of malignancy, even the mushroom cloud—all these are thrown casually up on the screen of the mind. It's harder, trickier, perhaps impossible for us to visualize a better, richer, kinder life. Honestly, though, is paradise any more difficult to believe in than was that first mile?

Eden exists. And you can run there.

CHAPTER 24

The Runner's Agony— I Mean the Runner's High

"RUNNING IS THE GREATEST METAPHOR
FOR LIFE, BECAUSE YOU GET OUT OF IT
WHAT YOU PUT INTO IT."
—OPRAH WINFREY

The truth—when we glimpse it at all—lies in contradiction. The pleasure of the marathon comes from the largeness of the achievement, but also because we associate the long race with death, the death of Pheidippides.

We'd all rather not die, but it's death that makes life grand. The runner's high is built on a foundation of runner's lows. The joy is often paid for in advance.

In order to experience what George Sheehan calls the magnificent post-race lassitude, you need first to have the pre-race jitters, followed by the during-race agony.

New York Times science writer Gina Kolata has been running "since before there were running shoes," but was pulled back into the center of the sport by her son, Stefan, a graduate student. "About 2 years ago, he said, 'Are you running just to run, or are you running for some purpose? Do you have anything you want to train for?'"

There was a 5-K in 2 weeks, and so Gina timed herself over 4 miles, and was embarrassed to find that she was running 9 minutes per mile. Stefan gave her a plan, and at the 5-K, she ran 8-minute miles. "And I thought, *whoa, look at this. This is really amazing,*" she said.

"The first race was such a thrill. It was so exciting. You can't believe you're doing it. You think you're going to die. Especially a short race. And then, of course, I won my age group. Don't ask me how."

Up in Boston this year to watch Stefan run an impressive 2:35 marathon, Gina bought a pair of Reeboks. "And they gave me a shirt. On the front it said, 'Run Easy.' And on the back, it said, 'Run at the speed of chat.' Which I guess is okay," she said. "I mean you can talk while you're running, but I feel that it also sends the wrong message. If you want the runner's high, then, 'Run easy. Run at the speed of chat' may not do it for you."

I ran a 20-mile out-and-back once when the sky burst. It was a hot, humid day, and it seemed as if I'd been traveling under a gray canvas ceiling. Then somebody slit the canvas with a bayonet. I put my head down and splashed the last 2 miles. It was shortly after the about-face that God radioed in the heavy artillery. A metal trash can took a direct hit. The lid wobbled across the road in front of me. Put that in a movie, and it means the hero's going to die. Water was streaming into my eyes. *Ten, or a hundred, or a hundred thousand,* I mumbled to myself as I sprinted toward home. I couldn't exactly remember how many Americans lightning kills annually.

Turns out to be 67, and we're a big country, so the odds were in my favor, until you factor in stupidity. If I had died, I would have been blamed for it.

Nobody dies by accident anymore. I suppose there must be a tribunal up there, floating between the satellites.

"Yes, judge it looked like there might be a lightning storm. Yes, I knew

I'd be running along a ridge. I'd guess I have a dozen metal fillings. I do remember the woman who told me about the bodies she'd seen, and that their feet were burned."

Runners are pigheaded, though. We know not to worry too much about blood in our urine. We also know to expect bloody nipples. I once took a run in shorts when it was cold enough to freeze the end of my you-know-what. This was not painful. Then it melted. This *was* painful. I thought myself unusual. Since then, I have come upon several articles on the subject. They have a name for it: frostbite.

Talk about running to a nonrunner, and you have to redefine the word *fun*. You need to break down the walls in it, make room for punishing hills, biting cold.

If life is the problem, then running is the solution. Head ache? Go for a run? Hung over? Go for a run. I can only think of one time when 5 miles didn't work. I had an exposed root. That tooth hurt so much I couldn't sleep. So, of course, I suited up and went out for a trot. This was *not* helpful. The tooth hurt every time my heart beat. Speeding up the heart-beat sped up the hurt.

Most everything else, though, it works for. Not just physical pain, but also its trickier psychic cousin. Change your biology, and you change your mood.

When Fred Lebow was hospitalized with his brain tumor, he calculated that 67 times around the roof terrace near his room at Mount Sinai equaled a mile, and he walked his miles. If there was no other reason to love Fred Lebow, then I'd love him for that.

I think of Fred sometimes when I'm running. And how he is said to have beaten back his cancer for 2 years. Other days, I run because I had two desserts the night before. And there are fearful runs taken, because I'd like to live forever. Foolish me.

When life seems dreadful, you go for a run and make the run more dreadful still. You look at your watch. You've put in 3 minutes. Look again, and it's 3 minutes and 14 seconds. It hurts to breathe. Is that a stone in my shoe? Then I break through the invisible plastic shield that separates me from life. I don't care that I had three drinks last night and decided to be candid. I don't care if the basement floods. What if the story that was going to be snapped up like a salad crouton thrown into a pond full of sunfish hasn't gotten a response in 3 weeks? Maybe it was lost in the mail. It doesn't matter. I'm not myself. I'm all men, and I'm not a man at all. Just will. Just spirit.

If the feeling is elegant and joyous, it is also carnal and cruel. Jack London may have been projecting human emotions onto Buck in *The Call of the Wild*, but his description of the big dog's feelings while chasing a rabbit works for me.

"He was ranging at the head of the pack, running the wild thing down, the living meat, to kill with his own teeth and wash his muzzle to the eyes in warm blood.

"There is an ecstasy that marks the summit of life, and beyond which life cannot rise. And such is the paradox of living, this ecstasy comes when one is most alive and it comes as a complete forgetfulness that one is alive. This ecstasy, this forgetfulness of living, comes to the artist, caught up and out of himself in a sheet of flame; it comes to the soldier, war-mad on a stricken field and refusing quarter; and it came to Buck, leading the pack, sounding the old wolf cry, straining after the food that was alive and that fled swiftly before him through the moonlight." [1]

Running is good for you, but the runs I treasure are the ones I shouldn't have taken. The runners I like best are the ones who are always threatening the very health we're all supposed to be in search of.

Once in a triathlon, a guy got off his bike right before I got off mine. His running shoes weren't where they were supposed to be. He began the 15-mile leg of the race without shoes. My first thought, of course, was *there's a man I'll catch*. Somebody sprinted after him with a pair of New Balance, but there were those eerie seconds when that man headed up the paved road, wildly determined, white tube socks flashing. It was, well, it was beautiful. Gorgeous.

CHAPTER 25

Boston

"TO PUSH YOURSELF, AND CONSIDER YOURSELF
A RUNNER, YOU MUST MAKE A PILGRIMAGE
TO MECCA. THAT'S HOW IMPORTANT BOSTON
IS TO RUNNERS. IT'S A RELIGIOUS EXPERIENCE."
—KATHRINE SWITZER, FIRST WOMAN WITH A BIB NUMBER
TO COMPLETE BOSTON

This is the marathon for snobs. It's also the one you want. The Boston Athletic Association event was not the first held in this country (it was the second). But it has survived to touch 3 centuries. In the brotherhood of gargantuan distance festivals, Boston is the only one that requires excellence for admission. The other giants can be devilishly hard to find a place in, but—unless you're an elite athlete—you don't get in by running fast. You earn that coveted Boston number by laying down a quick 26.2 miles on another certified course. The qualifying times are so stringent that earnest and committed runners are routinely barred. This is about merit.

The race that now starts at Hopkinton and ends at the Prudential Center has a checkered past. Saying "I ran the Boston Marathon" in the 1950s was the equivalent of announcing yourself as a ham radio operator or an amateur taxidermist. You had established proficiency in one of the poorly drained and ventilated corners of human endeavor. Your very success declared you a social misfit, somebody who had taken a drubbing on the great battlefield of life. Or who had called in sick.

No more. "When I ran Boston" is now a face card in conversational poker. Not an ace, mind you. Not "In the caves of Tora Bora . . ." or "When I dated Jennifer Aniston . . ." but right up there with "We at Harvard."

Marathons are popular now, and Boston is the marathon with tradition. You can't buy tradition. That's what Fred Lebow said, even as he lured the star athletes away to the New York Marathon with cash.

Staged for 111 years in a row, Boston holds the record for consecutive marathons. But it was not the first. The New York Knickerbocker Athletic Club sponsored the first-ever marathon in this country in 1896. Thirty men started out from Stamford, Connecticut, and 10 reached the finish at Columbus Circle in Manhattan.

The Boston Athletic Association's inaugural event was held 7 months later, in April 1897. Grandiloquently dubbed "The Championship of America and the World," the contest drew a field of 15. They didn't even have a gun. Olympian Tom Burke drew a line in the dirt with his heel and then shouted, "Go!"

John J. McDermott, the New York lithographer who had posted a winning 3:25:55 when he crossed the finish line at Columbus Circle, also triumphed in Boston with a 2:55:10, losing 9 pounds along the way.

This helped spawn two of distance running's most cherished canards— that marathons are thinning and that runners improve with age.

McDermott was beaten for the first half of the race by Richard Grant, who wore an H on his shirt and got cheers of "Rah for Harvard" from the

Wellesley women at 13 miles. The New York Flyer came from behind and drew far enough ahead to leave time for his bicycle-riding trainer to dismount and administer a quick massage. Then McDermott went on to the finish. Thus Grant had helped establish another tradition—that those who lead in the first half of a marathon die at the wall.

Both these pioneering American marathons had been inspired by the first-ever organized race of its kind, which had been held in Greece in April 1896. Having traveled to Greece and seen the birth of the great race, America's participants in those games (Tom Burke among them) returned to this country excited by the prospect of holding similar competitions here.

Since McDermott's Boston time was better than the 2:58:50 with which Spiridon Louis won at Athens, the New York athlete was declared the marathon champion of the world, although it's hard to see how they knew that, since the Boston course was 24.5 miles and the Greek one 24.8.

Greece would have swept the medals in that initial ordeal if third-place finisher Spiridon Belokas hadn't ridden part of the way in a carriage, thus establishing the tradition of shortcuts. In Boston's 1909 race, Howard Pearce of New Bedford had the finish in view when a policeman tackled him. The apparent leader had been spotted getting a lift in a car from about 13 miles to a place very near the end of the ordeal.

There was also contention about the marathon held at the 1900 Paris Olympics, when American Arthur Newton (not to be confused with the South African ultrarunner of the same name) pulled into what he thought was the lead and kept it only to finish the race and find that he was in fifth place. Apparently, the course was complicated and not terribly well marked. Newton accused the winner, a Frenchman named Michel Theato, of cheating.[1] The native, though, had finished more than an hour before Newton in 2:59:45. Newton had run a 4:04:12, which is slow enough to indicate at least one wrong turn on his part.

A euphonious name coupled with an unusual force of character combined to make Rosie Ruiz famous after she claimed to win Boston in 1980. She crossed the finish line, climbed right onto the winners' podium, and accepted the laurel crown. The problem here was that she looked too good. Race officials had learned to expect sweaty, stinky, skinny survivors. Even that year's male champion, Bill Rodgers, a man famous for his charm and manners, let on that he suspected fraud.

Witnesses soon came forward who had seen Ruiz enter the course from the sidelines very near the finish. Rosie was alleged to have qualified for Boston by riding the subway for part of New York's course the year before.

Since Boston is the oldest annually repeated marathon in the world, it would be natural to assume that it was the most significant among the many long races staged in early 20th-century America. Not so. The Boston Athletic Association (BAA) ran a strictly amateur event. Races that offered large purses appear to have drawn much of the attention. The great old race was dwarfed for a time by others of its ilk.

I know from Michael Connelly's *26 Miles to Boston*[2] that in 1909, the temperature hit 97 degrees and that 91 of 164 runners dropped out. So I searched Newspaperarchives.com for Boston Marathon in April and May of 1909. My first hit was from the *New York Times* of May 3, 1909. The story was headlined: "French Trio in Big Marathon Race.... Crack Field will start in $10,000 International Competition." Didn't sound like Boston. My next hit was coverage of that race itself, run on the front page of the sports section for Sunday, May 9, 1909, with a big picture of the starting field. The winner was Yves, of France with a 2:44:05; third was taken by Crooks of the United States in 2:52:10. Fourth was Simpson, identified as a member of the Ojibway Indian Nation. Sixth place went to Dorando Pietri of Italy, the man famous for having taken so many falls in the 1908 London Olympics. The venue for this major international competition? New York's Polo Grounds, where some 10,000 paid to watch the event. On the same day, 4,000 fans watched the Red Sox beat the Yankees 6 to 4.

The same lead sports page of that issue of the *Times* reported that Al Raines had won the Bronx Marathon, "which started and finished on the Bronx Oval, 163rd Street and Southern Boulevard." Coverage of two marathons on one page of one newspaper? Never, sadly, in my lifetime. A piece in another newspaper of the time declared that the nation was suffering from a severe attack of "marathonitis."

Races were still of varying length, since an official distance had not yet been agreed upon. Edward VII asked that the course for the 1908 Olympics be run from Windsor Castle to the Olympic stadium and then around the stadium to the Royal Box. Perhaps because this made such a good story, that distance became official and over time, all other races calling themselves marathons fell into line, laying out courses of 26.2 miles. Boston reset its start at Hopkinton in 1924 to bring the course to 26.2 miles.

In or out of the limelight, the Boston was an annual event, with local heroes. John A. Kelley the Elder and Clarence Demar are both famous for winning it again and again. Demar, a linotype operator who trained by running to work, first won in 1911. He won again in 1922 and was victorious a total of seven times. "Mr. Demarathon" was 41 years old at the time of his last victory. John A. Kelley won his first race in 1935 and his second in 1945. Kelley finished the race 58 times.

Families who lived along the route got in the habit of going out on Patriots Day and watching. Many of these got caught in the net and one day ran the race themselves.

Competitors and even spectators grew to appreciate the three punishing Newton Hills placed just where a runner's glycogen stores are likely to be exhausted. It was on the last of these elevations—between 20 and 21 miles—during the 1936 race that defending champion John A. Kelley the Elder passed the race leader, Ellison "Tarzan" Brown. As Kelley went by on the hill, he gave Tarzan Brown a tap on the shoulder.

Tarzan evidently didn't welcome the gesture. He roared back into the lead and ultimately won the race. *Boston Globe* reporter Jerry Nason wrote that Brown had broken Kelley's heart on that hill, and so the last of the Newton Hills has been called Heartbreak Hill ever since.

Those who may have lost interest in the race because of the streak of foreign victors might recall that when Amby Burfoot won in 1968, he was the first American to do so in 10 years. If you bunch Amby with John J.

Kelley, his cross-country coach who won in 1957, you have a stretch of 23 years with only two American men first across the finish. After Burfoot, of course, we had a spate of American champions—Bill Rodgers and Alberto Salazar notable among them.

Way back in 1979, I had my heart set on Boston, when I spent $18 and change on a pair of marked-down Brooks running shoes, which were a size too small. I had to run under 3 hours, and clocked a 2:59:33 in New York. My father celebrated my acceptance by taking the whole family to spend the eve of the Boston Marathon at the Ritz-Carlton. For breakfast on race day, the Carlton waived the necktie requirement in the Grill Room. My father suggested I write a "casual" for the *New Yorker* about this.

I finished the race in 3 hours and 2 minutes and 2 seconds. When I came back to the hotel room, nobody was there. The phone rang. It was the Associated Press wanting to speak with John Cheever. The phone rang again. It was UPI wanting to speak with John Cheever. I drew a bath.

My father came into the hotel room and then into the bathroom. "You finished the marathon?" he asked.

I nodded. "And you won the Pulitzer Prize," I said.

I finished my post-race bath while he spoke with reporters. Walking near the Prudential Center afterward, he noticed all the other runners still conspicuous in their silvery capes. "Nobody knows that either of us did anything," he said.

In a letter to a friend he wrote, "Ben came in gallantly under three hours which is considered winning and when I returned to the hotel he was sitting in the bath-tub, holding in his teeth a wire from the Pulitzer Prize Committee."

He'd chopped 3 minutes off my time.

The *New Yorker* turned down my "casual," and although it hurts me to admit this, I expect their judgment was sound. Still it meant a great deal that my father had suggested that I try. Good writing was mistaken for good character in our family.

He seemed delighted by my emergence at last—approaching 30—as the athlete he'd always yearned for in a son. In a television interview shortly after I'd run Boston, he said that I had broken 2 hours in a marathon. Now he'd chopped an hour and 3 minutes off my time. And the man hadn't had a drink in years.

Boston had first started requiring qualifying times in 1971. In order to enter Boston, a runner had to complete another certified marathon in 3 hours and 30 minutes. Now, each age category has its own separate qualifying time. These qualifying times have changed over the years.

Will Cloney, a businessman, served as race director from 1947 to 1982. He and Jock Semple functioned as a two-headed Cerberus, excluding the slower runners, however worthy.

There was, of course, a tradition of "bandits," or unnumbered runners (which still exists today), but these were frowned upon by officialdom and regarded with mixed feelings by those who had struggled to make the cut. The love/hate relationship between runners and the Boston authorities was delightfully expressed in a story by Erich Segal.[3] In it, a runner sells his soul in order to win the Boston Marathon.

Since there is need for training, the Devil took his protégé out to a track—I think at an armory—so that the young man can practice the style and demeanor he will need when he crosses the finish.

The Devil keeps his word, and the man he's chosen wins the race, but Boston officialdom finds that their champion has not run a qualifier. If he didn't run a qualifier, they reason, he couldn't possibly have been admitted to the race. If he hadn't been admitted to the race, he couldn't possibly have won it. And so our hero's immortal soul was saved. The door to those eternal fires was held closed with red tape.

As the popularity of the BAA event grew, qualifying times were tightened. For the 1980 edition, I needed to break 2 hours and 50 minutes.

So Janet and I and a black Puli named Sophie traveled to the Aberdeen

Training Grounds in Maryland to meet my training partner Eduardo Castillo. There, he and I ran a course advertised as flat-as-a-pancake in a race called "The Last Train to Boston."

It was 6 degrees that morning. The men with beards and mustaches—Eduardo had a mustache—got to look like the tugs with frozen rope bumpers I'd seen in northern harbors. You could have taken a mustache in your hand and broken it off.

I finished in 2 hours and 50 minutes and change. I thought the extra seconds would keep me out. I was wearing a watch cap, and the foam of sweat that had formed on the hat had frozen. Janet was impressed with the spectacle of a man who had tried so hard, and lost, but who still didn't lose his temper. She had no idea at the time how familiar failure was to this particular boyfriend. But a kindly race official at the Aberdeen race wrote a letter explaining the unfavorable conditions, and Boston let me in.

Boston once excluded runners thought too old. When Peter Foley turned 55, the BAA turned him down. He ran anyway, unofficially, as a bandit, but a righteous bandit. That rule has changed, of course. Male runners 80 and over are welcome, though they need to have completed a marathon in 5 hours. It's 5½ hours for women.

Wheelchairs also used to be barred, and now they are a significant element of the race. The longest string of consecutive Boston Marathon victories, seven from 1990 to 1996, belongs to wheelchair competitor Jean Driscoll of Illinois.

Most significantly, for a large part of its history, Boston kept women out of the contest. It was not by any means the only marathon to exclude female runners, but it became the most notorious for doing so. Kathrine Switzer had her picture taken with race official Jock Semple trying desperately to pluck the race number off her sweatshirt.

Women will run Boston "over my dead body," Semple was supposed to have said. But Semple came around. In 1972, the race was opened to women. Semple and Switzer are now friends.

George Hirsch, president of the New York Road Runners Club and former publisher of the *Runner* magazine, ran Boston in 1978. He remembers it as one of his worst races and one of his best as well. The very best was the one he ran with the woman to whom he is now married. But this was second best. It was also—for several miles—the worst marathon experience he's ever had.

"A marathon is like a dream," he wrote for the publisher's page of the *Runner*. "If you don't start to recount it pretty quickly afterwards you find massive stretches of the race you've totally left behind. Perhaps that is why each of us wants to tell anyone who will listen about our own 26.2-mile journey. I ran much of this year's Boston with the fastest women on the course. . . . Within the first mile I tied up with Sue Krenn, a glowing, blond pig-tailed runner from San Diego. . . ."

Later, they were joined by Joan Benoit, whom Hirsch recognized but hadn't known before. The three ran together, and were passed by Patty Lyons, who went on and out of sight to take the lead in the woman's race.

"At about ten miles Joan took off her T-shirt, and her pace quickened noticeably; she meant business," Hirsch wrote. "She was running easily as we came into Wellesley." Here, Hirsch was able to tell Joan that he and champion Miki Gorman had been together "at the same point two years ago and that Miki won the race. Joan flashed a big grin."

Later in the race, abandoned by his women friends, Hirsch would be struggling alone, having lost the ability to figure out his pace. No matter how often he did the math, he was coming in over 3 hours. The time would have been a painful disappointment. Hirsch slogged on, though, in despair. Although tired and dispirited, he was unwilling to slow his pace.

"Don't make a decision on the uphill" is one of his rules for life and running. When he passed Bill Rodgers's running gear store, which Bill had told him was exactly 4 miles out, and knowing that Bill would be precise on the course he had run so often, Hirsch tried the equation again and realized that his math had been way, way off. A personal record was still within reach. Then Sue Krenn appeared.

"All right, Sue," Hirsch remembers yelling. "She looked explosive. She pulled me through those last few miles. She carried herself proudly, living off the roar of the crowd. I was running well over my head, but stayed with her into the chute at the Big Pru. (She ran 2:38:50, four seconds ahead of me—PRs [personal records] for both of us.) We found Joan at the finish. The three of us clung to each other—the first, third and 'fourth' women in the Boston Marathon." Joan Benoit won the race and went on to win the first-ever Olympic Marathon for women at Los Angeles in 1984.

Some years, the Boston has had far too many applicants. Other years, the BAA had too few. Back in 1918 with America just getting into the First World War, it looked as if there might be no race at all. A military relay was set up. The course was covered, the streak maintained. The contest has outlasted more spectacular events. Nobody ever runs a marathon in Madison Square Garden anymore.

As time passed, Boston became less and less restrictive, although it kept time requirements, thereby moving away from prejudice and toward meritocracy.

The Boston Athletic Association has traditions. Sometimes—as in the case of that relay that kept the string alive—we are thankful for the foresight of those responsible. Other times—as in the decision to exclude women, wheelchairs, or older men—we are not so thankful.

When changes were essential, changes were made. From its origins, the race offered no prize money. When in the early 1980s, the rest of the sport turned professional, Boston was left behind. Upstarts like New York, London, and Chicago were luring the big-name athletes away with cash. Now Boston has a total purse of $525,000 with the top man and woman getting $100,000 each. The Boston Athletic Association event has reclaimed its position at the top.

The Hopkinton-to-Pru event is part of the recently launched circuit of Marathon Majors. The other gargantuan festivals included are New York, Chicago, London, and Berlin. The Olympic Marathon and the IAAF World Championships Marathon will also be scored.

Athletes get 25 points for first place, 15 for second, 10 points for third,

5 for fourth, and 1 point if they come in fifth. Each athlete's four best performances over a 2-year period will be added up, and the leading man and woman will each win $500,000. Each 2-year period will overlap, so that prizes are given out every year. The first contest includes marathons run in 2006 and 2007.

Boston swelled to almost 40,000 for its 100th anniversary outing in 1996, but the field averages 20,000. So the festival has grown, but it is not the largest. It is by far the largest race that requires speed for admission. The people at the top in the Boston Athletic Association have figured out when beloved traditions need to be preserved and when they should be smashed.

Runners prize Boston for the quality they value on the roads—this is, after all, the marathon with stamina.

CHAPTER 26

The Finish

"... WHERE WE HAD THOUGHT TO TRAVEL OUTWARD,
WE SHALL COME TO THE CENTER OF OUR EXISTENCE;
WHERE WE HAD THOUGHT TO BE ALONE,
WE SHALL BE WITH ALL THE WORLD."
—JOSEPH CAMPBELL, *THE HERO WITH A THOUSAND FACES*

I came up out of the polished bowels of Grand Central Terminal onto 45th Street and into the hush of Manhattan, which at this time on a Sunday morning was still fast, fast asleep. One ING New York City Marathon banner with its bemused orange lion had been roped to the Helmsley building. There was nothing else to indicate that this day was different from any other.

The stragglers on the sidewalk—some of whom had not yet been to bed—looked harried and out of scale as if they, and I, were visitors from a miniature civilization, different from and unrelated to the race of giants that must inhabit these enormous monuments of stone and glass. Steam poured up from the cracks around the manholes on East 45th Street, and the air was redolent of frying bacon with a distant, but distinctly recognizable whiff of urine on concrete.

Walking north up Central Park Drive with the Tavern on the Green to my left and the marathon finish up ahead, I knew that I was on hallowed ground, but I didn't have any sense of it. I tried to summon the emotions I'd had running those last yards in 1978. I could picture the clock reading 2:59 and remember how I yearned to break 3 hours, to qualify for Boston.

It seemed a sacrilege now to step across the finish, so I went around. A woman in a brown parka with multiple press tags of varying colors was up on the stairs to the photo bridge, talking into a cell phone. "This is not a good plan B," she said. "This is not a good plan B." I didn't know where I was supposed to go, so I waited for her to come down.

"I'm early," I said. "A volunteer."

"How did you get here?" she asked, and she wouldn't look me in the eye. I held out the green Media pass I had hanging from my neck. "You're not supposed to be here," she said and showed me where my pass read "You do not have access to: Finish Line, Photo Bridge."

I explained that I had volunteered to give out medals. She said I should go to the entrance of the park at 72nd Street. So I headed that way. The brown parka was clearly emblematic of high authority, like a general's stars. The marathon has a hierarchy, with the lowest level volunteers in mufti, and others in shirts or parkas of different colors, each seeming to indicate a level of command.

It's miraculous that the New York Road Runners Club has held this race—in one form or another—since 1970 without a serious mishap. I appreciate the need for structure. And yet one of the joys of running is that it shatters hierarchical expectations. Anyone with a number can win the race. It's simple, really. All you need to do is run fast.

I found my way to 72nd Street and waited in a group of other would-be volunteers. A man in jeans and a fleece was starting up a conversation with another man in jeans and a blank T-shirt.

We were near the city's heart, but I could smell earth and see grass that still had green in it, even in November. There were canvas tents in the foreground, like the pavilions in the illustrated *Merry Adventures of Robin Hood* from which my mother used sometimes to read my bedtime story.

I leaned uneasily against the stonework at the 72nd Street entrance to Central Park and listened while two women, who were clearly veterans, initiated a new girl.

"You put the medal on them, and you can hug them," the first woman said. "It's very emotional."

"Is not," the second woman said.

"They kiss you," the first woman said.

"Do not."

"You get covered with sweat," the first woman said. "And blood."

"Do not," said her friend. "Or only sometimes."

Another volunteer, quite a sweet-looking young woman, said that she'd never given out medals before, and she'd never do it again "unless my fiancé runs the marathon. I'd like to hang a medal on him."

Giving out the finishers' medals is a plum, and I'd started to inquire about it weeks in advance, failing to get a rise out of my contacts at the New York Road Runners Club. I'd finally just signed up online as myself, but not as a member of the press. You can do that.

"That's fine," I told Wayne Coffee. "If I show up, and if they don't let me give out medals, I'll write about *that*."

At his insistence, I sent one last e-mail to the coordinator of volunteers announcing myself as a writer. So when my name was called out by one of the staff seated under the tent, another woman, apparently the supervisor said, "I need to see who he is."

"I'm Ben Cheever," I said.

"Are you the one who wrote the e-mail?" she asked.

I said I was.

"Was it a nasty e-mail?" one of the other organizers asked.

"It wasn't a nasty e-mail," I said.

"We want *everybody* to have a good time," said the supervisor, and she said it as if I'd asked for special attention. Which at first annoyed me. Then I remembered that I *had* asked for special attention.

Volunteering for the race is a great gig. We each got a T-shirt that said, "Where were you on November 6 of 2005? I was a volunteer at the New York City Marathon." Also a free yellow poncho. And lunch. But mostly we were given a chance to feel grand.

After everyone had checked in, we were called together and moved south in a body to the area beyond the finish. Here, a genial supervisor told us "runners get medals, and so do helpers who run the marathon. So if you've run the distance with a blind person, you get a medal, too. If a blind person runs with a dog, we give the dog a medal."

"Make sure everybody has a number. And make sure that it says 'New York Marathon 2005' and not some turkey trot from 5 years ago."

"People will ask for two medals. Usually, when this happens, you can see that they already have a medal. You'll see it in their shorts. Don't give anyone two medals."

When I told the man standing beside me that this seemed harsh, "I mean how much can these gewgaws cost?" he didn't argue but said that last year, "This guy asked me for a medal for his uncle. He said, 'It would mean the world to him.'"

"I said 'I can't,'" he said.

Then a woman standing at his shoulder chimed in with an explanation that settled the matter for me. "What would it mean to the uncle? He didn't run the race. If the man wants to give his own medal to the uncle, that would mean something."

Looking back on that afternoon today, I can't distinguish the tasks I actually performed from those that were done by specialists or other volunteers in my group. There were always enough of us, so that it was a treat to get a chance to carry a box, or pick up one end of something bigger.

Stands made of naked wood with dowels sticking out of them about sternum-high were set out in the road in two long lines. Then we sliced open boxes of medals and hung these from the dowels by their red-white-and-orange ribbons. The medals brushed together and made the jangly sound of wind chimes.

We were lined up beside the racks and told that the winners would go down another chute, but we'd handle all the rest. Since early finishers would be spaced out, our supervisor told us, we should each take a turn and then go back to the end of the line. "But don't worry, you'll all get to give out a medal today," we were told. "You'll all get to give out plenty of medals." But I worried. I was afraid I might somehow be the only one who didn't get a chance.

A hand bike came in first, and the young woman who'd become the sort of pet of the group stepped out from the front of our line and bestowed the first medal, and we all clapped and cheered, uncertainly at first, but then with rising confidence. The athlete bowed his head and cycled off.

I know this sounds bizarre, but there are a lot of handsome men on hand bikes, and gorgeous women. I had expected pity to be mixed into my response, but what I felt instead was awe. These were beautiful, agile creatures.

I was stagestruck my first time out and couldn't quite get the ribbon over the helmet of the man on the hand bike. There was an awkward pause, then he leaned forward, and I got it done. "Good race!" I said. "Way to go!" Our eyes locked. He nodded and rolled away. I filed back to the end of the line.

We heard helicopters overhead, and I saw a tall black man being led off to the side, and people were shouting congratulations at him. Then I heard he was Paul Tergat, and he had won the race in a photo finish against defending champion Hendrick Ramaala. I was pleased. Above my desk, I have a picture of myself and Tergat at a dinner party in Nairobi. I suppose it's foolish, but I think of Kenya as the home team with Paul Tergat and Lornah Kipligat as co-captains. Yes, I know Lornah's Dutch, but then I'm not Kenyan either. Nor am I all that fast.

Now the runners started coming to us. Some were too played out to even manage a smile, but they all paused and bowed to get the medal.

I was up for a blond man who had his hair in a brush cut, and when he straightened, the ribbon pulled back through his hair and I was showered with sweat. There was laughter, but I remembered how these days dentists, doctors, even policemen put on latex gloves before they'll touch a stranger.

Everyone else was getting splashed too with precious bodily fluids. The trickle of finishers had become a stream and many were soaked with sweat and bleeding at the nipples.

As a gadgetophile, I noticed that some finishers had digital cameras, and a healthy number had music players, and/or belts with water bottles. This is not a hard-and-fast rule, but the general pattern was that the extremely fast runners had the least equipment.

By now, I'd given out hundreds of medals, but I kept right on looking everybody in the face, and when I shouted, "Congratulations!" I kept right on meaning it.

I heard one Italian speaking to another. *Sono stanco alla morte.* And I remembered that poor Pheidippides actually had gotten so tired that he died. He brought the good news from Marathon to Athens. Then he died.

They'd all been on a journey, and a long one. Dave Barry reports that the word *aerobics* comes from two Greek words: *aero*, meaning "ability to," and *bics*, meaning "withstand tremendous boredom."

"After the dreadful tests," writes Joseph Campbell, "the challenges both to body and to mind, we as heroes tap our deepest unconscious and experience a marvelous expansion of our powers, a vivid renewal of life."

When I looked at these faces, I knew how they'd humbled themselves. They'd run hundreds, if not thousands of miles. They'd run tired, they'd run in the dark and in the rain. And out on the course that day, they'd been through the moral relativism of the middle of the race.

I was witnessing a ceremony, which seemed both public and private, less formal and yet as joyous as the most fortunate wedding, as chilling as the most unlooked for funeral. "The distance runner," wrote Dr. George Sheehan, "is mysteriously reconciling the separations of body and mind, of pain and pleasure, of the conscious and the unconscious. He is repairing the rent, and healing the wound in his divided self. He has found a way to make the ordinary extraordinary; the commonplace unique; the everyday eternal."[1]

Shouting out some greeting, locking eyes, giving a medal, and then moving on was difficult, like bringing powerful magnets together and then yanking them apart. These were nothing like the exchanges I ordinarily have with strangers. More like how I feel when my wife goes through the gate alone to board an airplane. Or when I was graduating from boarding school and drinking champagne out of beer steins with the four guys who'd been my best friends for a year, one of whom I'd never see again in this world.

"The human face is really an awesome primary miracle," wrote Ernest Becker. "It naturally paralyzes you by its splendor if we give in to it as the fantastic thing it is. But mostly we repress this miraculousness so that we can function with equanimity and can use faces and bodies for our own routine purposes."

The river of runners became an ocean. We were grabbing armloads of medals and wading out into the crowd. "Way to go!" "Good run. It was a hot day, too!" "Nice run!" "You did it!"

I looked into more faces that afternoon than I ordinarily do in a year. All those sets of eyes. All liquid.

If this many people will run a marathon, I thought, *then nobody can ever accuse the species of laziness. Really,* I thought. *If we want to do it, there is nothing we can't do.*

By now, the volunteers were a team of friends, backing each other up. Making sure each runner got a medal. Finishers stumbled by, some too dazed to notice that they hadn't gotten the medal. The man behind me had talent.

"Donald," he'd call out, somehow having recognized the name from the smudged magic marker on a T-shirt. "Donald, do you need a medal?" Or "Peter, you need a medal?" Then he'd pass the sacred token into the tide of humanity.

"You're good," I said. "Excellent technique."

"Yeah," he said, and smiled, "It can't be taught."

This had gone on for at least 2 hours before I began to notice that I was growing hoarse, and that my feet were hurting.

Now, like Thomas, I began to doubt. I lost faith. Not as we ordinarily use the phrase. I wasn't losing faith in the spiritual world, the world you can't see. I was having trouble believing in the actual material world. I was losing faith in reality.

A marathon is a regular event in my life, but then a marathon is never a regular event. *Was it possible that this many individuals had run that far? Maybe they stayed up all night and smeared ketchup on their nipples and then ran through a sprinkler.* That's what I thought.

But then they would have looked like Rosie Ruiz after she didn't actually run the Boston Marathon she'd claimed to have won. Fred Lebow said that if you want to know how you will age in the next 20 years, then run a marathon and look in the mirror. This is both true and untrue. The runner's face at the end of the marathon is often unguarded, open, the face of an innocent, a child. We're both beaten and triumphant, "But trailing clouds of glory do we come/ From God, who is our home ..."?

When Janet and I went to marathons together, I sometimes used to finish first and then go back for her. Races—even the big ones—were a good deal less formal at the time. We'd run the last 5 miles side by side. And I'd look down into her heart-shaped face. I had a chance to be with her—the only chance ever—to be with her when I knew exactly what was going on and she was the one befuddled.

Then she'd tell people afterward what I'd done. "He ran more than 30 miles." And we'd hug. We were so cute that many of our friends were nauseated.

In 2006, I underwent the ordeal myself. I ran the marathon at which I'd given out medals at the year before. I ran it with Rick Rennert, whom I often train with in the Rockefeller State Park Preserve. We decided to stay together. Our other regular running buddy, Dave Drucker, also ran the race, but he had the bad taste to run it quickly, which meant depriving himself of our sparkling conversation. And, yes, I would certainly lie to you about my own time, but then—unfortunately—you could look it up.

Rick and I stayed together. I finished in 4:08:04. But then I need to tell you that I had run a 3:33:17 only a few weeks earlier. Now, you see what a weak character I am. Matt Simms, a soldier who ran the "Boston in Baghdad" marathon, neglected to mention his victory when he spoke with me, and I was a reporter. Elite runners rarely boast or make excuses, but then I'm not an elite runner.

Crossing the Queensboro Bridge, I remembered that, until I was 3½, my family lived in an apartment in Manhattan near the end of that bridge. When I was quite young, 6, or 8, I used to dive for those memories, but I couldn't distinguish the pleasures I'd experienced and those I'd only imagined.

The inside of the bridge is a study in dull gray slabs of metal. It looked and sounded like a big and antiquated factory. Every surface was covered with grime, and the grime was hairy with dust. I was cold. We were going uphill. We had more than 10 miles left to run.

A man was up on the guardrail shouting into his cell. "Where are you! Where are you?"

Rick Rennert told me that a week after his first New York City Marathon, he had a nightmare. "It was dark and loud. There were beams and girders. I woke up in a cold sweat. I called the friend I ran the marathon with and he said, 'The Queensboro Bridge.' And he was right. It was. It's also why we came here, Rick said, alluding to the throng of onlookers that collects at the foot of the bridge.

You come down into Manhattan, and the crowd—as Spenser told me almost 30 years ago—the crowd will suck you right up First Avenue. When I crossed that bridge in 1978, I thought I was on schedule for a sub-3-hour race. And I was delighted. I remember the yellow Frank Shorter shorts I'd bought for the occasion. I remember the Brooks Vantages with the varus wedge. I remember thinking "this is how it feels to do something important. This is how it feels to be happy."

Not exactly how I felt in 2006. Although I thought, quite mistakenly, that I could speed up later, run negative splits, come in under 4 hours.

A marathon is a time capsule. Every year, the shoes change a little, the watches get bigger, the T-shirts have different messages. I ran my first races in a shirt provided by the *Reader's Digest*. Now I wear my shirt from *Runner's World*. I've seen the logos and slogans of huge corporations and of bars and corner delis. I've seen shirts worn in support of political candidates. In 2006, I saw a shirt that read "Impeach Cheney."

The disabled— once excluded—are now center stage in the drama. In 2006, I ran for a while beside a blind runner and his guide. Then he proved faster than I was.

Some runners wore red shirts announcing themselves as members of Fred's Team, a cancer-fighting charity named after Fred Lebow, who founded the race. The group, which is associated with Memorial Sloan-Kettering, had raised $28 million by June 2006. Memorial's slogan: "Imagine a world without cancer."

I ran the marathon in 1992 keeping company with Gerry Krovatin, whose unbroken streak is now approaching 15 years. He was injured, so we took it easy. At one point, we heard this great explosion of cheering. Fred was running nearby and had been spotted. He had come back from cancer to run the race with Grete Waitz as a 60th birthday present to himself.

On 90th Street and East Drive, there's a life-size statue of Lebow, which is moved each year to a spot near the Tavern on the Green, so that his likeness can see the finish.

Fred's Team had a decent turnout, and there were many T-shirts announcing many other brigades in the war on cancer. Just the presence of the shirts marks a victory.

When I wrote obituaries for the *Rockland Journal News* back in the early 1970s, families asked that Sloan-Kettering not be mentioned: They were ashamed of their association with the disease. We couldn't even say the "C" word. Now we're calling the monster out.

Since runners on race day are often hypochondriacs, you won't be surprised to learn that on the night before the 2006 New York Marathon, I thought I had the flu.

Which you should distrust, as I would distrust you with the same news. I've been soundly beaten by men who told me—minutes before the starting gun—that they had a bad cold, or a torn ligament. A friend once called out "Knee's gone," as he flew by in a race.

But still, I thought I had the flu. Ask me why I ran at all.

I've always felt that you can run through a light cold, keep it from getting worse. My theory, and I'm sticking with it, is that a hard run boils the blood, murders the virus.

So I went out for my scheduled 13 miles once, with a whisper of a sore throat. Showered, changed, and drove into Manhattan for a date. By the time I reached the girl's apartment, I was reeling. Fell into bed, her bed. I stayed there for 3 days, without ever achieving consciousness. She kept me watered, listened to my ranting, and dodged parking tickets by moving my car. It was a shift. She hadn't known how to drive a shift.

We've been married now for 25 years. Something else precious I owe to running. You die to one life and wake up in another.

I'd guess that a significant slice of those 37,000 people out running New York every year are making some sort of transition. Deciding to get married, go to law school, buy a Labrador retriever puppy. What's central, though, is not the improvement of self, but the escape, the jailbreak from the prison of ego. You don't run to generate self-esteem, but to render it beside the point. This any religious man will tell you. Practical considerations, however worthy, limit and can mar the experience.

"Once you have made the world an end and faith a means," writes the devil to his junior devil in the C. S. Lewis masterpiece *Screwtape*, "you have almost won your man. And it makes very little difference what kind of worldly end he is pursuing."

At its best, the sport shatters that shell of self. Just starting to cross the Verrazano-Narrows Bridge, I once overheard one woman telling a friend, "I am doing this to honor my body." I thought she had it exactly wrong. The poet William Butler Yeats said that all happiness "depends on the energy to assume the mask of some other self; that all joyous or creative life is a rebirth as something not oneself, something which has no memory and is created in a moment and perpetually renewed."

I was slow all right. I did finish. And reeling away from the line, I was stopped by a woman, a volunteer. She looked me in the eye and draped a medal around my neck. "Congratulations!" she said and meant it.

One runner had "4 u dad" written on his back in marker, and he asked a volunteer to take a picture of it, "for my dad." Then a second runner, a girl, used her own camera to take a picture of this same guy's back. "For my dad," she explained.

I sympathized, but I couldn't quite keep myself from wondering what her father would think when presented with a picture of the naked back of a perfect stranger.

"Love" has become a battered old painter's tarpaulin of a word. We've thrown it over so many different emotions, that it's lost much of its usefulness. And all of its precision. The word is used to call on the great and often forgotten brotherhood of man. It's also used for carnal and illicit unions. We "love" our children, our motorbikes, and chocolate chocolate chip ice cream. We also use the word to indicate a passion to protect or to be protected.

My own most intimate attachments have at their base a confusion of identities. I'll find myself thinking idly that Janet might miss a meal, and I'll open a yogurt and eat it, even though she's miles away in Manhattan. "Put on a coat, or you'll be cold," I tell my son Andrew, when he heads off to school in February in a white undershirt. And when I say, "*you'll* be cold," *I* feel the chill.

What happens in the best families was happening now to a crowd of strangers in Central Park. Your marathon, my marathon. Your dad, my dad.

Milling toward the baggage buses, Rick thanked me. I thanked him. "Good race." We hugged. Runners were trading times, sharing disappointments, shyly announcing victories, and calling out excuses in a half a dozen languages. Rick and I marched along in silence, and I noticed that the mass of humanity has a post-race murmur very like recordings I've heard of whale songs. It's as if we're a single organism, not a sophisticated one either, maybe a giant sponge. We seemed more tide than crowd. Unrestrained, my brain kicked out phrases lodged deep in the gray wrinkles. "Time held me green and dying, though I sang in my chains like the sea." "James, James, Morrison Morrison, Weatherby George Dupree took great care of his mother, though he was only three. James, James, said to his mother, mother he said, said he . . ." "It is a far, far better thing I do than I have ever done; it is a far, far better rest I go to, than I have ever known."[3]

"Wherever wheels are turning, no matter what the load, the name that's known is Firestone, where the rubber meets the road."

These were my people. I adored them all. I caught the sharp smell of excrement in the air. We were packed so tightly that if I'd died, my corpse would have been carried for yards, like a cork in the ocean. I crushed a paper cup under my shoe. We gimped along in our silvery capes. "Good race," we told each other. The air was thick and had substance to it, as if the runners had been set in aspic. I was hurting. I was ecstatic. I was serene. I was wide, wide awake, but also deep in the folds of an ancient dream.

Coming up Central Park South, I had passed a man in boots—I think they were unlaced—and fireman's hat. He was cheering the runners through a bullhorn. "But can you do it in real life?" he shouted. "Can you live that dream? Can you achieve that goal?"

'Yes," I mumbled. "I can. I have." And for an instant, I was thankful, happy to accept encouragement from this stranger, this man who—for all I knew—hadn't run a step.

Wait a minute, I thought. *What's he talking about? This IS my real life!*

AFTER THE FINISH:
26.2 GREAT BOOKS
ON RUNNING

My wife looked across the marital bed to ask what I was reading.

"One of the five best books on running," I said.

"Seems you've already read 10 of the 5 best books on running," she said. And she had a point. Runners often write. They often write well.

For *Runner's World*, I made a list of five. But there aren't five running books you should know about. More like 50. Here, then, are 26.2 books I enjoyed. Doubtless there are many others I didn't get to, or never heard of. And others, such as Kathrine Switzer's *Marathon Woman*, which I haven't read yet. *Indian Running*, by Peter Nabokov (Santa Fe, NM: Ancient City Press, 1981), was an essential source, and belongs here. I just ran out of slots.

But what a crew! I can't think of another sport—unless you count alcoholism as a sport—with anything like this yield in prose.

This is complete happenstance, but while I was working on this essay, *Newsweek*'s cover story (March 26, 2007) was titled "Exercise and the Brain: We know that working out is good for the body. But now research says it also makes us smarter...." The article reported that vigorous exercise, long known to bring more oxygen to the brain, can also encourage the growth of new cells there. Add to this the propensity for solitude displayed in the classic runner's personality, and what do you get? Writers.

Jim Fixx's *The Complete Book of Running* (New York: Random House, 1977) is an evergreen. The science is creaky in spots, but the book still works as inspiration and as the autobiography of a man who died for our sins.

The pre-running boom story *The Loneliness of the Long-Distance Runner*, by Alan Sillitoe (New York: New American Library, 1959), contains stunning passages on how it feels to run and race, but the plot revolves around the English class system and the clash between authority and talent. I left it off the list, though, because for decades, it was the only book about running that anyone could name. No more. Even excluding the how-tos—by far the largest single category—there are now whole shelves of excellent texts.

1. John L. Parker Jr.'s novel ***Once a Runner*** (Tallahassee, FL: Cedarwinds Publishing, 1978) is a young man's fable. There are pranks and oafish college administrators. I first read it when I was in my fifties, and yet I was not alienated or saddened by the passage of time. Instead, I thought again about how it might be to train hard. Written by an elite athlete, the novel is crammed with information—"It's as if I poured my brain out," Parker explains. And yet it functions less as a manual than as inspiration: "Running to him was real, the way he did it the realest thing he knew. It was all joy and woe, hard as a diamond; it made him weary beyond comprehension. But it also made him free."

2. Roger Bannister's recently republished memoir, ***The Four-Minute Mile*** (Guilford, CT: Lyons Press, 2004), is the intimate self-portrait of a champion who trained less than I do, probably less than you do. He went hiking, took stretches of time off, and when he ran, he ran for half an hour or 40 minutes a day. This edition includes photocopies of Bannister's workout log. "Training across the year," the editor notes, "amounted to between 13 and 53 miles per week in sessions of up to 40 minutes' duration." The medical student's diary Bannister kept shows 5 days off before the slot for May 6, 1954. Here he wrote "3.59.4," in a scrawl so crooked, you just knew he was going to be a doctor. You need to love him for the jagged marks on the page, and for having labeled "May" as "April," in this historic document.

3. ***26.2 Marathon Stories***, by Kathrine Switzer and Roger Robinson

(Emmaus, PA: Rodale, 2006), is a gift in every sense of the word. First, it's just that, the ideal gift. While the text is superb, a giftee too harried to read "the whole thing" needn't feel cheated or guilty. The pictures are worth the price of admission. And if your eyes should stray, the text is excellent. Yes, one of the writers is Kathrine Switzer, who in 1967 was the first woman to run the Boston Marathon with numbers. She's been married for 18 years to coauthor Roger Robinson. A nationally ranked runner, Robinson is also a professor of literature and has written several books on the sport and masses of magazine articles.

4. *The Runner's Guide to the Meaning of Life: What 35 Years of Running Has Taught Me about Winning, Losing, Happiness, Humility, and the Human Heart* (Emmaus, PA: Rodale, 2000) is written by Amby Burfoot. Don't be alarmed by the long subtitle; the book is short, and small enough to tuck into a Christmas stocking. Best, or first, known for winning the 1968 Boston Marathon, Burfoot has been a member of the runnerati since almost before there was a runnerati, serving as executive editor of *Runner's World* since 1985. When asked about his life, he says how lucky he was to come to running, when so many great people were involved—John Kelley the Younger, Bill Rodgers, Frank Shorter, Joan Benoit. In this book, a lifetime of participation and study is mined for gems. "On Bouncing Back: Losing isn't contagious. It's not a fatal condition, and it's not forever. It's more like a cold that makes you miserable for a week but then goes away, and you're fine."

5. *Duel in the Sun: Alberto Salazar, Dick Beardsley, and America's Greatest Marathon* is written by John Brant (Emmaus, PA: Rodale, 2006). Brant teases a wealth of information out of a single race without ever stopping the action. Americans took first and second place in the 1982 Boston Marathon: Imagine that. It's been 22 years now since an American has won. This book is not a lament, but an exaltation studded with facts and observations. Did you know that the press bus actually struck Beardsley, while passing the competitors on a route impossibly narrowed by spectators? That's right, he was clipped by the rearview mirror, and Beardsley, ordinarily a sweetheart, "snarled and punched the bus in frustration." Did you know, for instance, that Salazar had a second career as an ultrarunner that was enabled by Prozac? He came back after years of burnout and won the 54-mile Comrades Marathon in 1994.

6. *Running Through the Ages,* by Edward S. Sears (Jefferson, NC: McFarland and Co., 2001). Sears begins his dedication "To everyone I have ever run with. . . ." Massively researched, profusely illustrated, a single volume takes us from the fossils of early runners through the races of the 1980s. Sears has an eye for delectable detail, giving, just for instance, the nicknames of the leading pedestrians of the 19th century. These include George "the Suffolk stag" Frost, William "the American Deer" Jackson, and a Seneca named Louis Bennett who ran as "Deerfoot." Sears ends his epilogue with a quote from miler Herb Elliott. "I think we're only on the border of understanding the interface between mind, spirit and body."

7. *Bowerman and the Men of Oregon,* by Kenny Moore (Emmaus, PA: Rodale, 2006). This is the life of Oregon's legendary coach and cofounder of Nike. He made the first waffle-trainers on his wife's waffle iron. Bill Bowerman coached Steve Prefontaine, himself the subject of many books and at least three full-length movies. The great coach seems to have been the sort of alpha male who always thought he was right. Often he was right, when everybody else was wrong. At Munich before the tragedy in 1972, Bowerman had the foresight to complain about the security. He was, of course, ignored. The athletes he brought along are too numerous to list. One of these—Kenny Moore—turned into a world-class writer. Advice to Moore from Bowerman: "'If you go out to race,' he said, 'and know you'll lose, there's no probability involved. You'll lose. But if you go out knowing you will never give up, you'll still lose most of the time, but you'll be in the best position to kick from on that rare day when everything breaks right.'"

8. *The Lore of Running,* by Tim Noakes, MD (New York: Oxford University Press, 1984; 4th ed., 2001). If you're heading to a desert island—large enough for a 2-mile loop, of course—and restricted to a single book, this would be the one. There's medicine. Dr. Noakes has been on the cutting edge of the science of exercise for decades now. There are tips on injuries that are still current today. There's a history of the sport. Plus, you'll find enough motivational prose to spark a running boom, if we didn't already have one. His eighth rule in the section titled "Staying Injury Free" is "Never Accept As Final the Advice of a Nonrunner (MD or Other)." During his medical training in the 1970s, Dr. Noakes informs us, "I was reliably informed by my teachers that exercise was dangerous for human health. . . . It now seems that regular physical activity might be the cheapest and most effective preventive medicine yet discovered."

9. *Running in Literature: A Guide for Scholars, Readers, Runners, Joggers, and Dreamers* (Halcottsville, NY: Breakaway Books, 2003). An elite runner and English professor, Roger Robinson has pulled long, choice quotes from the classics past and present. It's a book you'll race through, but also recall with relish. When I visited the Agora in Athens, I was shown the great naked rock on which visiting dignitaries used to speak. Because of Robinson, I was able to imagine how it might have looked when Saint Paul appeared. One of the great poets of the New Testament, Paul might also have been a runner. In any case, Robinson declares him the best running writer in the Bible.

10. *First Marathons: Personal Encounters with the 26.2-Mile Monster,* by Gail Waesche Kislevitz (Halcottsville, NY: Breakaway Books, 1999). The subjects—each reporting his or her own combination of agony and joy — include Bill Rodgers, Grete Waitz, Ted Corbitt, and John Kelley the Younger. I interviewed Allan Steinfeld for the *New York Times* on the 10th anniversary of his ascension to the position as the director of the New York Road Runners Club. He wanted to talk about Fred Lebow. Finally, I got him to talk about himself. He'd gone out too fast for his first marathon, the 1966 Boston Marathon. He covered the last miles in the backseat of a good Samaritan's car. I was delighted with my find, until I looked Steinfeld up in *First Marathons,* and there was the whole story told in a slightly better version than the one I had so laboriously recorded and transcribed.

11. *Running and Being,* by George Sheehan, MD (New York: Simon and Schuster, 1978). When I started running in the late 1970s, Jim Fixx was thought the Parish Priest of running, while Sheehan was the Bishop. It was splendid back then to have a doctor in our corner, a doctor just as nutty about running as we all were. Sheehan groaned so noisily during races that other runners would write him to complain and ask him to compete elsewhere. He seemed—on the page at least—to be quite naked. And devoted to the sport. He once said, half joking, that life was composed of "those annoying spaces of time in between races." "In seven years of writing a medical-advice column for runners," he wrote, "I have yet to hear from an injured runner who regretted his jogging." "Those well-meaning articles about the dangers of jogging serve little purpose except to expose the inadequacy of orthodox medicine when faced with a human being trying to be all he or she can be. Nevertheless, the proper care for these 'diseases of excellence' is available."

12. *Going the Distance: One Man's Journey to the End of His Life,* by George Sheehan, MD (New York: Villard, 1996). Diagnosed with terminal cancer, Sheehan seems actually to have been excited. Now he had a new subject to write about. "In the aging game," he wrote, "I must be all I ever was and am yet to be. What has gone before is no more than a learning period. A breaking in. Life, someone has said, is boot camp. If it is, age is the combat for which I was trained. Now I must make good on the promise of every dawn I am privileged to see." He wrote almost right up to the grave. Too weak to type, he dictated. "The cancer, like the bull, advances, retreats, charges with élan. It draws blood, staggers me...."

13. *Chasing the Hawk,* by Andrew Sheehan (New York: Random House, 2001). In this loving but sometimes scorching memoir, one of Sheehan's sons tells the story of the family, and how his father's fame was not always peachy for the rest of them. The title is taken from a Henry David Thoreau description of a hawk seen in Concord. "It appeared to have no companion in the universe and to need none but the morning. It was not lonely but made all the world lonely beneath it." Andrew reports as Sheehan himself had written, that the death sentence was taken as a challenge. "When someone asked my sister Sarah how my father was doing with his cancer, she replied, 'Oh, he loves it.'" "After my father died, it surprised me how empty I felt," Andrew writes. "I run the trails in Schenley Park, and on hot days I sometimes make a hard push up a final hill that climbs on for half a mile. I hear myself groan, and it is his groan—an elephant's groan—emanating from my chest and filling the air."

14. *Train Hard, Win Easy: The Kenyan Way,* by Toby Tanser (Mountain View, CA: Tafnews Press/Book Division of Track and Field News, 1997; 2nd ed., 2001). "If you insist on having a Kenyan 'training secret,' try this one...." Tanser writes. "A large percentage of the Kalenjin runners are circumcised by traditional methods, i.e., without anesthetic and with no crying. The 13-to-15-year-old sits in silence while the elders perform the ceremony." "Whenever I think I am in pain during running, I remember the pain of my circumcision," says a Kipsigis runner. "The pain when running does not compare."(The Kipsigis are a subtribe of the Kalenjin).

The second edition of the book has two forewords by John Manners, which alone are worth the price. The close-up of Kenyan culture has vivid moments, but the book's a hybrid, part how-to and part how-they. On the other hand, there's an extraordinary epilogue in which Tanser tells of being beaten almost to death on the beach in Zanzibar, Tanzania. The medical treatment was almost as bad as the attack. "Finally a doctor arrived and after dowsing me with a bucket of water, he lay me on the concrete floor. Apologizing for having no anesthetics, he sewed my head and wrist up...." Tanser came back, and 11 months after brain surgery to remove a blood clot, he placed 31st in the New York Marathon. That was in 2000, and he ran a 2:26.57. I know, I know, I wouldn't believe it either if I hadn't met and read of a lot of runners. Tanser closes his book with the line: "Four separate doctors told me I should have been dead in January, and I probably would have been if I were not a runner."

15. *The Courage to Start: A Guide to Running for Your Life,* by John "The Penguin" Bingham (New York: Fireside, 1999). I'm a sucker for self-help books, and so I hate them. Each is a miniature orthodoxy. You must first abandon your own reason, because you—it goes without saying—have been doing everything wrong. I follow the rules, then I stop believing, and whatever gains I've made are gone, along with my self-respect. From his nickname and a few columns more glanced at than read, I had the impression Bingham was saying he *wanted* to run slowly. And he was going to tell *me* how to run. But he doesn't tell me how to run. The book is honest, helpful and—here's the kicker—often funny. "Even in running shorts and shoes, I still am trying to portray an image of someone who I rarely am—someone who knows for sure what he's doing."

16. *Running Cultures: Racing in Time and Space,* by John Bale (London and New York: Routledge, 2004). Bale writes that his book is an examination of running "crafted in the humanistic-geographical writing of the Chinese-American geographer, Yi-Fu Tuan."

So you might think that in order to read the book, you first had to make a run at the works of Yi-Fu Tuan, but I just kept going. But Bale—once a runner himself—seems to have read, or at least dipped into—a thousand books. And from each, he's extracted a pearl or three. This from the aforementioned Yi-Fu Tuan, who wrote about the women's 100-meter final at the 1948 London Olympics: "The athletes *looked* beautiful to me from a distance, but if I could see their faces, I would no doubt see them twisted and ugly. But then the same could be said of ballet—how elegant the dancers look from a distance, how ugly from up close. And how close this elegance is to violence! At the end of a performance, the ballet slippers are stained by blood."

Plus every page is iridescent with opinion. Just for example—Chapter 4 is titled "Athletes as Pets." He's not a true believer, and finds many flaws in the sport and its participants. Still, the passion is transforming. He's an agnostic, but writing endlessly about the life of Jesus.

17. *26 Miles to Boston: The Boston Marathon Experience from Hopkinton to Copley Square,* by Michael Connelly (Guilford, CT: Lyons Press, 2003). "The Boston Marathon is life itself. For a hundred years the Mecca of all running events, it is a metaphor for the world around it." Connelly watched the race for 30 years. At 32, "the lessons that bored me in philosophy class years ago started to have relevance. Now Socrates' famous warning that 'the unexamined life is not worth living' took on meaning." Connelly had to undergo heart surgery before the race. This book is both a history and a memoir. "I ran from Hopkinton to Boston both to run a race and to prove myself worthy of my gift of life."

18. *The Quotable Runner: Great Moments of Wisdom, Inspiration, Wrongheadness, and Humor,* edited by Mark Will-Weber (Halcottsville, NY: Breakaway Books, 2001). "I had only one problem with my running, and that was in prison. I was in nine different prisons, and in one of the prisons we could only run in the yard," said G. Gordon Liddy. Now an actor and radio talk show host, Liddy was behind the Watergate break-in, which—with the subsequent bungled cover-up—led to the resignation of President Richard Nixon. The willingness to include Liddy and other unlikely joggers lends the collection unusual depth and range. The book has training tips as well, and motivational quotes. This from Oregon coach and Nike cofounder, Bill Bowerman: "If someone says, 'Hey, I ran 100 miles this week. How far did you run?' Ignore him.... The magic is in the man, not the 100 miles."

19. *The Fast Men,* by Tom McNab (London/New York: Simon and Schuster, 1986). Roger Robinson has picked this as his favorite running novel. I haven't read *The Fast Men*, but I have listened to it on cassette. Set in England and in the Wild West, the main characters are actors. There's a lot of running, scamming, and gambling. There are also Indians and guns. Also beautiful and sexually voracious women. This is a full-fledged wish-fulfillment novel. Even when stark naked, one man keeps his knife concealed ... well, you need to read the novel to find out where. What makes the novel unusual is that while it's fiction, it's also full of history. Genuine history. A lot of research was done by this storyteller.

20. *Best Efforts: World-Class Runners and Races,* by Kenny Moore (New York: Doubleday, 1982). All but one of these pieces ran before 1982, and you might expect them to read like yesterday's newspaper, but then you'd have forgotten Kenny Moore's talents. Take this from his account of the 1972 Olympics: "I finished fourth. Frank [Shorter] was waiting beyond the line to catch me; he was the first American to have won the Olympic marathon in sixty-four years. We walked on the grass outside the track, leaning on each other. Photographers screamed incomprehensibly from their moat. Bobbie was there, holding me, and I came apart, pain and frustration forcing out tears. 'I tried so hard,' I said. She just held me. In a few seconds I knew it was all right. She was more important than any medal and it was over and it didn't matter if I cried. I was amazed at having the moisture."

21. *The Other Kingdom,* by Victor Price (Halcottsville, NY: Breakaway Books, 1996). It's a coming-of-age novel, and the man coming of age is a runner. The larger themes, the ordeal, the defeat, even the love story, are all familiar to those of us who still read coming-of-age novels, but Victor Price writes with force and beauty. The main character's father—now dead—was a famous academic. His father's old friend confronts our runner and hero. Colin, the protagonist, has stopped running after losing a big race and finding a girl.

"At your age any temporary defeat means humiliation. I know that. But when you are as old as I am you will no longer be sure which events in your life were defeats and which were victories. The taste of humiliation will become familiar; it will cause you no more than the faintest malaise. You will not worry about defeat. You *will* worry about turning away from what you know you must do. Because that is cowardice."

22. *God on the Starting Line: The Triumph of a Catholic School Running Team and Its Jewish Coach,* by Marc Bloom (Halcottsville, NY: Breakaway Books, 2004). Former editor-in-chief of *The Runner*, Bloom, a lifelong runner, has been writing about the sport everywhere, and for as long as I can remember. This book makes the case that running is a splendid way to set religious differences aside. "Yet, at Saturday meets, I do feel a tug of ambiguity.... It's the Sabbath and I wonder if I should be in prayer with Jews at service. I wonder if I should be wrestling with Jewish issues, and saying Kaddish, as the rabbi intones 'for the six million.' My wife and I go to temple on Friday nights, but on Saturday, God's day of rest and reflection, I am hard at work coaching Catholic kids on running.... Sports psychologists talk about running through pain to a higher consciousness, and I believe in that. Conquering pain in a race combines courage with faith, and we have to count on prayer to work some magic. As St. Ignatius Loyola wrote, 'Pray as if everything depended on God, and work as if everything depended on man.'"

23. *Olympic Marathon: A Centennial History of the Games' Most Storied Race,* by Charlie Lovett (Westport, CT/London: Praeger, 1997).

Almost every year provides a thrilling little narrative much, much quicker to read than 26.2 miles is to run. Often these stories are both dramatic and humorous. The marathon at the 1904 St. Louis Olympics had been started late. It was hot. Thomas Hicks had a lead of a mile and a half. He "asked to lie down. Instead his handlers gave him a dose of strychnine mixed with raw egg white. Three miles later, he was given another dose of strychnine, more eggs, and some French brandy. His handlers also used water warmed on the engine of one of the automobiles to bathe him."

24. *The Sweet Spot in Time: The Search for Athletic Perfection,* by John Jerome (New York: Summit Books, 1980; republished in 1998 by Breakaway Books). Jerome's prose was a staple for amateur athletes. He wrote the text for a training diary for runners, and also about skiing, swimming, and even stretching. "Paradoxes abound," he wrote at the end of this book. "When a cell divides, it multiplies. Taking time to finish a move makes more time for the next move. Most shocking of all, the expenditure of energy creates more energy. At the same time that the laws of physics seem determined to grind us down, the paradoxes of the cell—the laws of life—point toward new possibility. They point upward."

25. *The Olympian,* by Brian Glanville (Tallahassee, FL: Cedarwinds Publishing, 1998). Written by a veteran sportswriter, this novel is built around the relationship between a miler and the irascible coach who takes him on. First published in 1969, it's a period piece, but fun, and also a thriller. Here's a speech—one of many—that coach Sam Dee makes to his boy: "A plant needs water, and a body needs exercise. If you deprive a plant of water, it dies. If you do not exercise a body, it corrupts, and the mind corrupts with it. Look at the politicians and the scholars and the business-men. Look at the people who rule our world and tell us what to do. What a travesty of logic! These people who have no bodies only heads."

26. *Anything for a T-Shirt: Fred Lebow and the New York City Mara-thon, the World's Greatest Footrace,* by Ron Rubin (Syracuse, NY: Syracuse University Press, 2004). This is a valentine to the man born Ephrian Fishl Lebowitz in Transylvania in 1932. We read of the highlights of the in-your-face showman who went to the White House in sneakers. Stricken with cancer, Lebow came back and ran the marathon one last time on his 60th birthday. The disease would ultimately kill him, but Rubin tells us how tough the great impresario was, and apparently willing to be kidded even in dire circumstances. After treatment had reduced Lebow from 144 to 124 pounds, "He ran in the park with a hood over his head so he wouldn't be recognized. He had no hair, no beard, and no reason to call attention to his illness." But his friends would spot him and tease him. Which he is reported to have enjoyed. He wasn't just loud and original and committed. He was courageous as well.

For that last, terrible two-tenths of a mile that always seem to be unfair, I need to return to *The Complete Book of Running*, by James F. Fixx (New York: Random House, 1977). Jim Fixx has been treated unfairly. Fixx didn't have his name blackened because his book was inaccurate. He had his name blackened for dying. This doesn't seem fair to me, not until the word "mortal" falls out of language. Not yet an antique, the volume is certainly a "collectible." Fixx suggests that you run with a dime in your pocket in case you need to make a phone call. But this book's great heart is still beating. The writer seems to have known what was going to kill him, and it's fascinating today to read him on hereditary heart disease, like Captain Hook cocking his head to hear the clock in the belly of the crocodile that had eaten his arm and wanted the rest.

Fixx died at 52. His father had died of a heart attack at 42. Before taking up jogging, the writer himself had been overweight and a heavy smoker. Running almost certainly extended his life. But this is all forgotten.

His was the heart attack heard round the world. I'll be sod, you'll be commuting to the office with a jet pack, and folks who are out of shape will still be passing the news of Jim Fixx's death—like a glittering gold Krugerrand—from sweating palm to sweating palm.

NOTES

CHAPTER 1

1. From the 1879 poem "Pheidippides," by Robert Browning. The battle to repel a Persian invasion in 490 BC was real and significant. The 20-plus-mile run from the Plains of Marathon to Athens to deliver the news of victory seems not to have taken place. Or not the way Browning imagined it. In any case, the poem inspired the race. The first marathon ever was run at the rebirth of the Olympics in 1896. It started at the Plains of Marathon and ended in Athens. It was 24.8 miles long and the last event of the games.

CHAPTER 2

1. Alan Sillitoe, *The Loneliness of the Long-Distance Runner* (New York: New American Library, 1959), 11. This book was republished by Plume in New York in 1992.
2. Tom Lashnits, "A Run All the Way to Self Pride," *New York Times*, October 4, 1981.

CHAPTER 3

1. John Jerome, *The Elements of Effort* (Halcottsville, NY: Breakaway Books, 1998).
2. John L. Parker Jr., *Once a Runner* (Tallahassee, FL: Cedarwinds Publishing, 1978).

CHAPTER 4

1. John Bingham, "Running Dialogue: When You Want to Get to Know Someone Fast, Try Going for a Slow Run Together," *Runner's World*, February 2007, 59.

2. Crossword puzzle genius Will Shortz, of the *New York Times* stages the American Crossword Puzzle Tournament at the Stamford Marriott, which was featured in the movie. He spoke at the June 2006 screening at the Burns Film Center in Pleasantville, New York, which I attended. When I asked him afterward if he liked people who did crosswords, he said, "I can't figure out if doing crossword puzzles makes people nice, or if nice people are drawn to crosswords." I told him I was working on a book about running. "The complete book of running?" he asked and smiled. "No," I said. "It won't be complete."

CHAPTER 5

1. Bernd Heinrich, *Racing the Antelope: What Animals Can Teach Us about Running and Life* (New York: Cliff Street Books/HarperCollins, 2001). This book was republished by Ecco, also a HarperCollins imprint, as *Why We Run* in 2002.

CHAPTER 6

1. Rulers such as Shulgi of Ur began to claim divinity early on, and some still cling, though unconvincingly, to shreds of this antique glory. Which reminds me of one of Napoleon's great fits of pique. He'd convinced the Pope to crown him emperor, but when the pontiff was not quick enough, the little corporal snatched the headgear and put it on with his own hands. And yet he was disappointed in himself. "I have come into the world too late," he wrote. "There is nothing great left for me to do. I do not deny that I have a defined career, but what a difference between me and the heroes of antiquity. Look at Alexander for instance. After he has conquered Asia, he declares himself to be the son of Jupiter, and the whole East believes him, save only his mother and Aristotle and a handful of Athenian pedants. But if I today were to declare myself the son of the Father Eternal, every fishwife would laugh in my face. There is nothing great left for me to do."

2. Running is like breathing. Men and women have always done it, just as they have always gulped the air. And like breathing, running is not always noticed. Hammurabi—also of ancient Mesopotamia—gave his name to one of the first sets of public rules ever. There were 282 rules (see Hammurabi's Code of

Laws—translated by L. W. King). Running isn't mentioned at all unless you count runaway slaves (Rules 16, 17, and 20) and runaway husbands (Rule 136).

Swimming, on the other hand seems to have been an exotic and useful skill. Rule 2 goes like this: "If any one bring an accusation against a man, and the accused go to the river and leap into the river, if he sink in the river his accuser shall take possession of his house. But if the river prove that the accused is not guilty, and he escape unhurt, then he who had brought the accusation shall be put to death, while he who leaped into the river shall take possession of the house that had belonged to his accuser."

3. Jack W. Berryman and Roberta J. Park, eds., *Sport and Exercise Science: Essays in the History of Sports Medicine* (Chicago: University of Illinois Press, 1992), 13.

4. Lines taken from *The Iliad*, rendered into English prose by Samuel Butler (1898).

5. If starting the Olympics to celebrate the death of your father seems harsh, it's worth noting that Zeus had cause. Having cut off the genitals of his own father, Uranus, with a sickle, Cronus was told that he would be undone by one of his sons. He came up with a plan. The moment a son was born, Cronus would swallow the baby.

Again, this seems unnecessarily violent, but Cronus and Rhea, his queen, ruled during the Golden Age, when there was no need for law, because people just always did what was right.

Despite the fact that she was queen in a paradise, Rhea was still angry at her husband. And he was still swallowing all her boys. So she came up with her own plan. When Zeus was born, she took a big stone, and wrapped it in swaddling clothes. She gave this to Cronus. He fell for it and swallowed the stone. Zeus survived and went on to oust his father and become the king of the gods.

6. William O. Johnson Jr., *All That Glitters Is Not Gold: An Irreverent Look at the Olympic Games* (New York: G. P. Putnam's Sons, 1972).

7. David C. Young, *A Brief History of the Olympic Games* (Malden, MA: Blackwell, 2004).

8. Charles Russell, *Wonders of Bodily Strength and Skill in All Ages and All Countries* (New York: Scribner Armstrong and Co., 1873). This book was a translation and enlargement of an earlier history written in French by Guillaume Derping.

9. Johnson, *All That Glitters Is Not Gold,* 12.

CHAPTER 9

1. Edward S. Sears, *Running Through the Ages* (Jefferson, NC: McFarland and Co., 2001).

2. Printed for C. Davis in Pater-Noster-Row; and T. Green at Charing-Cross. MDCCXXIX.

3. William Heywood, *Palio and Ponte: An Account of the Sports of Central Italy from the Age of Dante to the XXth Century* (n.p.: 1904).

CHAPTER 10

1. Elie Wiesel, *Night,* Oprah Book Club Edition (New York: Hill and Wang, 2006), 72.

2. Greg Easterbrook, *The Progress Paradox: How Life Gets Better While People Feel Worse* (New York: Random House, 2003), 46.

3. Michel de Montaigne, *Essays*, translated by J. M. Cohen (New York: Penguin Books, n.d.), 384.

4. Real Time. Scotiabank Toronto Waterfront Marathon results. Whitlock came in 26th overall.

5. John L. Parker Jr., *Once a Runner* (Tallahassee, FL: Cedarwinds Publishing, 1978), 117.

6. It's a vast understatement to identify Wayne as a sportswriter. He is an award-winning journalist, but also the author of many books, the most recent of which, *The Boys of Winter: The Untold Story of the 1980 U.S. Olympic Hockey Team*, now in paperback from Three Rivers, was a *New York Times* bestseller.

7. Sheehan ran in his backyard (26 loops to a mile), according to Wikipedia and Sheehan's own Web site. Although in *Chasing the Hawk* (New York: Random House, 2001, p. 79) his son Andrew says it was only eight times around the yard to a mile. Just the sort of figure I'd expect a runner to notice.

CHAPTER 11

1. Edward S. Sears, *Running Through the Ages* (Jefferson, NC: McFarland and Co., 2001).

2. Pierce Egan, *Sporting Anecdotes, Original and Selected* (Philadelphia: H. C. Carey, and I. Lea, Chestnut Street, 1822).

3. Sears, *Running Through the Ages*, 71–73.

CHAPTER 12

1. Bruce Weber, "Losing Patience Not Weight: Guidelines on Exercise May Discourage Activity," *New York Times*, April 21, 2005.

2. The article ran in 2005, and I interviewed Dr. Morris that year. Closing the book, I contacted his office again. Now almost 97, he was still going to work twice a week.

3. Walter Thom, *Pedestrianism; or an account of the performances of celebrated pedestrians during the past and present century; with a full narrative of Captain Barclay's public and private matches ; and an essay on training* (Aberdeen, 1813), from the introduction.

4. Ibid., 33.

5. Ibid., 255.

CHAPTER 13

1. Renee Askins, *Shadow Mountain: A Memoir of Wolves, a Woman, and the Wild* (New York: Anchor, 2004), 55–56.

2. David McCullough, *Truman* (New York: Simon and Schuster, 1992).

CHAPTER 14

1. I had read the story, but it was Garth Batista of Breakaway Books who spotted the quotation, saved it, and when he heard I was writing about running, he sent it to me.

2. Robert Le Roy Ripley, *Ripley's Giant Book of Believe It or Not!* (New York: Bonanza Books, 1976).

3. Tom McNab, *The Fast Men* (New York: Simon and Schuster, 1986).

4. William O. Johnson Jr., *All That Glitters Is Not Gold: An Irreverent Look at the Olympic Games* (New York: G. P. Putnam's Sons, 1972), 121.

CHAPTER 15

1. Taken from a paper by Jean P. Lindsay (2000). He took it from Henry Chadwick's *The Consolations of Music, Logic, Theology, and Philosophy* (Oxford: Clarendon Press, 1981).

CHAPTER 16

1. William O. Johnson Jr., *All That Glitters Is Not Gold: An Irreverent Look at the Olympic Games* (New York: G. P. Putnam's Sons, 1972), 58.

CHAPTER 17

1. Jeff Galloway, *Galloway's Book on Running* (Bolinas, CA: Shelter Publications, 2002).

CHAPTER 18

1. *Running Cultures* (Routledge Taylor & Francis Group, 2004), 68. Attributed to *Die Finnen, das grosse Sportvolk* (Berlin: Wilhelm Limpert Verlag, 1936) translated into English by Ruth Bale.
2. Gail Waesche Kislevitz, *First Marathons: Personal Encounters with the 26.2-Mile Monster* (Halcottsville, NY: Breakaway Books, 1999).
3. Gabe Mirkin and Marshall Hoffman, *The Sports Medicine Book* (Boston: Little, Brown, 1978).

CHAPTER 21

1. Gina Kolata, *Ultimate Fitness: The Quest for Truth about Exercise and Health* (New York: Farrar, Straus, and Giroux, 2003).
2. Joyce Carol Oates, *The Faith of a Writer: Life, Craft, Art* (New York: HarperCollins, 2003), 29.
3. Lawrence Block is author of more than 100 books. The most dazzling are part murder mystery, part thriller, and part comedy. The best come as close to literature as genre fiction ever has. Anna Quindlen is a friend. I always she knew was talented, but I wasn't aware of just how talented, until I stumbled on her piece in Phyllis Theroux's magnificent collection of eulogies and realized that Anna's essay was my favorite. Ralph Waldo Emerson and William Styron were among the writers I thought she had outclassed.
4. I find the assertion that the Croton Dam is the second largest mortised stone structure in the world confirmed on the Web, but I do wonder about the Great Wall of China.
5. Diagnosis is a tricky process. The more subtle the tests, the more likely the false

positive. The definition of a perfectly healthy man? A man who has not yet had a full medical checkup.

CHAPTER 22

1. *The Long Hard Road: An Autobiography by Ron Hill, Part Two: To the Peak and Beyond* (Ron Hill Sports Ltd., 1982), 208. David Smith at the New York Public Library found the book for me, but I wouldn't have known to look this section up had John Bale not referred to it in his book, *Running In Culture.*

CHAPTER 23

1. John Cheever, "Signs of Hope," *Reader's Digest*, May 1982. Held for some time, this was the last writing my father published while alive.
2. David Nieman, *The Exercise-Health Connection* (Champaign, IL: Human Kinetics, 1998).

CHAPTER 24

1. Jack London, *The Call of the Wild* (first published in 1903; Bantam's first publication was in 1963), 48–49.

CHAPTER 25

1. As of June 14, 2007, Wikipedia reported that although Theato ran for France, he was born in Luxembourg and maintained Luxembourgian citizenship.
2. Michael Connelly, *26 Miles to Boston* (Guilford, CT: Lyons Press, 2003).
3. Erich Segal is best known as the author of the screenplay for the 1970 movie, *Love Story*, which gave us the line: "Love means never having to say you're sorry." His novel of the same title was a huge bestseller. Segal wrote many other books and was a classics professor at Harvard, Yale, and Princeton.

CHAPTER 26

1. George Sheehan, *Running and Being* (New York: Simon and Schuster, 1978), 28.
2. William Wordsworth, "Intimations of Immortality."
3. I know I've changed the line from *The Tale of Two Cities*. The original is too stately to be said out loud.

ACKNOWLEDGMENTS

I ran into a new world. My wife is the greatest treasure I found there. She'd probably deny it, but I doubt Janet would have twigged to the sad, portly, defeated man who meant to be a writer but rarely finished a story. Back before running, I was funniest off the page and most eloquent when cataloguing my own spectacular failures. I use the word *spectacular* advisedly. I presumed—quite mistakenly—that I'd cornered the market on melancholy.

Gorgeous, witty, open to the world, and the mother of our two boys, John and Andrew, Janet is the cornerstone on which my life is now built. She ran eight marathons. She's more apt to walk now than run, but for my 59th birthday, she went out again, and I met her on the trail behind our house. When I told our older son, John, about this, he said, "Now *that's* a great present."

I have long been fortunate in my friends, but at this juncture in my life, I am in the astonishing position of having friends who are talented editors.

The first of these is Terry Bazes, himself an astonishing novelist. I don't just admire Terry's judgment, I trust it.

Rafael Ygesias was my first writing friend, and he's still the best. My sister Susan is also a pal and ally.

I am indebted to Tish Hamilton and to *Runner's World* editor-in-chief David Willey, who assigned her to work with me on this book. I doubt I'll ever forget the glee excited by a note from Kathy Robbins asking if I'd ever met Tish Hamilton, because she would be working on *Strides*. Not only had we met, Tish and I had been in the same van for the Hood to Coast Relay, but more significantly, she'd handled the half-dozen pieces of mine published in *Runner's World*.

I rushed downstairs and found Janet. "Tish!" I said breathless. "Tish is going to be the editor of the book. So that was the second gift from Kathy Robbins, who had first connected me with the project. And for this, I am deeply grateful. Writing *Strides* has been the most gratifying editorial experience of my life.

When Tish had to return to her magazine responsibilities, I heard I would get a new editor. I don't mind admitting that I was filled with dread.

But this project seems to have had a charmed life. My new editor was— is—Kevin Smith. And if you're wondering, then the answer is no, he is not *that* Kevin Smith, anymore than I am *that* Cheever.

Kevin's brought the project the distance it needed in the last stages, suggesting structural changes I couldn't have imagined but now applaud. He's smart and enthusiastic. The pleasure he takes in his work is infectious. And yes, he too is a runner.

As always, I am thankful to Marilyn Johnson, Esmeralda Santiago, Larkin Warren, and Kate Buford, the other members of the weekly writers' group to which Terry and I both belong. Marilyn's husband, editor Rob Fleder, is my Wednesday run, or I'm his. Rob's encouragement has been precious in the extreme.

John Manners checked and double-checked the Kenya section and the chapter on the Boston Marathon, correcting and amplifying the facts and often distilling the prose as well.

Amby Burfoot has been extraordinarily helpful. No question was too petty for his time and attention. He even suggested a cure for a bout of Achilles tendonitis that included the purchase of a Strassburg Sock and a course of stretching and self-massage that was supposed to make me cry out in agony. Amby's wife, Cristina Negron, is a natural humorist and a talented writer.

I owe a great debt to the librarians of Westchester County, particularly the reference staff at the Town of Mount Pleasant and Chappaqua Public Libraries. I've always been in awe of the New York Public Library at 42nd Street in New York. I've used the collections there in the past. For this particular book, though, I had the great good fortune of getting to know David Smith, who was unfailingly helpful, encouraging, and humorous. Original sources are not just the most convincing, they're also the most fun to read.

Agent Andrew Blauner inspired the two chapters about coaches, an earlier version of which ran in his collection, *Coach: 25 Writers Reflect on People Who Made a Difference*. Lettie Teague of *Food and Wine* has given me several delightful assignments, most significantly, though, she sent me to France to run a marathon where wine is served at the water stops.

I'd need to be drunk to capture the warmth and humor I have shared on the trails and roads. But instead, let's all go for a run soon.

The first trips Janet and I took together almost always featured marathons. If I can run one soon with John and another with Andrew, my life will be complete.